MODEL RAILROADING

A FAMILY GUIDE

MODEL RAILROADING
A FAMILY GUIDE

BRUCE GREENBERG

Prentice-Hall, Inc.

Englewood Cliffs, New Jersey

Model Railroading
Bruce Greenberg

Produced and prepared by
Quarto Marketing Ltd., New York

Designed by Connie Sherman

Editor: Anne Ziff
Associate Editor: Nancy McNally
Production Manager: Tammy O'Bradovich

Copyright © 1979 by Quarto Marketing Ltd.
and Greenberg Publishing Company

Quarto acknowledges with thanks
the assistance of Ed Schneider and Ruth Kolbert

Library of Congress catalog card number 78-61847
ISBN 0-13-586149-7 (hardcover)
First American edition published
by Prentice-Hall, Inc., 1979
Printed in the United States of America.

This book is dedicated to my wife Linda whose continuing
support and assistance helped create this book.

ACKNOWLEDGEMENTS

This book grew out of discussions between the author and Michael Friedman of Quarto Publications. Michael was very enthusiastic about the need for an introductory-to-middle level book for the Lionel enthusiast. The author agreed, but wondered how he would find the time to write the book. Michael said it would be easy. Well, two years, much correspondence, and many phone calls later, the book is finally together. Michael's never-flagging enthusiasm, the skilled editing of John Bell, the managerial effort of Ed Schneider, and the photography of Rhoda Baer and Neville Long provided invaluable support. Special thanks also go to Tom McComas and James Tuohy.

Several other people made important contributions: George Stanton spent many hours, with unfailing good humor, to help us photograph and describe his toy train fantasy world. His world boasts over 500 square feet of layout with oil fields, industrial sidings, operating accessories, as well as a Wild West shoot-out between Indians and Cavalry. Not only do the Indians win, but the General (locomotive) arrives in the melee and is dramatically captured. Another whimsical section of George's layout features The Enchanted Forest, a Baltimore area storyland-amusement park. There an American Flyer Franklin provides service from the city to the park. In the park are: Jack and Jill, Humpty Dumpty, Brer Rabbit and numerous other story book favorites, all skillfully and creatively blended into the train layout.

Ralph Barger graciously permitted the author and photographer to record his handsome layout which models a big railroad mainline with dual tracks for up to 50 car trains! Ralph also shared his years of experience in designing and constructing scenery. The 600 square foot layout rises dramatically from 42 inches to 66 inches at the mountain pass.

Stan Shantar made a major contribution to the text with his discussion of cab control and multiple train operations. Harold Moore and John Hubbard also contributed information.

FOREWORD

Model Railroading is written for the Lionel, Marx, and American Flyer operator who is either resuming an involvement with trains or who is just beginning to collect and operate them. It is intended to provide easy to understand, thorough information that will help keep trains rolling without derailments.

The book discusses the planning of the layout as well as the building and operating of one or many trains. Train operations are discussed as a family activity; numerous suggestions are made for the sharing of building projects.

An unusual but important aspect of the book is its detailed analysis of the toy train marketplace. Such information is useful for purchasing rolling stock and train equipment as economically as possible.

INTRODUCTION

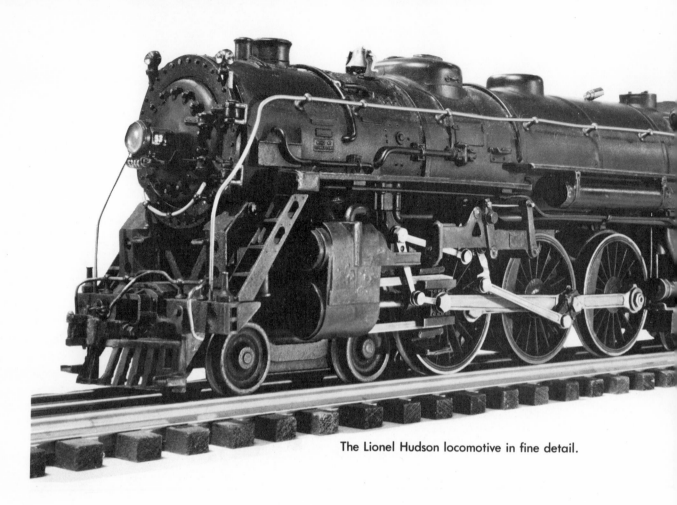

The Lionel Hudson locomotive in fine detail.

What is model railroading?

For ages, men and women and children have been fascinated by miniaturization. In fact, in the pyramids of Egypt, 4,000 years ago, well-crafted models of boats, breweries, granaries, and butcher shops were placed with the deceased.

Model railroading involves miniatures of real objects, a concept that is time-honored, and it provides hours of creative involvement for its enthusiasts. Model railroading focuses on trains and the train environment. Forty years ago an author might have stressed that model railroading has lured millions of enthusiasts because of the dominant role of railroads in the American transportation network. This clearly is no longer the case, yet model railroading is thriving more now than at any time in its history. Today, more people are buying more trains and building more layouts than ever before.

Model railroads involve motion: in particular, *controlled* motion. The operator can control the speed and direction of his or her train. Certainly, speed and direction can capture interest (as they have in toy "slot" racing cars) but there is more to toy trains. Very often, enthusiasts decide to build a railroad "empire." Train layouts frequently exhibit not just trains on the track with a few associated buildings, but entire communities with retail stores, manufacturing centers, and residential areas. Model railroaders are building small worlds which they *control*.

Model railroading may be seen as little more than a hobby activity that focuses on models of true-life railroad equipment: engines, rolling stock, and related buildings. Some people prefer very small models—some as small as $1/100$ the size of the original. Others prefer larger models, up to one-third the size of the original prototype. This book is concerned primarily with the models in the $1/48$ scale and $1/60$ scale known as O-gauge and S-gauge respectively.

2

Model railroading may involve "scratch-building" in which the hobbyists construct most or all of their equipment and miniature structures from basic raw materials (wood, metal, and plastic). Others prefer store-bought kits in which the manufacturer provides the design work and some of the production work. Still others prefer to use mainly ready-to-run equipment. This book is primarily concerned with ready-to-run equipment and related kits.

Model railroading may involve the construction of very elaborate and large layouts, with many hundreds of square feet of scenery—or it may involve the annual assembly of the train layout around the Christmas tree. This book concentrates on permanent layouts, although temporary installations will be discussed and suggestions offered.

Some model railroaders devote the bulk of their energies to building and operating a layout. Others have only a modest layout and are interested simply in *collecting* trains.

Model railroading involves working with electricity, wood, metal, and various tools. It can be as fundamental and basic or as complex as you wish it to be. There is an intrinsic pleasure in designing and creating objects; the process is self-expressive. Indeed, the true "builder" may infrequently operate his layout. He is always constructing a new piece of equipment.

Traditionally, model railroading has involved parents as well as children and adolescents. Parents often buy trains for their children and join in the enjoyment. Children, of course, love toy trains. They are captivated by a train running under its own power around a track.

Model railroading is a social activity. Train shows and train clubs provide meeting places for persons sharing your interests. A common interest in trains can provide the basis for beginning new relationships. In fact, train enthusiasts report that many of their enduring friendships developed from their mutual involvement with trains.

Model railroading is exciting. Watching a model train pound along the rails at track level is great fun—it gives a slight rush of excitement to even the most veteran operator. And witnessing the night operation of a well-crafted, complex layout—from smoke and whistle to switchyard maneuvering—can produce durable memories.

As a hobby, model railroading embraces diverse motivations and interests. It provides the basis for family activity, the basis for forming friendships, a means to exercise your creative and imaginative impulses, and it offers the chance to create a miniature world in which *you* are in control.

Model railroading is a diverse field. There are very small models (N-gauge), small models (HO-gauge), medium size models (S-gauge and O-gauge), and large models (Standard-gauge, Nos. 1 and 2 gauge). The relative widths of the tracks are shown in Figure 1. In model railroading, the gauge of the track refers to the size of the model track as compared with the prototype track. American railroads use a two-rail system in which the rails are 4′ 8″ apart. O-gauge trains use a track where the distance between the rails is about 1¼ inches. This is approximately 1/48 the prototype size.

Some people are interested in modeling the earliest trains from the 1830s and 1840s; others are interested in late nineteenth century equipment. Still others are fascinated by the great steam engines of the 1920s and 1930s, and some

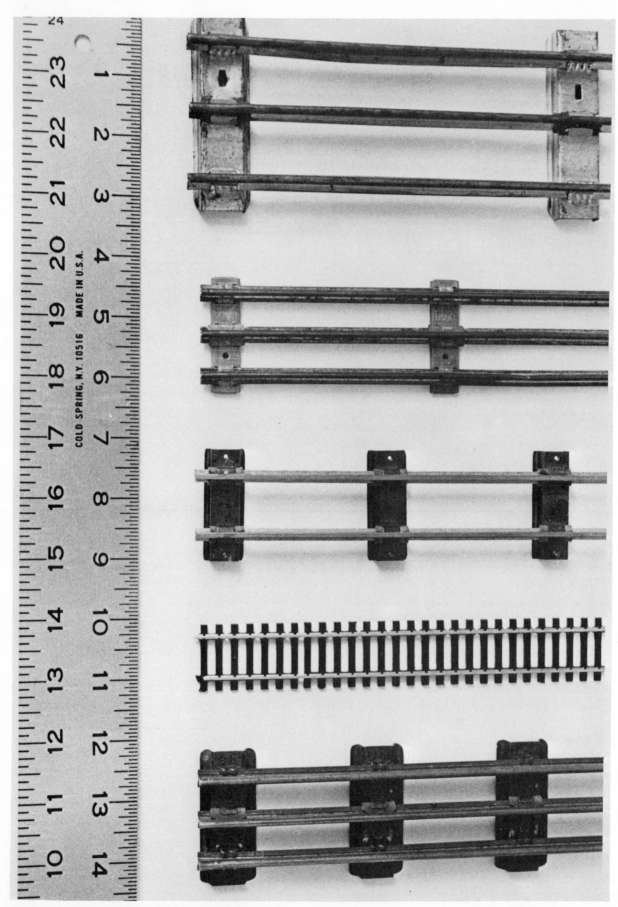

The relative widths of toy train track sizes with ruler: from the top of the page to the bottom—Standard gauge, O-27, S gauge, HO and O gauges.

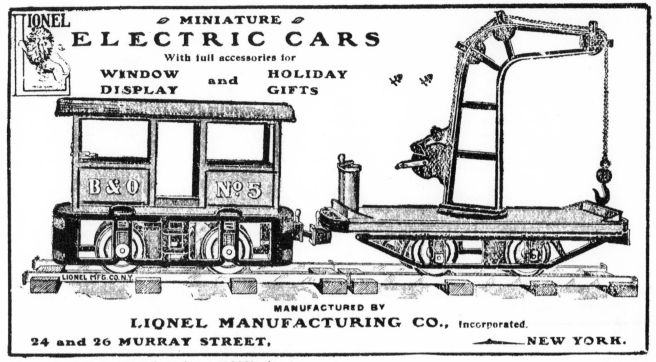

No. 931

MINIATURE
ELECTRIC CARS
With full accessories for
WINDOW and HOLIDAY
DISPLAY GIFTS

B&O No. 5

MANUFACTURED BY
LIONEL MANUFACTURING CO., Incorporated.
24 and 26 MURRAY STREET, NEW YORK.

The cover of the first Lionel catalogue (1903), showing
early 2⅞ gauge equipment.

choose to model contemporary equipment. Many model railroaders purchase from a variety of eras, depending on their fancy. On a given layout, you might see an old-time engine such as The General (from the 1860s) running on a track not far from a model of the Metroliner. Since model railroading exists for the enjoyment of the hobbyist, the model railroader should do whatever is most pleasing.

Some model railroaders believe that every possible detail of the entire layout should be in exact proportion to the prototype. Of course, any model railroad will necessarily depart from exact prototype scale. It is extraordinarily difficult (but not impossible) to find items as small as the bolts on rail joiners in exact prototype scale. Most model railroad people make compromises. Some (including this author) enjoy running Standard-gauge and O-gauge trains on the same layout. Do what you please.

This hobby also provides a wide variety of pocketbook options. In O-gauge (the focus of this book), there is an enormous range of available equipment at four different price levels. A Marx Co. locomotive with an electric motor can be purchased secondhand for less than $2. It

also is possible to spend more than $400 for an excellent copy of Lionel's No. 773 engine built in 1950. Or you might spend $700 on a finely detailed brass O-gauge loco. If you have *any* nonessential income, model railroading is a hobby you can afford.

Model railroading also requires widely diverse investments of time. Some people spend about 10 hours per year on their trains; others spend five hours per day. Since trains do not need to be fed, watered, combed, or exercised, the intermittent demands are quite manageable. When the spirit of the iron horse moves you, then do your trains.

LIONEL LINES

Since this book primarily is concerned with O-gauge and O-27 gauge, you probably will want to know more about the Lionel Company, the world's largest producer of toy trains in these two gauges. Joshua Lionel Cowan, the founder of Lionel, began producing toy trains in about 1900. The earliest powered equipment was made for track with a 2⅞-inch gauge, and included a powered gondola and tunnel engine. The track consisted of two metal strips fastened

5

The 1970 and 1971 Lionel Fundimensions catalogues.

in wooden ties (or "sleepers"). It was not particularly satisfactory. In 1906 Lionel introduced what his company called (in a stroke of advertising inspiration) "Standard-gauge" track, with about 2⅛ inches between the outer of three rails. Standard-gauge track came soon to be the "standard" American size, and was adopted by American Flyer and Ives, which called it "wide-gauge." Standard-gauge trains dominated the Lionel Line until the early 1930s. By the mid-1930s Standard-gauge trains were on the decline and O-gauge trains took over the Lionel catalogue. The last complete Standard-gauge train sets were catalogued by Lionel in 1939.

O-gauge was introduced in the United States about 1900 by the Ives Company, the major producer of American model trains at that time. American Flyer began to manufacture mechanical (clockwork) O-gauge trains about 1907. Lionel did not start producing O-gauge until 1915. By the mid-1930s, O-gauge trains were Lionel's main feature and in 1937 the com-

pany achieved a major innovation in the hobby by introducing the first mass-produced O-scale locomotive. For its prototype, the Lionel company wisely chose the New York Central Hudson, a 4-6-4 steam locomotive. The Hudson prototype remains widely admired for its sleek appearance and its excellent design. Lionel's Hudson was a superior product, with remarkably fine detail work which modelers today still hold in high regard.

After dropping its toy train production due to the war effort from 1942 to 1945, Lionel resumed production and enjoyed spectacular growth and sales from the late 1940s through the mid-1950s. An amazing array of engines, cars, and accessories was introduced. The operating cars (such as the milk car with its worker pushing milk cans onto a platform, and the cattle car with tiny cows marching from the corral into the car) caught the imagination, and dollars, of millions of Americans. These were complex and inspired toys, sophisticated in design and manufacturing. Lionel accessories, such as the No.

45 gateman who leaves his shack to warn motorists of passing trains and the No. 97 operating coal loader, were quite successful.

In the late 1950s, the Cowan family sold its interest in toy trains, about the same time as the toy train marketplace went into a decline. Road race sets and the relatively low prices of HO-gauge train sets had lured the enthusiasm of many parents, sons, and daughters. Hard times hit not only Lionel, but American Flyer and Marx as well. The recession of 1958–59, the deepest in a decade, also cut demand for expensive toys such as Lionel trains. The decline is clearly evidenced in the Lionel catalogues of the period. By 1960, the once glossy and handsome catalogue had slumped to an inexpensive hurry-up pulp job. Matters continued to decline and in 1967, for the first time since 1903 (discounting wartime) Lionel failed to issue any catalogue at all. In 1968, only one complete Lionel train set was offered to consumers.

Time and money were running out for the Lionel Toy Corporation. They simply could no longer manufacture trains profitably. Then the General Mills Company, apparently looking for diversifications in the great American conglomerate game, determined that toy trains still had substantial potential. In 1970, a subsidiary of General Mills named Fundimensions secured a license from the Lionel Toy Corporation to manufacture Lionel trains. Fundimensions took over Lionel's Irvington plant and moved production to Mt. Clemons, Michigan. Fundimensions began aggressively to merchandise Lionel trains.

In the early 1970s, there was another significant development: a generation of boys from the 1950s, who had owned and enjoyed Lionel trains, now were fathers and uncles looking for trains to enjoy with their children. Sales soon boomed. Today, toy trains are decidedly back in business.

AN OVERVIEW

This book seeks to highlight some of the joys and skills involved in model railroading and toy trains. The following section, chapter 2, provides the basic information you need to get started in this hobby. Here will be considered track gauge, electricity, motors, and transformers. There will also be outlined the basic decisions you will want to make in beginning this hobby—how much money you might spend, where you might construct your layout, how much time you may wish to spend on your layout. Provided, too, will be basic hook-up instructions for getting your first temporary layout operating rapidly.

Chapter 3 focuses on children and toy trains. Here there is an explanation of why O-gauge and S-gauge trains are the wisest choices for a family. There's a discussion of how you can involve your children in your hobby—and what expectations you might have regarding their skills and aptitudes. It is explained how you can provide your children with their own trains at minimal cost, and how you can help your children enjoy these trains.

Chapter 4 focuses on the contemporary toy train marketplace, which competition has made remarkably diversified. A major marketplace issue is the role of the discount department stores, the mail order discount firms, and the independent local hobby shops. A subdued struggle is now going on between these different types of seller. Several of the mail order discount houses are seeking total dominance of the marketplace. These firms have disrupted the usual flow of goods from the manufacturer to the distributor to the retailer, and have made dramatic gains in their sales.

These are perhaps ominous signs for the future of model railroading. The mail order firms cannot provide the ancillary services necessary for the enjoyment of the hobby. It is hard to envision a thriving toy train industry with only mail order links between consumers and manufacturers. Toy trains are a commodity for which the interaction of the customer and the knowledgeable salesperson is a crucial ingredient.

An unusual characteristic of the toy train marketplace is the predominance of the amateur dealer at train shows, which now can be found across the country with increasing regularity. These shows are staffed mainly by men and women who have surplus trains and who support their operating and collecting activities by selling to others. Such people lend a neighborly quality to train shows, where questions are asked candidly and advice flows freely. The level of integrity is quite high, particularly in comparison with other secondary markets. The market, however, is becoming more professional. More people are entering whose primary livelihood is the buying and selling of toy trains, perhaps a regrettable development.

The toy train clubs, particularly the Train Collectors Association, have played a major role in the revival of toy trains in the 1970s (along with Fundimensions). These clubs and associations were created to enhance the enjoyment of toy trains and to provide facilities for people to meet each other and share their common interests. While these clubs have grown, the average member still is given ample opportunity to meet other train enthusiasts and to find bargain prices or additional toy train paraphernalia. These clubs foster a form of market capitalism at its best: easy participation by many individuals and substantial competition among the sellers so that profit margins are kept to a minimum.

In chapter 5 the possible types of train layout tables and surface designs are explained, and solid suggestions are offered as to which combinations of construction designs might be most appropriate for your circumstances. This chapter also provides in detail and at considerable length a survey of track layout designs and wiring schemes to be considered once you have built your table.

In chapter 6 actual techniques for table construction are considered. The suggestions and step-by-step instructions here will help you build your table, even if this is your first attempt. There are also suggestions for accomplishing the fundamental procedures of laying track and soldering, as well as creating insulated sections of track to operate various accessories.

Model railroad scenery construction is the theme of chapter 7. A number of scenery construction techniques are detailed, including how to work with papier-mâché, how to mold screening for the construction of mountains, and (for the more daring) how to use real water in your layout riverbeds and lakebeds. You will be shown how to make your own trees, how to build an O-gauge turntable, how to construct buildings and roads, and how to modify store-bought kits.

Chapter 8 provides operating instructions on a wide variety of Lionel accessories. Included are sections on various crossing signals, the gateman and the semaphore, and bulb-type accessories. A collection of tips is offered on operating and maintaining your layout and equipment once it has been made operable, and you are given an introduction to operating a variety of Lionel transformers.

Chapter 9 concentrates on repair techniques and how to avoid potential problems before they develop (such as steel wool particles on the tracks). You will be shown how to "troubleshoot" your equipment—all the way from milk cars and gatemen to "E-units" and dirty commutators. There are a lot of money-saving tips here to save you from needing the services of repairmen.

Chapter 10 will be quite useful to most model railroaders: it provides the names and addresses of the nation's major suppliers of Lionel, Marx, and American Flyer equipment. Since relatively few hobby shops carry extensive lines of equipment, this information should prove valuable. This chapter also includes the addresses of the nation's major model railroading clubs and the appropriate officers for you to contact.

In chapter 11 you will find a glossary of terms to help your understanding of the codewords and railroad lore which permeate this multidimensional hobby.

GETTING STARTED

Testing a locomotive by touching one lead to the center rail pickup roller and fastening the other lead to the metal truck frame. The engine would then be turned right side up.

Trains can be enjoyed regardless of the size of your chosen investment. Trains can be enjoyed at $10 per month (which is difficult) or you can lavishly indulge yourself at $1,000 a month. Obviously, these are extremes. What you will spend depends on your income. What kind of money do you have available? Can you afford $25 a month or $100 a month? Consider these questions carefully; the answers will place your expectations in line with your budget, and foster peace and tranquillity in your home. The train budget can be an unnecessary source of family disunity. Once agreement is reached by interested parties and accommodations made, toy train budgeting can promote family cooperation.

Naturally, the size of your train budget will dramatically influence how much equipment

you buy and where you buy it. Frequently, people with limited budgets do have substantial amounts of free time. And time can be a substitute for money in this field. If your budget is limited, local train shows will be events where you can stretch your train dollar. Used or "previously owned" trains are much less expensive than are new trains. For example, a well-running die-cast 2-6-2 locomotive (No. 2026) from the late 1940s or early 1950s can be purchased with its tender for $30 at many train shows. A No. 2046 or 2056 4-6-4 die-cast steam engine can be bought in excellent used condition (with smoke, whistle, and magnetraction) for less than $55. Lionel's current top-of-the-line die-cast steamers (roughly comparable in design and quality to the No. 2046) have list prices greater than $100.

Used track is an excellent value. Used O-27 gauge track of good quality often can be bought for 10¢ a section or less, while good used O-gauge track runs up to 25¢ a section. New track costs at least two or three times these rates. Track that is tarnished or even dirty is readily made clean and usable. Little can go wrong with toy train track; either it is straight or it isn't. The insulator is either there or it isn't. Used track may be your best bet.

Used switches also are good values. At train shows, used O-27 switches bring $15 a pair with a warranty of operation from the seller. Good used O-gauge switches bring about $25 to $30 a pair with two controllers and the switch direction indicators. Unless you are mechanically inclined and/or have access to *Greenberg's Repair and Operating Manual for Lionel Trains*, do not buy "bargain" O-gauge or O-27 gauge remote switches unless you can test them for operation, or unless the seller guarantees that he has cleaned and tested them for reliable operation. "Bargain" switches are usually broken and are difficult for the beginner to repair.

The least expensive route is to buy trains from people who own trains and no longer want them. Sometimes trains can be bought by the set (or cardboard box) for only one-tenth of what they would cost at a train show. (For a report on the train show values of toy trains, see *Greenberg's Price Guide to Lionel Trains from 1945 to 1977*, and the companion volume *Greenberg's Price Guide to Lionel Trains 1906–1942*. The latter volume covers both O-gauge and Standard-gauge. When trains are purchased in accumulated amounts, frequently there are mechanical and electrical problems. Often, these problems frustrated the original owner and resulted in the trains being stored away. Sometimes you can be very fortunate and purchase first-class merchandise at third-class prices.

The next cheapest way to buy trains is at train shows. Such shows are sponsored either by clubs or enterprising individuals and attract the surplus equipment of collectors and operators. Prices usually are quite competitive and bargains are available.

When buying used equipment, it is always advisable to have it tested for operation before you pay for it. Most train shows now provide test tracks for testing equipment. When buying trains in "accumulated" form, ask permission to plug in the transformer and touch the wires from the transformer to the loco (one wire goes to the center-rail pickup and the other wire to the wheels). Hold the engine right side up. The loco light should glow and the motor should make some effort to run. If these two things do not occur, you may wish to ask for a price reduction. You still may wish to purchase the equipment even if it does not run—given a sufficient price concession by the seller. (In most communities there are train collectors and operators who help to finance their hobby by performing repair work for other train enthusiasts. Generally, their fees are quite reasonable; in fact, they are often bargains. The best method of locating such repairmen is to inquire among other enthusiasts, particularly at train shows.)

Certain kinds of equipment at train shows are true bargains, depending on the types of sellers and buyers at each specific show. Train shows evolved primarily to fulfill the needs of train collectors. Train operators also have discovered shows as real sources of value.

Train show sellers usually have bought several sets of trains en masse and usually have great quantities of track, which is rarely in demand and usually low-priced. Even if the track is missing pins, you can substitute nails, which are cheaper and work just as efficiently. Good used ZW transformers, which run four trains, cost between $60 and $75. A model 1033, which runs one train, can usually be found used for less than $10 at a train show. Four 1033s for $40 or less provide more power than one ZW. While new, top-line Lionel cabooses can cost $8 each (and scarce Lionel cabooses from the 1950s can run to $50) there are dozens of common cabooses available at most train shows for less than $1.

Clearly, budget-minded train enthusiasts can purchase much more "hardware" if it has been previously owned. Many people are hesitant to buy used goods, but used Lionel and American Flyer trains are dependable in most cases and can represent excellent investments. At train shows, the seller often will guarantee the operating condition of the equipment. (You should request the seller to write out a brief statement along the lines of "I hereby warrant this 736 locomotive and tender to be in good operating condition." He should add his name, address, and phone number. If asked politely, nearly all ethical sellers will consent to this.)

Regarding the train maintenance structures, factories, and residences for your layout, current Lionel kits cost about $7 to $12, while Plasticville structures run from $2 to $4. Old cardboard Skyline buildings sometimes can be found at train shows for under $1 each. Buildings also can be hand made from materials found around the home: cardboard, small wooden blocks, paper, pencils, and glue. With sufficient time and patience, extremely realistic structures can be built, although a single structure can easily consume 30 hours of your free time.

If you wish to purchase brand-new trains and equipment, your choices are not limited to hobby stores. New trains also can be purchased from discount department stores and mail order discount operations. For further discussion, see chapter 4.

Let's assume that you have decided to spend about $25 a month on your hobby. First you will need a place to build your layout, preferably a location where the layout may be permanently mounted. And you will need lumber for the layout. New lumber is expensive; a sheet of 4' × 8' plywood (½ inch thick) costs as much as $12. Wood to skirt the edges of the plywood sheet can cost another $6. In other words, your first month's budget can be entirely consumed by the cost of lumber, nails, screws, and other miscellanea.

An alternative is to acquire used lumber, which sometimes is slightly warped or has nails in it, but can be considerably less expensive than new lumber. Construction sites are usually reliable sources for used lumber. Find the

superintendent on the construction site and explain that you are building a train layout and want to reduce your costs. Ask him if there is any used lumber you can buy (or accept for free). He will either ignore you, urge you to depart, or be quite helpful in your effort to cut costs this month.

A sanitary landfill is another likely source for lumber (this site used to be called the dump). Today, the dump is not a particularly smelly or unhygienic place; the federal government requires that waste materials be promptly and properly buried. If you go up to the "work face" of the sanitary landfill (the trench where materials are being buried) and discuss your goal with the machine operator, frequently you can secure your plywood and other construction materials without charge.

Our suggested cost of $25 for a plywood table, of course, is only an estimate, based on 1978 East Coast prices. Regardless of where you live, one certain way of reducing this cost is to use the "open top" construction technique. This method uses much less lumber and little, if any, plywood. The cost of new materials could be as low as $12. See our further discussion on table construction techniques in chapter 6.

HOW MUCH TIME DO YOU HAVE?

Model railroading can be time-consuming. It will be helpful for you to recognize that time, just like dollars, is a limited commodity. How many hours each week do you want to spend building your layout? After construction, how many hours will go into operating your railroad? What other obligations and commitments do you have to your family, your job, your house? What about those nagging little chores and obligations which have always eaten up your free time in the past—the doctor and dentist, shopping, car repairs, and so on? Can you spare 20 hours a week on your layout, at least during the construction stages, or is 10 hours more realistic? Can you involve your family in these hours? Do you want to involve them? While they are sunk in the morass of evening television upstairs, you can be building your own brave new world in the basement.

Fortunately, most model railroad projects can be stopped and started easily at your convenience without significant penalties in either time or money. When you get tired of laying track, you can lay down your drill and screwdriver and head for the bunkhouse. Wiring can be left dangling, in most cases, until the next evening, as long as you keep note of your intentions. Even painting projects can be interrupted, as long as you clean your brush and wrap it well. Your railroad will wait for you; it's all yours.

A MATTER OF SPACE

Where will you put your train layout? There are a number of important considerations here. First, how much space is available? Second, what type of space is available? Third, what are the atmospheric conditions in these locations—primarily, what is their humidity level and temperature? Fourth, how does your appropriation of this space affect other family members?

As a general principle, not surprisingly, it is preferable to have more space rather than less. Thus, assuming all other factors are equal, if there is more space in the attic than in the basement, opt for the attic. Train layouts have a tendency to grow and demand more space.

Your chosen location may be best suited by a free-standing train table; or a perimeter layout around the sides of the room may be more appropriate. You may prefer the perimeter approach, which generally affords more operating time from starting point to stopping point and is easier to work on (since you do not have to cope with stretching across three feet of train table). The short depth of the perimeter layouts sometimes results in very narrow track right-of-ways, thus limiting the construction of a residential community, an industrial complex, or significant scenery. It is possible, however, to combine a narrow perimeter layout with one which is much wider at several places. For more on layout design see pages 35 to 59.

Atmospheric and climatic conditions are important. If your attic registers 120 degrees Fahrenheit in July and August, you will not want to melt along with your Plasticville buildings.[1] However, if the addition of a window fan, air conditioner, or insulation can eliminate climatic concerns at an affordable cost, then go with the attic. If your basement has a pleasant temperature for most of the year, but becomes too damp in June, July, and August, you can consider purchasing a dehumidifer (small ones are usually available for less than $100). Used dehumidifiers are often good values, and if you have less than 800 square feet in your train room, you can probably get by with a small one.[2] The alternative to a dehumidifier in a damp room is rust—which is not only unattractive, but can damage your train equipment.

An unheated garage can also be used for a train layout. Here the principal problems, in most parts of the country, are the cold winters and the damp weather of the spring and fall.

Insulation and an electric space heater will solve your winter blues and the dehumidifier is usually effective in the other seasons. Garages are relatively easy to insulate. Rolled batts of insulation can easily be stapled to the underside of the ceiling or roof and the sides of the walls. (One major caution: fiberglass insulation is an irritant to the skin and eyes. Protective goggles should be used; old work clothing should be worn and not washed after use, as washing will disperse the strands.) Garages can accommodate both cars and toy train layouts, if there is sufficient headroom above the car. The layout most commonly used is suspended above the car by a block and pulley. In the absence of the car, the table has its own folding legs which are extended when the layout lowered toward the floor.

People also have constructed small train layouts on plywood sheets or boards mounted on casters, so that the layout may slide beneath

---

[1] The melting point of Plasticville units actually is much higher.
[2] Dehumidifiers take water vapor from the air and condense it into water. The water can drain into a pail, which periodically you will have to empty, often once a day. With most humidifiers, you can attach a garden hose and run the hose "downhill" to a basement drain. The latter method, clearly, is preferable.

A Lionel transformer with the cover removed to show the iron laminated core and the whistle rectifier disc. Note that the transformer should *not* be operated with its protective cover removed.

a bed. They must make sure they have sufficient clearance to avoid damage to those items permanently mounted on the layout (such as platforms that accompany the milk car and the cattle car).

Finally, you should dwell on the obvious: train layouts take up space, and for many families disposable space in the home is a prized commodity. It is best to involve the whole family in the decision as to which room will be used. There will be noise and dust generated in the construction of the layout, as well as occasional noise from subsequent operation and visitors. People should not have to pass through a bedroom to reach the train layout. And if your children are under the age of five, you probably will want to protect them from the train layout—and vice versa. Unsupervised access of toddlers (and grabbers) to your train layout must be prevented; your prize steamer falling to the floor can be a terminal trip.

THE POWER SUPPLY

There are two major kinds of electric cur-

rent: alternating current (AC) and direct current (DC). Electrical current flows from the positive pole (+) to the negative pole (−). Direct current is graphed with an instant rise to the voltage and an instant drop when the voltage is discontinued. Alternating current is graphed with a reversal of poles many times a second. The standard alternating current found in the United States is 60 cycle (or 60 Hertz AC). This means that the poles reverse themselves 60 times a second.

Nearly all Lionel equipment can run on either AC or DC. However, several starter sets sold in recent years will run only on DC. Operating these sets on AC will rapidly burn out the motor.

Domestic current in your home is usually between 110 and 125 *volts*. Think of the flow of water in a streambed: the voltage is the pressure behind the waterflow. *Amperes* are used to measure the amount of the flow of electricity and *ohms* measure the amount of resistance to the flow. House current, as it comes from the wall receptacles in your home, is too powerful

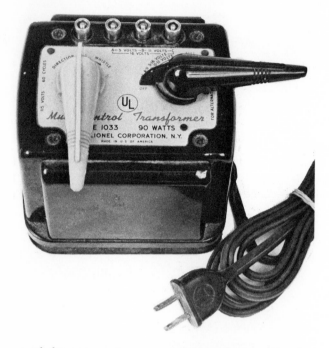

A Lionel 1033 transformer with 90 watts maximum output. This transformer will adequately run one train. It features a separate whistle control and direction control lever. It provides for two different variable voltage ranges—5 to 16 with posts A and U, 0 to 11 with posts B and U.

and dangerous to use on the exposed rails of a model railroad. Thus, a device known as a transformer is used to reduce the voltage from 110–125 volts to 6–20 volts. Transformers are very simple devices, consisting of an iron core (usually a series of laminated iron plates with insulation between each plate) and two coils of wire, one wrapped around each end of the core. One coil is plugged into the wall receptacle. Through a process known as induction, current is "induced" through magnetic fields into the second coil. The ratio of windings on the two coils determines the output (or secondary coil voltage).

The above is a necessarily crude explanation of the power which makes your toy train run. It will be helpful to you—and to your children—to know more about how your transformer functions, so that you can view it as something more than that little black box of magic.

CHOOSING YOUR GAUGE

The model railroader has several gauges (or sizes) of trains from which to choose. We will look first at O-gauge and O-27 gauge, for they have long been favorites among American model railroaders. These two gauges have track which is approximately 1¼ inches between the outside rails. Lionel produces O and O-27; Marx made O-27 trains from the mid-1930s to 1975; American Flyer made O-gauge from 1907 through 1941. O-gauge can be three-rail or two-rail; all three of the above manufacturers made three-rail track. While O-gauge trains are approximately 1/48 the size of the prototypes after which they are modeled (or a scale of about ¼ inch to the foot), the manufacturers have occasionally taken significant liberties in scale and proportion.

There are several differences between the O-gauge and O-27-gauge track, including the slightly greater height and heavier gauge of steel in O-gauge track, as well as its thicker track pins. Usually, Lionel has classified its better locomotives and rolling stock as O-gauge, although the only difference between an O-gauge engine in one year and an O-27 engine the next year can be an engine number change (from No. 675 to No. 2035). Most O-gauge equipment can be operated on the tighter O-27 curves if run slowly enough, especially if straight pieces are added in the curve areas. The large aluminum passenger cars, however, will not pass through O-27 switches since they catch on the motor switch housings.

Between 1946 and 1965, American Flyer manufactured S-gauge trains, based on a scale of three sixteenths of an inch to a foot. S-gauge track has only two rails, both of which are insulated from the track ties. Although the two-rail track appears more realistic, it is slightly more difficult to wire when switches are being used.

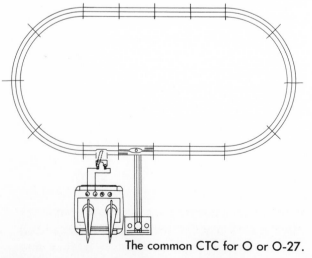

The common CTC for O or O-27.

The S-gauge track rails are T-shaped, as are prototype railroad tracks, unlike Lionel track, which is rounded. Although American Flyer equipment is no longer manufactured by the Gilbert Company, which has been purchased by Lionel, the equipment remains quite available and reasonably priced.

HO-gauge trains have taken a large share of the toy train market in recent years and are popular among all age groups. The trains are much smaller than the larger gauge trains; indeed, "HO" stands for "half of O-gauge." They are about $1/87$ of prototype size, or a scale of 3.5 mm. to the foot. All American HO trains are designed to run on direct current and have permanent magnet motors. The track, while small, is not exactly to scale. HO trains generally are more demanding to operate. It is necessary to have a higher personal level of perseverance to maintain operation, and the small HO engine motors are more susceptible to stoppage from oil and dirt than are the large-gauge motors.

N-gauge trains also have gained in popularity recently. Even smaller in scale than HO, these are truly miniature trains, as opposed to toy trains. Their track is not exactly to scale, and their motors are similar to those of HO-gauge trains. Dependable operation of N-gauge trains requires scrupulous cleanliness.

The size and gauge of your train set is a matter of personal preference, especially since the costs of equipment in the different gauges will not differ greatly. Some people prefer large trains, others prefer small ones. Clearly, more track and more buildings can be packed into a $4' \times 8'$ HO layout than into an O-gauge layout of the same dimensions. Clearly, too, O-gauge equipment is likely to be more durable and dependable. Small differences in track height or width will bring HO engines to a halt, while O-gauge trains can surmount such hindrances. O-gauge equipment also is more readily available at train shows and easier to repair. All in all, then, this type of equipment is to be preferred.

SETTING UP YOUR TRAIN LAYOUT

First, carefully read the instructions, if any,

which came with the equipment. Then read and follow the instructions in this book.

To make a toy train set operate, you will need a transformer, an electric wall outlet into which the transformer will be plugged, two pieces of light, insulated "bell" wire, and a device known as a lock-on or track clip to carry the power from the transformer wires to the track. Enough track will be needed to form an oval or a circle, initially, so that the train may travel continuously. Finally, you will also need a working locomotive or other motorized rolling stock.

It is highly recommended, even for temporary efforts or your first toy train layout, that you invest in the purchase of a large piece of plywood for mounting your track layout. A $4' \times 8'$ sheet of ½-inch thick interior grade plywood is adequate; masonite is too hard, and homosote or other insulating board must be used with reinforcement. For laying the track on the plywood and installing several accessories, you will need:

- Box of 100, No. 4 wood screws, about ½ inch long.
- Pair of needle-nose pliers (buy a good grade for $7 or so; the cheap ones will break under stress).
- Small screwdriver with screw-holding attachment. The split-blade version (in which the blades are forced together by a shank to tighten in the screw slot) sold by Sears and Vaco is recommended.
- 50' of No. 18 bell wire, red covered.
- 50' of No. 18 bell wire, white covered.
- Small hand drill (or ¼- or ⅜-inch power drill) and three $1/16$-inch drill bits, or hammer and several 4d finishing nails.

Your first step should be to form an oval with the track. Use track clips to hold the track together, especially if you are not mounting the track on a board. If you do not have a board and track clips, operation will be difficult if not impossible. Examine the track pins and make sure they are tightly positioned in the rails. If not, take your needle-nose pliers and gently squeeze between the flanges on the bottom of the rail and the pin. Move the pliers in a bit further and

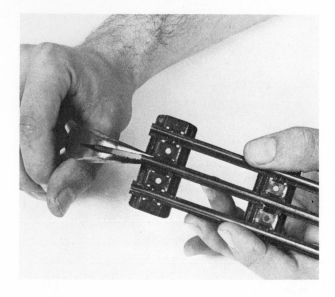

Before putting your track together examine both ends. Check the track pins for snugness in the rail. Check the open end for hole size. The holes should fit the pins snugly. If they don't, take your needlenose pliers and gently squeeze between the flanges on the bottom of the rail and the widening area. Don't overdo it—leave enough room for the track pin to enter the rail.

squeeze again. Repeat until the track pins are not loose.

Now examine the ends of each track section which will receive the pins. Using your pliers, and placing the pliers between the flanged base and the rolled top, gently squeeze to make the rolled top slightly smaller so that the pin from the other section will fit tightly. The two sections of track are now ready to be fit together, if they are clean.

Track which has already been used may well be dirty, in which case, use of a nonflammable liquid cleaner is suggested. Emery paper and extra-fine sandpaper will put small scratches in the track; these abrasives should only be used to remove rust from the track. (Badly rusted track can be cleaned with the wire brush on a power grinder or a hand-held steel brush mounted in a power drill. Do not use steel wool; steel strands will adhere to locomotive engines and damage them.)

TRANSFORMER HOOK-UP

After two sections are fitted together, connect your transformer to one of the two sections of track using the lock-on and insulated wiring. Notice that the transformer posts are labeled. Most Lionel transformers use combinations of A-U or B-U for train operation. The relevant voltages usually are printed on either the front or the top of the transformer. The train set's instructions also should indicate the proper connections between the lock-on and the transformer. If you notice sparks or a change in the sound pitch of the transformer, then you may be assured that you have misconnected it to the track. By convention (but not by necessity)

either post A or post B is connected to the middle rail, while post U is connected to either of the outside rails.

Your track clip or lock-on should be snugly fastened to the track; it also must be fastened to an area on the track that is clean and bright as a result of a little emery paper effort. The wires from the transformer will usually fasten to the lock-ons by a spring-clip. Check to make sure there is enough spring tension to hold the wire tightly. At the transformer end, the wires are usually held in place by small stud nuts. The looped bare end of the wire should be placed on the stud shaft going clockwise—the same direction in which the nuts tighten. Hence, when the nuts are tightened, the wires remain firmly around the shaft. To provide a more secure connection to the transformer, purchase a package of "solderless connectors." These are illustrated on page 18 (purchase a size which will fit wire gauges No. 18 through 22 and fit No. 6 or No. 8 machine screwposts).

To use these solderless connectors, strip the wire between one fourth and three eighths of an inch, place the bare wire in the open end of the connector, and crimp the open end so that the wire is securely fastened. To crimp the open end, use a wire cutter or a "nipper," or the crimping surface of a wire stripping device.

Wire stripping is an important skill which you will use countless times. It is easy to master. You may either buy your own wire stripper or learn to strip wire with a small knife. A wire stripper resembles a pair of pliers fashioned with round holes of various sizes in its jaws which remove the insulation from the wire while leaving the core of copper or aluminum uncut. A light-duty pair is available for under $2. These will be satisfactory in most instances, since the most common wire is a lightweight 18- or 20-gauge. Professional quality strippers cost $6 to $8 and strip a wider range of wire diameters. Some of the so-called professional strippers, however, do not strip the most common toy train gauge wires.

The alternative to the wire stripper is a very sharp penknife or paring knife. An appropriate

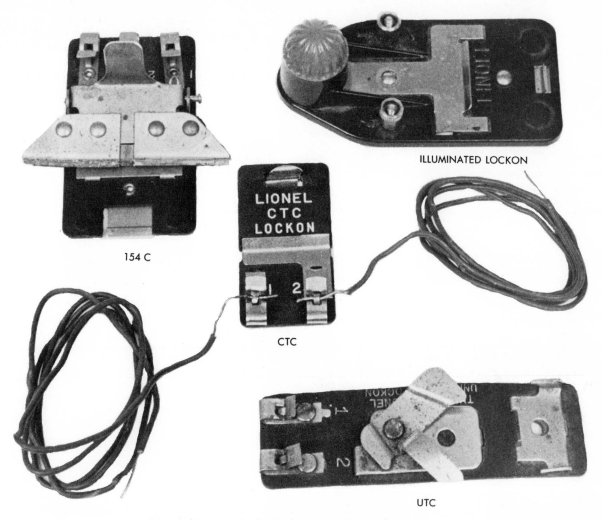

How train controls should be grouped together.

Four different lockons are illustrated. The most common is the CTC lockon which is designed to fit O and O-27 track. To put the wires in the slots, gently depress the spring just above the slot where the wire will go. The wire should then slide easily into the slot. No. 154C is a special lockon for use with No. 154 crossing signal with two flashing red lights. UTC lockon is designed to fit O, O-27 and Standard gauge track. The pressure contact that swivels has two positions—one for the smaller track and one for the larger. The illuminated lockon is designed for O, and O-27. It provides an additional indication as to whether all is well.

stripping method is to lay the wire across the edge of a flat surface and use the knife to scrape in a plane parallel to the wire. Since you do not want to nick the wire, scrape the insulation in a parallel direction *away* from you. If the wiring has cotton fibers beneath the outer plastic or rubber coating, be sure to scrape or trim away these cotton fibers, as they will interfere with electrical contact.

If you are using older wire, it may have become oxidized. Oxidation, which usually appears as a dull and darkened glaze on the aluminum or copper, interferes with the transmission of electricity. It is therefore strongly recommended that you gently scrape the wire core with your knife to make it shiny again.

After the transformer has been connected to the first section of track, you will want to determine that the connection is firm and that there is no significant voltage loss. The best way to measure voltage is with a volt-ohm-meter. These devices are available for as little as $10 (for an unsophisticated model) or $20 to $25 for a relatively sensitive model. Radio Shack and Lafayette stores offer them.

A much less expensive but adequate tester can be easily fashioned at home from a miniature light socket with an 18-volt bulb (GE bulbs 1447 or 432). Alligator clips should be attached to the ends of each wire lead.

To check track continuity, take your test lamp or volt-ohm-meter and connect the leads

To fasten a wire to the transformer, first strip the insulation from the end of the wire. Then form a loop with the bare end. Place the loop on the transformer terminal or stud such that the loop is going clockwise— the same direction that the knurled nuts will tighten.

An assortment of wire connectors. On the top row are shown plastic cones that are used to cover wires that have been spliced and wrapped together. Note that the very small sizes are usually the most useful for the model railroader. The bottom row shows a variety of solderless connectors that require a crimping tool for effective fastening of the wire. Note that the connectors come as male and female pairs—as shown on the far left—as well as with holes for fastening on to the transformer or accessory terminals.

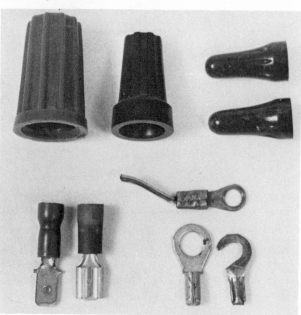

to the two transformer posts which are being used. (Most transformers have alternative sets of posts to which the wires may be attached.) Usually, one or more pairs of posts will provide a variable voltage, such as 9–15 volts or 10–19 volts. (Often, on the face of the transformer, the manufacturer will list the voltages obtainable from various post combinations.) Depending on the size of your locomotive and the number of cars to be pulled, and assuming that your transformer offers a choice, you may decide to use either the lower volt range or the higher one.

First, check the voltage at the post with your meter or bulb and socket; then test the voltage again on the piece of track that should now be hooked up. There should be no significant voltage loss. If there is a substantial voltage loss (or difference in bulb brightness), check the wire contact at both ends until you locate the

source of the voltage drop. Next, check the voltage on the first piece of track. Having tightened the track pins in the second piece of track, connect the two track pieces. Then check the voltage on the second piece. If it is satisfactory, tighten the track pins on the third piece and connect it to the second piece. Continue with this process of connecting and testing until you have completed your oval or circle. This will save you the grief of attempting to locate a voltage drop after a large number of track sections have been laid.

Having completed your circle or oval, and having tested the voltage, it is now time to test run your equipment. Turn your transformer speed/voltage knob to the "off" position. Carefully position your locomotive or diesel on the track. If there are leading or trailing trucks, be sure that these are properly riding on the track. Then turn on the transformer. Hopefully, the light in the loco or diesel will shine and the equipment will either emit a pleasant humming sound or actually run along the track, backward or forward. If the loco light does not shine and the transformer begins to make a different sound (starts to hum loudly or make a throbbing sound), turn the transformer off. You probably

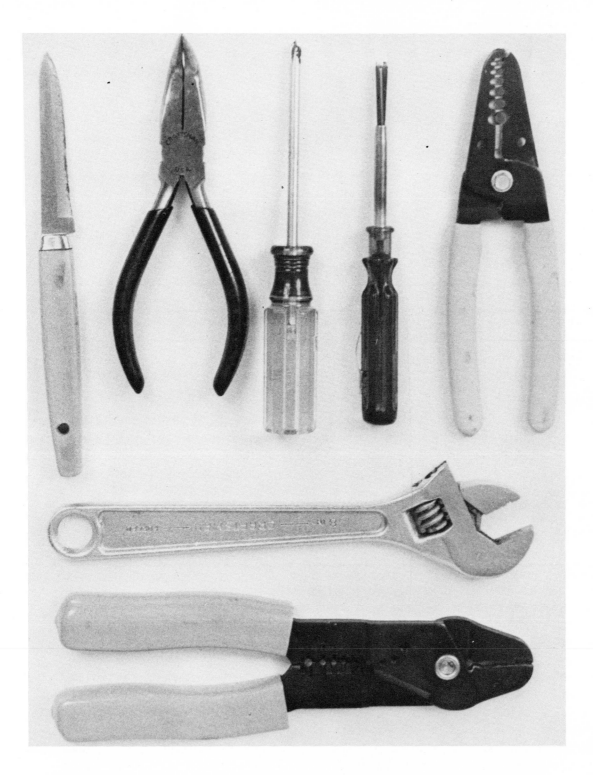

An assortment of useful tools for building your layout. From the left: a paring knife which is useful in scraping wire insulation, a pair of needlenose pliers for tightening track pins, a small Phillips head screwdriver for removing loco chassis from the superstructure, a screwdriver with screwholding attachment, and a wire stripper. The bottom row shows an adjustable crescent wrench and a crimping tool for use with solderless connectors. This crimping tool is essential for proper tightness.

have a short circuit. If the loco light does not shine, and the transformer does *not* change its steady hum as you increase the voltage flow to the track, then you do not have a short. The engine bulb may be loose, burned out, or even missing.

Occasionally, shorts will result in visible sparks; with other shorts there will be no sparking. With a major short (one in which there is too much current flowing) the transformer's hum will be altered. Learn to listen to your transformer; it has many secrets to tell you.

Short circuits occur in toy train operation when there is an excessively heavy flow of electricity. The current flows too heavily between the two poles, positive and negative. For example, a piece of metal or wire between the center rail and the outside rails will cause a short; a piece of wire touching posts A and U (or B and U) on Lionel transformers will cause a short. Since a great deal of electricity is involved in this flow, such a short circuit will generate considerable heat. This heat can cause damage. Inside the transformer, the heat will melt the thin coating of enamel insulation on the copper wire windings. This will cause additional shorting, with additional heat, until the transformer begins to get very hot and starts to smoke.

Testing the voltage using a bulb socket with bulb. This technique will help you rapidly identify the problem in your layout. You can test the transformer, then you can test a section of track and then another section of track.

Usually by that point, your transformer is ruined. Transformers often have circuit breakers which are supposed to prevent too much current from flowing. These circuit-breaker units, however, are not always dependable. Small circuit breakers suitable for your model railroad are readily available at an electrical supply store.

If your loco light shines brightly but the engine does not go either forward or backward, generally one of three situations is involved. Most likely, the locomotive reversing unit is in neutral and by breaking the current to the locomotive, the reversing unit will sequence to either forward or reverse when the current flow resumes. The solution is to interrupt the current flow by briskly turning the speed controller to zero and then back on again—or by pushing the direction button (if your transformer is so equipped). If all is well, the loco will then begin to move either forward or backward. (Note that pushing the direction button, or turning the speed control off and on, will cause the loco to return to neutral. Interrupting the current again will cause the loco to move in the other direction.)

Most Lionel and American Flyer engines have a three-position reversing mechanism. The sequence is: forward, neutral, reverse, neutral, forward, neutral, reverse, etc. Thus, when you place the engine on the track it may be geared in forward, neutral, or reverse. If in neutral, all that is required is interruption of the circuit to continue the sequence. The current may be interrupted by turning the speed control to "off" and then turning it back on. Or, the current may be interrupted by pressing the direction button that can be found on most transformers.

Most Lionel and American Flyer engines with three-position reversing units also have a mechanism—usually a lever—for locking the engine in either forward, neutral, or reverse. When the engine is in the desired phase, the lever is simply pushed to its other position, locking out the sequencing device. It is possible that if your engine refuses to go through the normal sequence of motions, it may be locked into one

position. If so, you should locate the reversing sequence lever and push it to the other side.

Most Marx engines, and some Lionel engines, have a two-position reversing unit (forward, reverse, forward, reverse, etc.). The Lionel engines usually have a lever for locking the reverse unit in one direction or the other.

Let's assume that your locomotive engine is functioning properly. It reverses on command and accelerates smoothly as power is applied. At this point, you should also place the tender (coal car) and the remainder of your rolling stock on the track. Turn the power off and push your train by hand around the layout. You may have inadequate clearance (either on the sides or overhead) or a track curve may be too tight; it's better to make these discoveries through a slow-speed encounter rather than a high-speed wreck.

Toy trains—just like real ones—will derail on many curves due to excessive speed. The crucial issue is determining the appropriate speed for a given curvature. For example, Lionel O-27 gauge trackage has tight curves. *Some* equipment will derail at any immodest speed. Other equipment (such as the GM 1000 series switch engines) will take these curves at a relatively fast speed without derailment.

A solution to curve derailments, obviously, is a more gentle curve. O-gauge track with its less severe curvature (31-inch diameter) is less prone to derailments. Train stability with both O-gauge and O-27 gauge can be improved by placing straight track sections in between the curved sections. Another solution is to use Gargraves brand of "flexible" track and bend it into a gentle curve. (Satisfactory results will require considerable patience and practice.)

A third solution is to use Lionel O-72 gauge track (or the O-72 gauge track currently being manufactured by Andrew Kriswallis of Endicott, New York). A circle of this track has a 72-inch diameter, rather than the 31-inch diameter of regular O-gauge. It mates perfectly, however, with O-gauge. With O-72 gauge track it is possible to run most toy train equipment at "wide open" speeds without derailment prob-

	SHORT CIRCUIT	Operate transformer 10 seconds or less	Check for derailed cars	Check wires to track	Check power on track with test bulb or lighted car.	Change loco E unit position	Check loco bulb	Push train on track
Transformer hums normally. Loco does not light; loco does not run.				X	X	X	X	X
Transformer is THROBBING and not humming normally. Loco does not hum and does not run.	X	X	X		*Find source of short!*			
Transformer hums normally. Loco lights, does not run, does not hum.						X		
Transformer THROBS. Loco lights dimly, loco hums, does not run.	X	X	X		*Find source of short!*			
Transformer hums normally. Loco runs, does not light.							X	
Transformer hums normally. Loco runs only one direction; loco lights.						X		
Transformer hums normally. Loco lights and hums, does not run.						X		

lems. It can be quite exciting to watch your trains move so rapidly—even if they are not performing a "scale" operation.

The Marx Company at one time made 34-inch diameter track of the height and weight of O-27 gauge. This track is occasionally available at train meets and is very useful, especially since it may be acquired quite reasonably.

Just prior to World War II, American Flyer manufactured O-gauge track with a 40-inch diameter for its large sets.

Finally, it is possible to buy Standard gauge curve track very inexpensively—at less than 25¢ per section—and remount this 40-inch diameter curve track in O-gauge ties. Some rail end trimming will be necessary, however; use a hacksaw for this function.

Once your track has been tested and your

train has gone through its first trials, you will want to fasten the track to your board in a semipermanent manner. Before fastening the track, you may wish to paint the board a grass green and to paint a brown stripe for the simulation of trackbed.

To fasten the track, use the drill with the $1/16$-inch bit to make "starter holes" for the track screws. This is important since the screws are small and the plywood is hard. It is very difficult to drive in the screws without starter holes. Often the screwheads will become distorted. An alternative to drilling starter holes is to use a small nail (a 4d finishing nail) to start the hole. Tap the nail through a hole in the track tie and then pull the nail out. If you drive the nail too far into the plywood you will have difficulty in pulling it out, and may damage the track section.

CHILDREN AND TOY TRAINS

NEW RECRUITS IN YOUR FANTASY WORLD

Toy trains have great potential as a valuable family activity. Children can share your fantasy in creating the world in miniature. They can learn the use of household tools while working on a genuine project. They can be trained in safety measures, train construction, operation, and repair, and learn the virtues of cooperation in a "construction" project.

Children will love sharing your fantasy world; they are probably already expert make-believers. They can help you create a story for your model railroad. Where is the train going? you can ask them. Where are all the people going after they ride the train? Is Mr. Smith going to see his niece and nephew? Is Mrs. Jones returning from a business trip to her country home?

Toy trains provide the potential for involving children as young as two years old. Reversing train direction and operating horns and whistles produce glee in children. Four year olds can be permitted to control speed and direction with adult supervision. The lure of speed, however, is too much for unsupervised four-year-olds. By the time children are eight or ten years old they are often ready for unsupervised use of the family train layout, if they have been previously trained. It is crucial to remember, however, to train them to turn off the power supply when a derailment or other malfunction occurs. Otherwise, short circuits may cause severe damage to the transformer, or cause fire or other hazards to your children and your toy train layout.

You know that construction of a model railroad layout involves the use of a number of tools: hammers, saws, screwdrivers, measuring devices, wire strippers, soldering irons, etc. The period in which you are constructing your layout is an excellent time to introduce these tools to your children, as long as they are old enough. Obviously, you should first assess each child's dexterity, degree of natural caution, and the level of risk involved. Some seven year olds have the dexterity and sense of caution to use potentially harmful tools such as pencil soldering irons with adult precision. Others do not.

Remember that children must be taught to follow directions. Children do not instinctively know how to use tools, nor do they instinctively know how or where a tool can hurt them. As a preliminary principle, children must be taught to follow your instructions precisely; this must be the prerequisite to participation.

Obviously, the larger gauge trains are more appealing for use with children than the small HO- or N-gauges. The track itself is larger and more durable, and rolling stock is easier to place on the rails, just as it is easier to couple. Toy train track is strong stuff: one classic Lionel ad from a half-century ago claimed that their track would support up to 50 pounds without buckling. The track withstands assembly and disassembly with only an occasional loose track pin. Most large trains also feature automatic uncoupling—an important aide for children.

As you plan the scenery for your model railroad, talk with your children about your plans. Explain that you want to create in miniature the buildings and other sights that are found along real railroads. Suggest that your model will not be exactly the same as the real thing but will be constructed to give the impression of the real thing. Try to explain the concept of an illusion.

Dollhouses, play schools, and airplanes, are illusions; they are "make-believes" made as real as possible. The dollhouse has a stove and refrigerator, but they do not cook or cool. Draw further analogies to toy cars and trucks. Toy cars are both similar to and dissimilar from real cars. Toy car tires are solid rubber; real car tires have air inside. Toy car headlights do not function. Toy car engines do not pollute our atmosphere with hydrocarbons.

Design your train layout so that your children can operate it with you. In chapter 8, which covers multiple train operation, the use of track "blocks" and cab control is discussed. This approach, with a transformer controlling each train, provides the maximum potential for shared operation with your children.

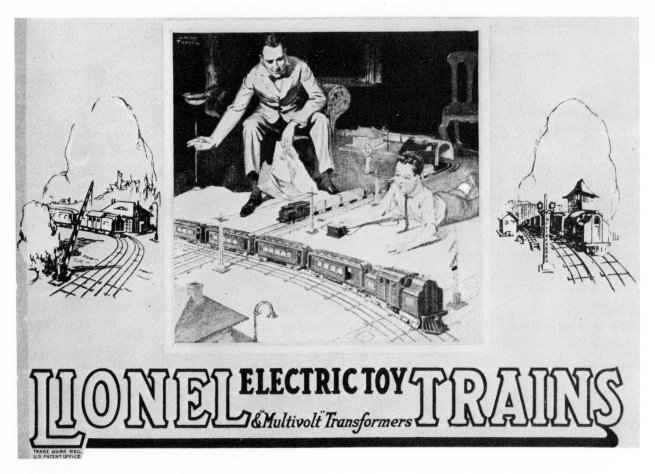

A classic Lionel catalogue cover warmly presenting Lionel's perception of model railroading as a desirable family hobby.

Switchyard operation—the "building" of trains through the shuffling and coupling of cars—is an ideal family activity. You and your children can prepare a list of cars to appear on the train and assign responsibilities: cab control of the road engine to one person, cab control of the switchyard engine to another person, and control over the switches and uncoupling sections to the yard tower to a third person. The train car roster can provoke a lively discussion. What is the cargo in the Conrail boxcar and who is receiving it? And what about those Santa Fe tankers? Now that the coal strike is over, who is getting that first shipment of UMW coal in our Burlington-Northern coal cars?

CLOCKWORK TRAINS FOR THE ROOKIES

In involving children with toy trains, it is crucial that the project demands be consistent with a child's capabilities. It is also most important that all items handed over to young children be impervious to damage. A mechanically powered train set (in which the engine is powered by a wound spring) is the wisest choice for a child of four years or younger, as long as the child can wind the spring alone. Trains powered by electrical transformers are definitely *not* recommended for children under eight. The combination of responsibility and operational complexity is simply too great a burden to place on

24

younger children. A transformer-powered train draws its power from regular house current, and short circuits can rapidly cause severe damage to the transformer. Even worse, a short can cause a fire. Unfortunately, situations which cause transformer shorting occur often, principally with the derailment of a train. Nevertheless, we urge you to let younger children operate your electrically powered trains—but in *your* presence, under *your* supervision.

Mechanically powered trains require only moderate preparations for track assembly, since the track fits together with relative ease. In contrast, transformer-powered track requires considerable care during installation (see chapter 2) so that the electrical current is carried around the entire track plan without interruption. Fortunately, Marx Trains for many years made clockwork sets ideally designed for children aged three to seven years. Many older Marx clockwork trains (so named for their internal spring-and-gears motor) from the 1930s through the 1950s, featured the Commodore Vanderbilt design. This was a streamline locomotive with a heavy-gauge stamped steel body. This loco came with three or four light tin lithographed cars. A new set, complete with a circle of track, sold for $1 or so when the set first came on the market, and last sold for less than $4. The stamped steel shell proved to be nearly indestructible. The cars, because of their box-like shape, survived well. The couplers were a sturdy metal hook-and-slot type which also were durable. Today at many train shows you can find a well-sratched set for less than $3, or a set which looks almost new for under $10. There still are great values in toy trains.

Sometime in the 1950s Marx replaced the Commodore Vanderbilt clockwork set with several others. The most common is a black plastic switch engine of 0-4-0 wheel arrangement which was available until the late 1960s in discount stores for about $5 (including three freight cars and a circle of track). These are still available nearly new in the original packing box for $5 to $7 at train shows, or for $1 and $2 in used and somewhat battered shape.

There are other clockwork and small battery sets available, but generally they do not have the durability of the Marx sets. Battery-operated sets are not recommended for children because of the relatively high operating costs of dry battery cells.

The Marx mechanical/clockwork sets originally were equipped with O-27 two-rail track (without a center rail); there remains no reason why these trains will not operate quite satisfactorily on O-gauge or O-27 three-rail track. If the seller does not include track with the set you buy, then you should buy three-rail O-27 or O-gauge track for your child's train layout (since this track will be usable later for electric trains).

When your children are seven or eight years old they will probably be ready for an electric train, particularly if you have your own train layout and have spent time together operating the equipment. Lionel today makes inexpensive starter sets, which can be purchased at discount department stores (or from mail order firms) for $25 or less. The starter sets manufactured by Lionel 30 years ago, however, can be purchased today at train shows in good used condition for between $10 and $15. Lionel also produced a "Scout Series" of locomotives and train sets; some of the Scout sets from 1947 to 1950 included heavyweight die-cast locos with motors on which maintenance and repairs were easy because they were not sealed-unit motors. Some of these loco numbers include 1001, 1010, and 1020, while the Lionel 240 series included equivalent loco models. With a little bargaining, these locos are available for between $2 and $10.

The original Scout sets came with "man-umatic" couplers, mechanically operated plastic coupler units. These were rather clumsy to operate, but were designed to be readily convertible to remote control (electromagnetic control). For this reason you may not find the original manumatic couplers on all Scout Series freight cars. A Scout set usually consisted of a locomotive, a tender, a gondola (usually No. 1002), a boxcar (usually No. 1004), tank car (usually No. 1005), and a caboose (usually No.

Marx made dependable and durable mechanically powered engines for many years. These are often available for a very nominal sum in good used condition at train shows. Three different varieties are illustrated here with the necessary key.

1007). These freight cars are exceedingly common and hard to sell at a decent price; they rarely cost more than $1 at train shows.

Children should be encouraged to respect their toys, to play with toys in a manner consistent with their design and function, and to put the toys away after use. For some children, this comes naturally. For many others, adult supervision, particularly at the beginning, is necessary to promote good and safe play habits.

You may find that your child plays very nicely with toys, including the train, when playing alone. However, when another child or several other children join the play, the quality of play may deteriorate and the toys become endangered. As a parent promoting good play habits you should plan to assist your child when other children are present.

HELPING YOUR CHILDREN TO HELP YOU

When beginning to construct your child's train layout, you may wish to assemble the track on the floor of the child's bedroom. If you do, track clips are an enormous help in holding the track together and preventing derailment. Lionel track clips are available both for O-gauge and O-27; Marx used to make track clips with a slightly different design from O-27, due to differing tie-design. Make sure you purchase the appropriate set of clips. (American Flyer also made clips for its S-gauge.)

Your child's train can be run around the bedroom and under the bed. It is delightful to watch the train disappear and then suddenly reappear at the other end of the "bed tunnel." Your child can easily integrate the toy trains with cars, trucks, Lego construction sets, doll houses, and so on. Children commonly are less inhibited than older folks in integrating what seem to be disparate game units. Children often use trains as part of their storytelling worlds.

Marx mechanical trains will climb modest grades. Show your children how to make grades using pieces of cardboard and small pieces of wood beneath the track. They may spend hours experimenting to determine the maximum grade their loco can climb, loaded and unloaded.

Children's layouts can involve engine houses made from shoe boxes, water towers consisting of a Quaker Oats box and a straw, a passenger station fashioned from a cardboard box with windows and doors cut out. (The Greenberg Publishing Co. offers a number of very inexpensive cardboard buildings and figures which children can cut out and place on their layout.)

Children can help you on your own layout, especially in such routine tasks as laying track. First, the track must be prepared, and young children can commonly handle the process of polishing rail and removing rust with fine emery paper. However, children should not be allowed to use the track cleaning solvents—even those which claim to be harmless. Children often put their fingers in their mouths and could easily transfer solvent to their mouths via their fingers. Solvents which are harmless to adults may be quite harmful to children, who metabolize foreign substances at much higher rates than adults.

Energetic seven- or eight-year-olds can handle a pair of small needle-nose pliers and apply the skill frequently since the track pins in used track regularly need to be tightened and replaced. Even a four-year-old can assist in the process of fastening track to the layout table by hammering the nail which is used to start a hole for the track screw. By the time a child is seven, he or she can hammer the nail and pull it out without your assistance. Even though your four-year-old may slow you down, he or she will immensely enjoy this participation. Your seven-year-old should be able to complete the process of screwing the track down to the surface.

THE FAMILY LINE

We also suggest involving the entire family in the fun project of creating your own "private label" freight train. Start by purchasing some inexpensive Lionel freight cars and join together in the chore of cleaning them. Jointly decide the new colors for each car and the color for the label lettering. Then run with your imaginations; create the imaginary companies through family consensus, incorporating familiar personalities and relatives from the make-believe work world. Your local pet store owner can have her own box car or Aunt Nellie's noodles can be shipped in a newly painted old Marx boxcar. Personalize your railroad with your family's help.

Your children also can be taught to buy wisely at train shows. Marx freight cars in moderately battered condition are still available for as little as 25¢ each. You can discuss with children the kinds of accessories and cars they want for their train layout, and then give them a nominal amount of money to fulfill these planned acquisitions.

Involving your children in train show purchases has additional benefits, as this experience whets their appetite for numbers, counting money, and making change. Since there usually are several different items from which to choose within a given price range, your child will also have to learn to select the best values.

When your child is about to graduate to electric trains (particularly to a first Scout set), you could suggest the sale of the clockwork set to help finance the purchase of the electric set. Your child will then absorb the experience of being the seller and seeking the best market price by emphasizing the train set's positive features.

Everyone benefits when the entire family is involved in model railroading. Skills are learned, confidences grow, the joys of sharing are achieved, a life-long hobby is kindled, and family unity and harmony is promoted. If you don't have a family, go out and borrow one from a friend or neighbor and get them *involved* in your toy train layout!

THE TOY TRAIN MARKETPLACE

This is the highly desirable Lionel Mickey and Minnie Mouse handcar. This windup toy came with a circle of track and originally sold for $1.00 from 1934 through 1937. It was a best-seller at the time.

The toy train marketplace is remarkably diverse. There are hobby shops, discount stores with model railroad departments, mail order firms, train shows, and "basement operators," all competing for your attention and dollars. At first glance, you may think there is a shortage of supply outlets; after you have become involved in the hobby, you will be impressed with the generous variety of sources.

The hobby shop has long been the backbone of the toy train industry. Even small communities of 5,000 people or fewer may have a local hobby shop. Usually, these are "Mom and Pop" businesses owned and operated by the people who greet you by name from behind the counter. They offer personal service, information, and sometimes a genuine variety of merchandise. Some Mom and Pop hobby shops specialize in model railroading. These shops often have enormous inventories of trains, parts, accessories, scenery, and building materials. You are fortunate if there is such a railroad specialty store nearby.

Hobby shops do have competition, however. One source is the discount department store with a hobby department. These stores are usually able to sell all merchandise for an average of between 20 and 40 percent less than the small hobby shop. But compared to the hobby shop, the discount store normally stocks only a thin selection of train items. Many of the lesser materials—bulbs, accessories, hardware, and even track—are not to be found at the discount stores. Nor do these stores generally have the trained, informed personnel that the hobby shop offers. On the other hand, the lower prices can be quite attractive; the local hobby shop is essential to the hobby, but many of the big dollar purchases go to the discount department stores.

Mail order sources are crucial to the toy train hobby. Several of these operations had substantial mail order catalogues as early as the 1930s. Lately we have witnessed the emergence of aggressive price competition in the mail order business. Prices have been pushed down to the point where they commonly are the same as those paid by the retailer, i.e., wholesale prices. Price competition is most strenuous in the new Lionel equipment; on most other items, retailers are usually able to make a fair profit. But mail order firms offer a more limited range of materials than does the hobby shop, and often do not carry the minor items which the individual hobbyist may urgently need.

Some of the mail order firms provide very rapid service: two or three days to fill an order once received; regretably, others take three or four weeks to respond. And these firms do not always have all the items which they advertise; they, too, have supply problems. Most of the mail order firms are reputable and reliable operations. For references, contact the publishers of *Model Railroader* or *Railroad Model Craftsman* or consult a colleague.

Some mail order firms will hold your order until your personal check clears the bank; others do not have this policy. You may wish to ask your specific supplier about their policy. Of course, postal money orders or bank drafts are always gladly accepted; some firms even accept VISA or Master Charge. The consumer in these cases supplies his number, expiration date, and card type to the supplier in a letter or phone call (without actually relinquishing the card to the supplier). The amount of the purchase is then authorized by the shipper. Under federal law, as a consumer you may reject the billing if you are dissatisfied with the transaction. It is therefore probably safer to buy model train equipment using a charge card through the mail than it is to send a check or money order.

Some mail order firms deal strictly with new equipment, while others deal solely in used equipment, and others deal in both. The purchase of new trains by mail involves very little possibility of misunderstanding. If a new Lionel train is defective, the mail order seller will take it back and send you another.

Used toy train purchases through the mails, however, present a significant potential for misunderstanding. There are several types of problems. The seller may describe the exterior condition as "excellent" but the buyer may perceive it only as "good." (The Train Collectors Association has developed a set of categories for grading equipment.) The train may have replacement parts (not noted by the seller) rather than the original parts. Or the train may not run once it has been received. If the seller has been recommended to you, then you are taking no more than a "reasonable" risk in purchasing used trains through the mail. If you do not have a personal reference on the seller, however, you may be taking a substantial risk. You should be certain that in any mail order purchase you have the unconditional right to return the merchandise for a full refund of the purchase price if you are not satisfied.

The Train Collectors Association, the Toy Train Operating Society, and the Lionel Collectors Club each seek to help solve disputes between members over transactions. However, these organizations do not see their function as policing the marketplace; at best, their intervention should be viewed in the role of conciliator rather than referee.

TRAIN SHOWS

Toy train shows are a vital part of the toy train marketplace. In recent years, these shows have grown enormously in size, with several shows regularly attracting more than 5,000 people and offering many thousands of trains for sale. These events are in some ways a gathering of the clan, with train enthusiasts coming from all over the country for the large ones.

These large shows—such as the members-only show at York, Pennsylvania, twice a year, the Cal Stewart meet on the West Coast, and the public Greenberg's Great Train Show in Towson, Maryland, four times a year—are remarkable feasts for the eyes. They feature many thousands of trains of all descriptions, including O-gauge, HO, Standard, new and used, antique and modern.[1] The finest and rarest equipment often surfaces at these shows for sale. The large shows are ideal places to find common equipment as well as excellent pieces at modest prices.

In addition to these giant shows, there are

hundreds of small and medium-sized shows held each year throughout the nation. Sometimes these are advertised in railroad magazines. Sometimes local hobby shops will feature fliers in their windows or at their counters. In most cases, active collectors and operators will know the details on the next local train show. And at most shows there will be fliers heralding other nearby shows. In other words, once you find one train show, you'll be able to find the others.

Train shows have their own peculiar etiquette and customs. As with most "collectibles," it is expected that visitors will ask permission to handle an item. Although this varies from seller to seller, prices generally are negotiable. Some sellers set a price by which they stand "come hell or high water." Others are quite ready to negotiate, particularly as the time to pack up and go back home draws near.

Most of the train show sellers are honest people. Few of them engage in intentional deception, such as touting a common piece as a rare one or trying to sell a restoration piece as an original. The odds are quite high that such deception will work against the seller sooner or later. Nevertheless, the buyer should always be prudent. Look carefully at potential purchases, and be knowledgeable about price guidelines as published in *Greenberg's Price Guide to Lionel Trains*.

If you are making a major purchase, you should have the assistance of a more knowledgeable train enthusiast, preferably one who owns one of the same pieces that you are considering purchasing. Particular pieces have idiosyncracies—hidden parts, common flaws, particular operating difficulties.[2]

Many sellers at train shows are reluctant to take checks from strangers; it is wise to bring cash or travelers' checks. Some of the professional dealers do accept credit cards, especially Master Charge, VISA, and Bank Americard.

Train show prices are usually quite competitive since there often will be several of the same pieces in the hall or items which can readily be substituted for them. Prices are almost invariably lower, for example, than in hobby shops, discount department stores, or mail order firms—primarily because of the low overhead costs.

Train shows also are fun for nearly everyone involved. You meet people who share your interest for toy trains, shared interest being the prime ingredient that makes these events enjoyable. Literature is often on display, as are parts and tools in great variety.

Most of the sellers at train shows are amateurs. They are people who buy and sell trains and train parts to support their own collections. Some are semiprofessionals for whom profit is the prime consideration. A small number are professionals whose livelihoods are dependent on the toy train marketplace. The role of amateurs is very important in giving this marketplace a friendly character. The amateurs are there for fun, to have a good time, to make a few bucks. The professionals have an important role in that they provide new Lionel equipment at very low prices. Some professionals also specialize in rare and exotic pieces, providing buyer access to these pieces as well as an outlet for those seeking to sell major collections.[3]

The toy train clubs sponsor train shows frequently. The Train Collectors Association, the largest of these clubs, sponsors numerous shows every month nationwide. You must be a member or a guest of a member to attend these shows, however. The national office of the TCA in Strasburg, Pennsylvania, can provide you with the names of local members.

The Toy Train Operating Society, the nation's second largest toy train club, sponsors

[1] These shows commonly feature primarily "tinplate," (Lionel, American Flyer, Marx, or Ives) or they offer mainly HO scale with some O-scale; there is, however, occasional cross-pollination.

[2] Several years ago I myself bought an unusually fine and rare piece from a noted dealer. Unfortunately, I had never before owned such a piece, and I was sold a reproduction Lionel No. 7 locomotive as an original. Had I previously owned one, or benefited from the counsel of a previous owner, the subtle distinguishing marks of the reproduction would have been strikingly apparent.

[3] Test tracks are now a common feature at many train shows. Track strips of a variety of gauges are provided with power supplies, and prospective buyers are allowed to test equipment for operation. It is highly recommended that you use these tracks if available.

shows which are generally open to the public for a nominal fee. Admission to the shows sponsored by the Lionel Collectors Club of America (LCCA) is restricted to members only. Many other shows are sponsored by private entrepreneurs; in the New York City metropolitan area there are at least ten separate proprietary meets each year. Other frequent sponsors are the National Model Railroad Association and the Marklin Enthusiasts of America.

THE PAST AS GUIDE TO THE FUTURE

Toy train values have steadily increased over the last 30 years. However, the increases have not been uniform and some items have reflected much greater appreciation than others. Generally, the top-of-the-line pieces have shown the most appreciation; these pieces have mostly been the "most attractive" pieces, or at least the most ornate. Most collectors wanted these top-of-the-line pieces in their youth but had to settle for less. Some of them, now adults with regular incomes, have decided to fulfill their childhood desires; thus, demand for these top-of-the-line pieces exceeds supply and the price goes up.

Clearly, this "generational" source of the demand for toy trains is significant; the principal buyers today are men in their mid-twenties through late-thirties who are buying what they wanted as boys. Thus it is that the items showing the greatest appreciation at any given time are those that were manufactured 15 to 25 years earlier. The "hot" items of today are the top-of-the-line Lionel equipment from the early and mid 1950s. It is also suspected that the greatest growth in appreciation of the Lionel top-of-the-line Standard from the mid-1930s—the 400E, the 381, and the 408—is past.[4] The earlier Lionel Standard-gauge from the 20s and the preceding decade has shown relatively small appreciation in the last 5 to 10 years because so few new buyers are interested in this early equipment.

Substantial appreciation has been observed sometimes on low-cost items where there was a particular attractiveness to the item. The most dramatic examples are the Walt Disney handcar items from the 1930s made by Lionel, featuring Mickey and Minnie, Pluto, Santa Claus, and Peter Rabbit. These items, which originally sold for a dollar or so, now bring at least $250 each if they are in fine or excellent condition. But attractiveness is only part of the reason for this appreciation. Another source of demand is generated by collectors of Disneyana, who inflate the demand for these handcars. Also, these items were inexpensively manufactured and easily damaged or destroyed by children; hence the supply has been reduced.

Another factor affecting appreciation is whether the piece was popular when it was issued. For example, certain road names in the Lionel F-3 diesel series were not popular when they were made in the 1950s (such as the Illinois Central and Western Pacific), although they were top-of-the-line productions. Their lack of popularity and high production status, however, have now made these two engines among the most desirable of the era.

As we have indicated with the Disney handcars, demand which cuts across several collectors' fields creates pressures for strong upward price movement. A further example of this is the demand for the Lionel 700-E scale Hudson locomotive and the 773 scale Hudson. Both pieces appeal not only to toy train collectors but also to scale modelers. This aggregated demand has driven the price for an excellent-condition 700 E above $1,500, while the less detailed and later 773 brings $450 in excellent condition.

Even if they are not particularly popular, it is worth considering top-of-the-line items as possible investments. Do not select your investments solely on the basis of road-name popularity. The service station specials of the past five years (which were top-of-the-line items made in relatively small quantities) are now appreciating rapidly. Look for inexpensive items

---

[4] Of course, in the case of the 381 and the 408 there is a complicating factor, namely the fine reproductions which are manufactured by Williams Reproductions, Ltd., 7925 Hammond Parkway, Laurel, Md. 20810.

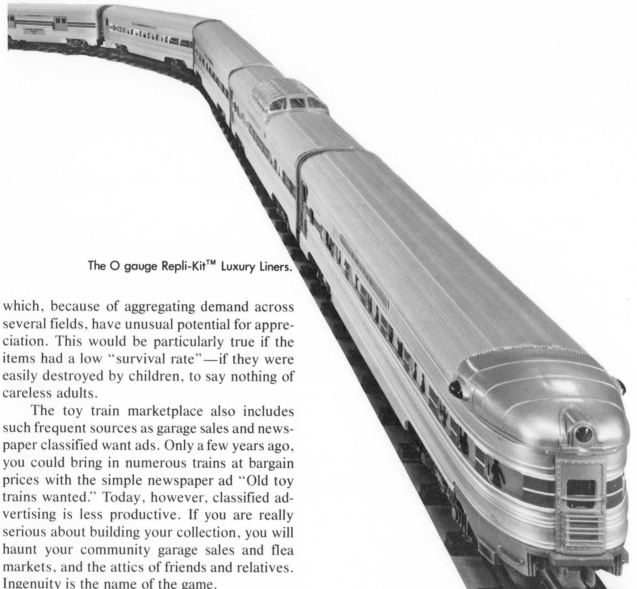

The O gauge Repli-Kit™ Luxury Liners.

which, because of aggregating demand across several fields, have unusual potential for appreciation. This would be particularly true if the items had a low "survival rate"—if they were easily destroyed by children, to say nothing of careless adults.

The toy train marketplace also includes such frequent sources as garage sales and newspaper classified want ads. Only a few years ago, you could bring in numerous trains at bargain prices with the simple newspaper ad "Old toy trains wanted." Today, however, classified advertising is less productive. If you are really serious about building your collection, you will haunt your community garage sales and flea markets, and the attics of friends and relatives. Ingenuity is the name of the game.

A basic dilemma arises from the fact that although there are many thousands of train sets stored in attics, basements, and garages across the country, people rarely want to sell them since they have learned that "trains are valuable." The truth is that while trains have increased in value (and a few locos are worth more than $500 each), most trains have only modest value. This illusion of swollen value, however, has fostered hoarding.

REPRODUCTIONS AND REISSUES

As in almost all fields of collectibles, when the price of the original becomes sufficiently high, an entrepreneur will offer a reproduction for sale, or the original manufacturer will produce a reissue. In the field of toy trains, Williams Reproductions, Ltd., of Laurel, Maryland, in 1973 issued a reproduction of the highly desirable and very scarce Lionel Standard-gauge No. 9 electric engine. The original was selling at that point for about $600; Williams's first-rate reproduction was an instant success at $160 (without a motor). Subsequently, Williams offered a reproduction of the desirable and scarce Lionel 381 Standard-gauge locomotive. This model by Lionel was a credible interpretation of the famous electric Olympian locomotive, with pleasant proportions and handsome trimmings. Since the Lionel original was selling for nearly $2,000 in excellent condition at that time, Williams's $295 reproduction was enthusiastically received. He rapidly sold out his 381's, made more, and quickly sold them out, too. Williams subsequently produced the dual-motored Lionel 408E which was the most powerful locomotive in the Standard-gauge line, and offered his reproduction at about $250.

Williams has been busy with O-gauge, too. In 1975 he reproduced Lionel's large, extruded aluminum passenger cars from the 1950s. These cars were offered in the less common road names (Canadian Pacific and Santa Fe) and in the special Pennsylvania Congressional sets. These cars are excellent reproductions but lack the operating couplers found in the originals. These items rapidly sold out to both collectors and operators, since the originals were going for nearly $100 each (in mint condition) and Williams's price was $30 or so. The handsome brown Pullman passenger cars named Irvington, Madison, and Manhattan have been excellently reproduced by Edward Kramer, of Fairfield, New Jersey, as well as by Williams, who sells his copies at about $35, half the market value of $70 for an original in excellent condition.[5]

In 1970, when Fundimensions began producing Lionel trains under license from the Lionel Toy Co., they continued making many of the items in the Lionel line, while changing some of the actual numbers in the Lionel series (e.g., the No. 6464 boxcar series became the No. 9200 series). Observing the growing interest in older Lionel products, Fundimensions in the early 1970s began reissuing items not manufactured for many years. Fortunately, this gamble proved successful and Fundimensions since has reissued many significant items.

Perhaps the most important reissue has been that of the GG-1 locomotive. The GG-1 is the long-lived and famous Pennsylvania Railroad electric engine which appeared in the Lionel line in 1947 as the 2332, in 1950 as the 2330, in 1955 as the 2340, and in 1956 as the 2360. Some of these models were bringing $350 to $400 in excellent condition when the GG-1 was reissued by Lionel as the 8753. (Williams has brought out a fine reproduction of the GG-1 at a somewhat lower price than Lionel's.) Lionel has reissued the Civil War era General from the late 1950s as the No. 3; the Virginian Rectifier Electric was reissued in 1976 and 1977 as No. 8659. The company also has reissued the Pennsylvania 2352 and the popular line of Budd self-powered passenger cars.

Some people object to reproductions and reissues in the belief that their investments will not continue to appreciate, and may even decline. It should be clear from this analysis of toy train values that the reproduction or reissue of an item *does* stabilize the price and even occasionally causes a short-term price dip.

In recent years we have witnessed the emergence of a mixed breed, the restoration repaint model. Many Lionel diesels from the mid-50s share the same bodies, differing only in coloring and lettering. Consequently, train rebuilders have refashioned Santa Fe F-3's into, for example, the more scarce and valuable Canadian Pacific and Western Pacific engines. One firm owned by Ed Kraemer has turned out many such pieces. Kraemer has provided a list of his products with instructions on how to distinguish them from the originals.

From the point of view of most consumers, however, reproductions and reissues are a great boon. These new items make available the great trains of the near and distant past at more affordable prices. More than 900 persons (this author included) now enjoy the elegant No. 381 with sparkling brass and copper trim, having paid a price which is equivalent to its original price nearly half a century ago which was one week's income for a middle-class family in 1929. The availability of a substitute at a more moderate price means that some of the demand for the original is absorbed, thus keeping the price of the original within the range of more consumers.

---

[5] Usually restorations are marked with identification tags, which can be TCA tags or even a piece of tape or other more casual indicator. However, there do exist unmarked restorations. If you are paying the price for an "excellent" original piece and have some concern as to its status as an original, it is wise to seek expert advice. (Several professional restorers, whose work is so good that it cannot be distinguished from the originals, do not use labels. It is therefore acknowledged that human greed can invade the fragile realm of toy trains.)

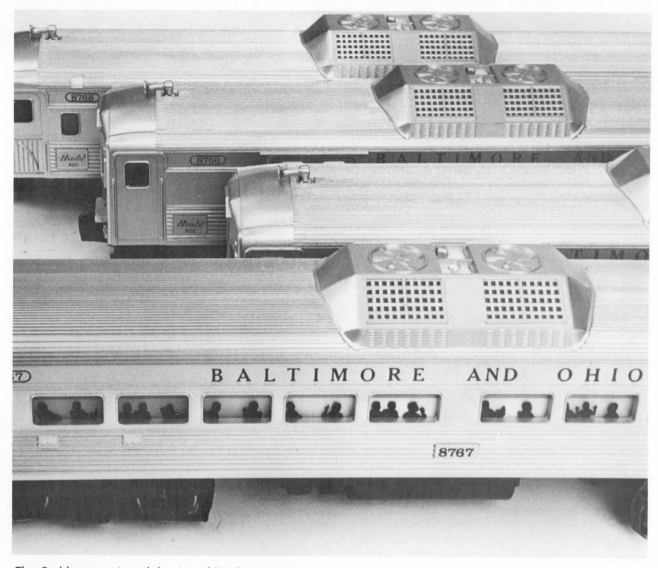

The Budd cars reissued by Lionel-Fundimensions in 1977. These cars carry the numbers 8766, 8767, and 8768. The original Budd cars were numbered 400, 404, 2550 and 2559. The originals are worth more than the reissues.

Finally, reproductions and reissues simply mean that more goods are available to more people (and the toy train items which are now being reproduced and reissued were of generally high quality and very popular when first manufactured years ago). The more these items become available, the more people can enjoy them, and the more our hobby of model railroading will grow.

Today, reissues and reproductions are a significant portion of the model railroad marketplace. It can be expected that the magnificent Lionel state cars from the 1930s will be reproduced. The Fairbanks-Morse diesels, the No. 746, and the scale model Hudson No. 773 are also likely to reappear in some form within the next few years.

Some items are likely *not* to reappear. One such item is the very powerful and useful "ZW" transformer made by Lionel. This large unit (rated at 250 watts) was capable of running four trains at once but now has been rated as "too dangerous" by the Consumer Products Safety Commission (although this author has yet to hear of any injury caused by this transformer).

IMAGINATION AND TABLE DESIGN

The well-known Lionel milk car. A worker, dressed in white, delivers the milk containers on the press of a button. This car was one of Lionel's most successful accessory items. If the milk cans are inserted incorrectly, it will jam. However, this is easily remedied by removing the car top either by taking out screws on the end or removing spring clips from the bottom.

It is helpful to begin this chapter by imagining an ideal model train layout. Take a theme and build a miniature world, along with suggestions as to how it might be outfitted. Then become familiar with the concepts of open-top and closed-top table designs and their pros and cons.

There is a relationship between the theme of your railroad and the type of layout table you choose, and some themes call for certain types of table construction. You should learn the concept of multiple train operation as it relates to layouts, and will hopefully appreciate the number of track plans provided in detail in this chapter.

There are four elements to consider here: theme, the appropriate construction technique (in relation to theme and available space), mul-

tiple train operation, and the appropriate track plan. You should integrate each of these elements into a well-considered building plan, and this integration should lead you to complete a highly satisfying layout.

One of the true pleasures of layout construction is in dreaming up your own railroad empire. You may decide upon an urban theme with a traditional grid pattern of houses, stores, and factories, with the railroad diagonally bisecting the community and with a large railroad yard in a setting of structures and motor vehicles. In this world there will be necessarily limited green areas. The pleasure lies in creating and admiring the building facades and street activities. A city will need a trolley line to carry local riders efficiently (several Lionel No. 60 trolleys would fill the bill). There also could be an elevated commuter line that stretches from the heart of the city to the suburbs (over the horizon), and Lionel "Budd" cars which are now again available commercially would be ideal for this line.

Some of the city's major industries could be dependent upon the Lionel accessories of 20 years ago, along with a sprinkling of some of the newer selections. There should be a coal yard, with one or more pieces of coal-moving equipment: the No. 397 coal tower, the No. 497 diesel loader, or the No. 356 coaling ramp. One or more sidings should be provided for servicing these facilities. You might use a Lionel diesel fueling station for your diesel locomotives; a bulk oil storage depot could be located in an adjacent area. Coal trucks and oil trucks from the appropriate period should be visible loading coal and oil from the yards and making deliveries to the city's furnaces and factories.

Your layout can easily reflect a particular period in American history; it could be in the Roaring Twenties or the Great Depression, the Korean War era or "modern times" in the 1970s. Once you've made this decision, then you can choose motor vehicles, building facades, and railroad rolling stock appropriate to your era. However, you can just as easily choose not to be bound by a historical period for your layout.

You might choose the 1930s, when coal was still king of the energy scene; you can construct a world centered around black gold. Imagine a huge coal-fired generating plant carrying the high voltage electricity to the city in the distance. You may be fortunate enough to own the magnificent Lionel No. 840 power station from the early 30s. The Standard-gauge electrical towers were recently reproduced and can be found in most toy train marketplaces. There should be a large coal pile adjoining the station and a siding for hopper cars to deliver the coal. With a little construction effort on your part, the siding could become elevated; the Lionel coal ramp No. 456 is commonly seen at train shows for between $25 and $30. The matching Lionel hopper car with doors opening from the bottom should cost no more than $10. If you do not feel

you need an operating hopper car, standard versions are available for $3.

As already mentioned, the energy focus of your railroad empire could be oil rather than coal. Oil derricks, an oil refinery, gas stations, fuel trucks, and a diesel fueling station could be just part of your industrial layout. Lionel manufactured a handsome operating oil derrick (No. 455) in the mid-50s, which is generally trouble-free and available for between $40 and $60 at train shows.

Building your own oil refinery can be a satisfying project. A refinery will need a number of large tanks for oil storage and many pipes will be crisscrossing the refinery acreage. Coffee cans or oatmeal boxes make great tanks, and soda straws can serve as pipelines. The "cracking" tower can be constructed from the cardboard tubes found in toilet tissue or paper toweling; the smaller cores from adding machine tapes also can be useful. Put a bit of glue on the bottom of your tube and fasten it to a heavy cardboard base. An oil refinery often receives raw materials from oceangoing tankers. In this case, an open-top table design will give you the opportunity to add a river or bay harbor to your layout, with tankers docked to unload their cargo. (Make sure that your model boats, however, are the same scale as your train set.)

You may prefer the prairie setting and the large open spaces of the Midwest and Far West. Sleek, modern passenger trains cross the prairie, rushing through the nodding little towns along the way. Cattle and horses graze in pasture along the right-of-way. Large barns and huge silos store the grains from the fields for winter feeding. Plasticville farm buildings would fit in here, as would Lionel's new grain elevator (No. 2796) priced at $10 to $12. Such small towns in middle America often consist of no more than a block of stores: commonly a dry goods store, a hardware store, a drug store, and a luncheonette. The Lionel diner or the Williams diner model would be appropriate in this setting. A church might appear along with some small houses on the street behind Main Street, and on the outskirts of town there might

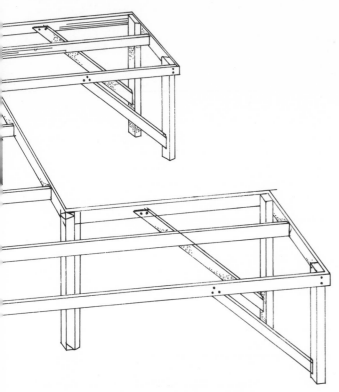

An open top "U" shape perimeter table.

be a large Victorian farmhouse. Mid-50s autos and trucks would add a nice touch.

These towns often serve as the marketplace for hogs, sheep, or cattle. Thus the Lionel cattle car and pen (No. 3356) could be worked into the slaughterhouse near the town. Dairy products could also be a staple of your local economy. A milk processing plant could be serviced by a string of Lionel operating milk cars with platforms (Nos. 3462, 3472, or 3482).

Alternatively, you might wish to model your layout after suburban America of the 1920s or 1930s. The Lionel bungalows and villas of the early 30s are quite attractive. The Skyline Com-

A closed-top table design.

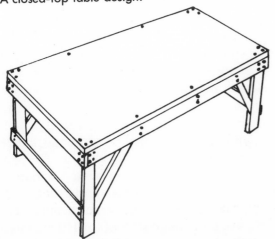

pany also made attractive buildings both of paper and metal relating to the same period. Lionel's handsome plastic kit of the Rico station (No. 2797) might be a welcome addition for $10 to $12. Your locomotives would be steam-powered and could include the early stream-lined locos and diesels (if you have moved into the late 30s) such as the Hiawatha, the Burlington Zephyr, or the Yankee Flier. Of course, your trucks and autos should match; some fine models of classic 20s autos are now being produced. The Lionel passenger cars could include the Madison, the Irvington, or the Manhattan (Nos. 2627, 2625, and 2678, respectively), or you could save money by substituting the Williams reproductions either in Pennsy brown or New York Central green.

DESIGNS FOR TRAIN TABLES

Basically, there are only two table shapes. There are tables which go around the perimeter of a room, and there are rectangular tables which stand to one side of the room (or occupy most of the room). Of course, the two can be combined within one room.

There are two basic table surface styles: the closed-top and the open-top. The former usually consists of a large piece of plywood laid upon a frame. Open-top tables consist of a frame without a top; boards are laid over the frame to support the track and large accessories, while the gaps are filled by scenery—screening covered with papier-mâché and plaster. Of course, it is quite possible to have a table top which is partly open and partly closed.

A variety of combinations is possible. The most common train table currently is a rectangular one with a closed top, although rectangular open-top tables are also popular. The rectangular tables may have an open top in one section and a closed top in the other. It is also feasible to build perimeter tables with closed tops and/or open tops, or sections of each.

Each style has its own peculiar advantages. A closed-top table clearly is faster to construct. There is a single flat surface on which to lay track, place accessories, and create scenery. But closed-top tables usually are more expensive since they use more wood per square foot of layout.

Perhaps the strongest argument behind construction of an open-top layout is the fact that the world is not flat, and you will want your layout to reflect reality. Even the Great Plains have dips and valleys, slopes, and hills. Such diversity dramatically enhances the appeal of your train layout. And with an open-top layout it is much easier to have multiple track crossings, in which one track glides on trestles or bridges over another track beneath. This is because the safe rate of climb or decline of most model railroad equipment is ½ inch per foot of track. If your Lionel equipment needs four inches of clearance over a track which is fixed below, the higher track will need at least eight feet to make the clearance climb. Open-top designs allow one track to fall while the other is climbing, thus requiring only four feet to accomplish a crossing.

Perimeter layouts provide longer operating runs. The train actually can take several minutes to complete its circuit. (A sophisticated timetable also can be developed in which one second equals one minute of real time and the entire trip represents perhaps two hours.) While one train is completing the layout circuit, you can be conducting switching operations in the freight yard and preparing a fast passenger train for departure. Furthermore, model trains function better on straight track as compared to curved track; you will notice that most derailments occur on curved track. Perimeter layouts also leave the center of most rooms free for other family activities. These layouts may be a bit more complicated to construct, depending on whether you can attach the layout to the room walls. If you can use the walls for support, then the perimeter layout will use less lumber and be easier to construct than a free-standing table.

Perimeter layouts, of course, do have their limitations. A relatively narrow layout greatly limits the amount of scenery you can fashion.

For example, a 24-inch-wide layout simply is not wide enough to develop a dynamic switchyard.

As you may have guessed, a combined strategy is preferable in dealing with these issues. Why not build a rectangular table at one end of your attic (or basement) and run a narrow perimeter layout around the rest of it? As few as six inches are needed for two perimeter tracks (as well as accomplished track work to avoid derailments and the consequent damage of trains landing on the floor). With a single-track line (and occasional passing sidings) you could have perimeter stretches as narrow as three inches! Indeed, you can tunnel under stairs and through walls (with the consent of your family). The train could even pass behind or over the washer and dryer in the laundry room.

Your rectangular table should have a piece of plywood covering part of its surface; the other section should be open-top. This latter portion could be utilized for mountain-building, and for a train overpass into a tunnel through the mountain. With your long, straight sections on the perimeter segment use a gentle grade to elevate the track so that it enters the mountain at an imagined height of 100 feet or so above the valley.

The closed-top section of your rectangular table could well serve as either a freight yard, a passenger yard, or both. If you construct a passenger terminal adjacent to your yard, you might consider elevating the terminal over the tracks, as is done in large urban terminals with the trains maneuvering at lower levels.

It should be evident that there is a solid relationship between the theme of your layout and the table shape and surface style. Clearly, if you wish to plan a large switching operation for complicated train movements, you will require a flat, open area. If you are planning to build a mountainous area with deep valleys and majestic bridges, then an open-top table is the only way to go. The Midwest prairie simulation would work well with a perimeter layout, complete with backdrop drawings of sky and grass.

Now that you know what goes into choos-

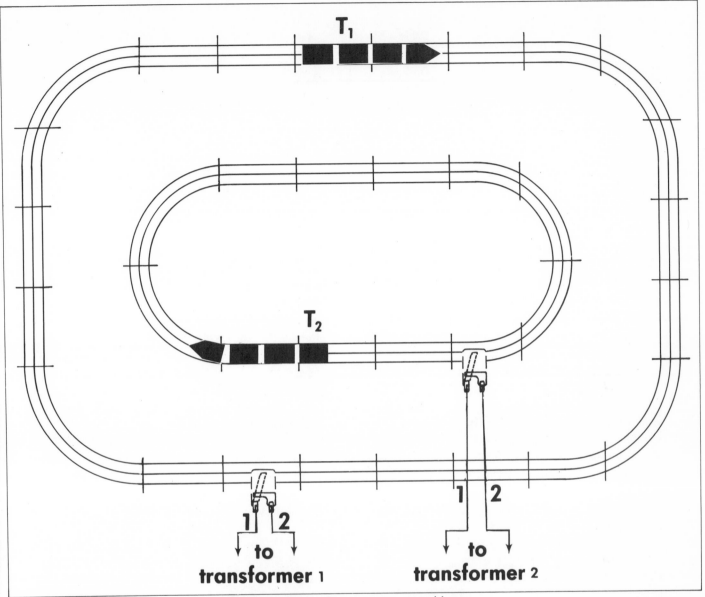

Figure 1   Simple track plan for two unconnected loops.

ing the appropriate table design, it's time to consider some track plans.

MULTIPLE TRAIN OPERATION
Part One

Perhaps the most universal requirement for a tinplate track plan is the ability to run two trains at one time. In this chapter we intend to introduce to you the basic concepts of wiring for two-train operation. Toward the end of the chapter the more complex track plans will be provided.

The simplest track plan for two-train operation consists of two loops that are not connected in any way (Figure 1). However, most people would surely get bored with running this layout in a short time. Therefore, the next logical thing

to do is to interconnect the two loops by adding two pairs of switches (Figure 2). Note that an insulating pin is needed only on the center rail where the two loops join if the two power supplies are wired in a "common ground" fashion. This is most easily accomplished by using a dual throttle transformer for both loops (such as the KW or ZW shown in Figure 2). It is also possible to use two separate transformers if they are both in phase. Phasing and other considerations for using transformers will be discussed in detail later in this chapter.

Adding the switches to connect the two loops makes swapping trains possible, but the simple wiring shown in Figure 2 makes it difficult at best. To see why, let's go through a swapping operation. Assume that the two trains

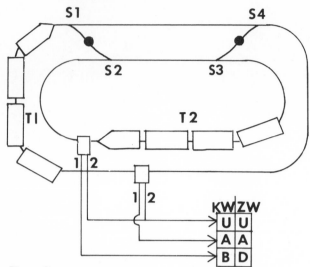

Figure 2

A track plan with switches to connect the two loops.

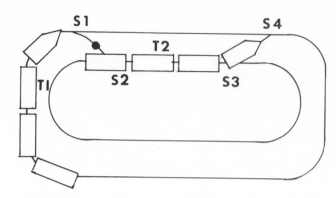

Figure 3   Train No. 2 at junction of the two loops.

are in the position shown in Figure 2 with the power to the outer loop off. Switches S3 and S4 are now turned to allow train 2 to move to the outer loop. When train 2 gets to the junction between the loops (Figure 3) the problems begin.

If the locomotive of train 1 does not have an E unit (such as the No. 55 tie jector or the No. 54 ballast tamper) or has only a two-position E unit (such as MPC Alco FA's or smaller steam engines) train 1 will begin to move when the outer loop power is turned on to allow train 2 to move onto the outer loop. If you plan to operate such locos, it is readily apparent that this type of wiring is not acceptable for swapping trains. However, to continue the discussion, let's assume that the locomotives of both trains have three-position E units. Then, when the outer loop power is turned on, train 1 will remain in place as train 2 moves onto the outer loop. When train 2 is past switch S4 the outer loop power is turned off (Figure 4).

Now we must move train 1 to the inner loop. However, when the outer loop power is turned on train 1 will be moving backwards. Therefore, one must *quickly* hit the direction button twice *and* turn switches S1, S2, and S3. This will result in train 1 moving forward into the inner loop and train 2 remaining in place. When train 1 is past S2, then S1, S2, and S4 can be turned back to their original positions. Both trains can resume continuous running now on different loops and under the control of different transformers or throttles.

Is this any way to run a railroad? It is extremely important that no short circuit occurs when making all of these moves as this would trip one or both of the E units. Once the E units are out of synchronization it will be extremely difficult to finish the swapping operation. A short circuit can occur if both the outer and inner loop voltages are not approximately equal when an engine is passing over the switches joining the two loops.

There must be a better way, you say? Fortunately, there are two better ways. The first method will be covered in the pages which follow, while the second, a preferable method, will be discussed later in this chapter. Figure 5 shows the wiring for an improved two train layout.

This requires one additional lock-on, two more insulating pins and two SPST toggle switches (X1 and X2). These switches may be purchased at any electronics supply store (such as Radio Shack), or you may use 364C controllers (available at Lionel Service Stations) if you believe in keeping things "all in the family." Let's go through a swapping operation with this new wiring. Assume the two trains and the toggle switches X1 and X2 are positioned as shown in Figure 6.

Because X1 is open, train 1 is at rest. As before, switches S3 and S4 are turned to allow train 2 to pass to the outer loop. However, this time when the outer loop power is turned on, train 1 is not affected since X-1 is open. After train 2 is past S4, train 2 can be turned on via X2 and train 1 can be turned on via X1 (Figure 7).

Now completing the operation is simply a matter of turning switches S1, S2, and S3, moving train 1 to the inner loop, restoring S1, S2, and S4, and closing X2.

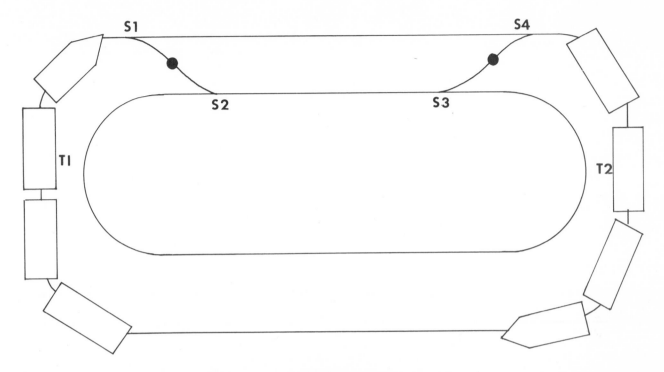

Figure 4   Train No. 2 past the switch, power turned off.

Note that using this type of wiring allows the use of locomotives with any type of E unit (or no E unit). Also, the possibility of error is decreased and a short circuit is not disastrous. However, the problem of crossing from one power circuit to another is still present. Next, a look at the second method for multiple train operation, called "cab-control," which solves this problem and gives better operational flexibility.

MULTIPLE TRAIN OPERATION
Part Two

The first part of this chapter discussed the problems of multiple train wiring and operations. Here is presented the cab-control wiring technique. This technique offers the most flexible and trouble-free operation of a multiple train railroad.

In order to understand the basic principle of cab-control wiring, it is essential to realize the simple relationship between the transformer, the track, and the locomotive in an electric train system. Strictly speaking, the transformer is connected to the *locomotive*. The track is merely a part of the connecting circuit. Earlier we saw the difficulty in operating layouts in

which the transformers were permanently connected to certain sections of track.

The cab-control wiring technique surmounts these difficulties by allowing a given transformer (or "cab") to be connected to any electrical section of track (or "block") at a given point in time. The idea is to assign a transformer to each of the locomotives on the layout. Then, as the locomotives move into the various blocks, each transformer must remain connected to its assigned locomotive. If the track is correctly divided into blocks, each locomotive may move over any part of the layout without causing electrical or physical conflicts.

To illustrate the wiring and operation of a cab-control layout, an O-27 track plan has been developed for a 4' × 8' space. This track plan and its wiring are shown in Figure 8. The same layout could be made out of O-gauge track by substituting equivalent track components. However, the resulting layout would be about 12½ percent larger due to the wider curves and longer straight sections of O-gauge track. Note: the two tracks at the bottom of the layout are spaced correctly for the No. 450 signal bridge.

On a cab-control layout one selector switch must be provided for each track block. On a

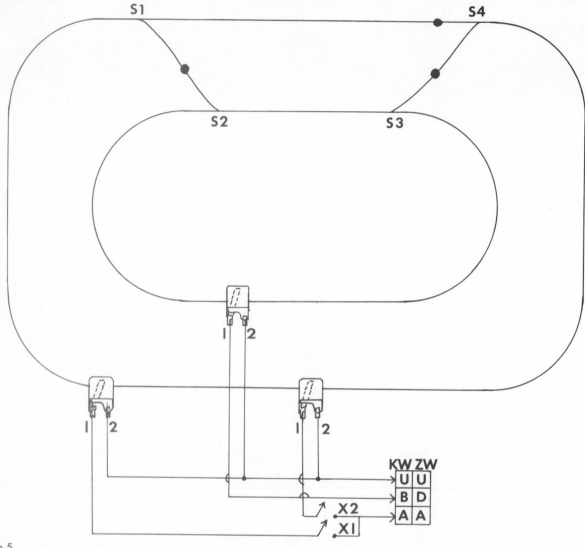

Figure 5

The wiring for an improved two train layout.

two-train layout these may be single-pole double-throw (SPDT) toggle, slide, or knife switches. In the layout diagram the selector switches (X1-X6) are numbered so that they correspond to the blocks (I-VI) that they control. For the sake of discussion, we will refer to the two throttles of the transformers shown as "transformer A" and "transformer B". As switching operations on our layout are discussed, when a selector switch is said to be in the A position, the block controlled by that switch is connected to transformer A.

The first operation that will be described is the exchange of two clockwise running trains.

Initial Positions, Operation No. 1:
Train 1: Running clockwise on the outer loop.
Train 2: Running clockwise on the inner loop.
Selector switches:
   X1—A position on transformer

X2—A position on transformer
X3—A position on transformer
X4—B position on transformer
X5—B position on transformer
X6—B position on transformer

Based on the positions of the selector switches, train 1 is under control of transformer A while train 2 is under control of transformer B. Throughout the entire operation these train-transformer assignments will remain constant.

Step 1, Operation No. 1:
Train 1: Held in block III
      (transformer A off).
Train 2: Moves to outer loop via track switches S3 and S4.
Selector switches:
   X1—B position
   X2—B position
   X3—A position
   X4—B position
   X5—B position
   X6—B position

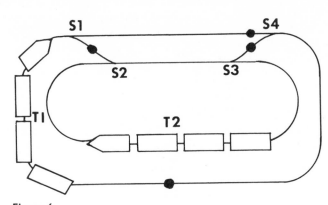

Figure 6

Two trains and two toggle switches positioned

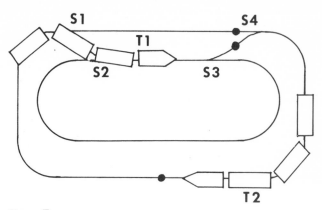

Figure 7

Further train No. 1 and train No. 2 positions

Step 2, Operation No. 1:

Train 2: Held in block II
(transformer B off).
Train 1: Moves to inner loop via track switches No. 1
and No. 2
Selector switches:
X1—A position
X2—B position
X3—A position
X4—A position
X5—A position
X6—A position

Step 3, Operation No. 1:

Train 1: Running on the inner loop.
Train 2: Running on the outer loop.
Selector switches:
X1—B position
X2—B position
X3—B position
X4—A position
X5—A position
X6—A position

Notice that at no time during the operation was it necessary for an engine to span blocks connected to different transformers. Since there is no reliance on holding one engine in neutral while the other is in motion, engines with any type of E unit may be used on a cab-control layout. Because our layout is symmetrical in design, Operation No. 1 could be performed with counterclockwise running trains as well.

One of the biggest advantages of the cab-control technique is that each train on the layout may utilize any part of the track. Applying this concept to our 4′ × 8′ track plan, the two inner loop sidings may be used by inner and outer loop trains. To illustrate this, let's go through a simple switching operation in which a clockwise running train on the outer loop will pick up a car sitting on the upper siding.

Initial positions, Operation No. 2:

Train 1: Running clockwise on the outer loop (pulled by
engine E1).
Train 2: Running clockwise on the inner loop.
Car C1: On siding connected to track switch S5.
Selector switches:
X1—A position
X2—A position
X3—A position
X4—B position
X5—B position
X6—B position

Step 1, Operation No. 2:

Train 2: Held in block VI
(transformer B off).
Engine E1: Uncouples from train 1 at uncoupler U3.
Selector switches:
In same positions as above.

Step 2, Operation No. 2:

Engine E1: Moves into the inner loop via track switches
S1 and S2 (E1 continues until it clears track
switch S5).
Selector switches:
X1—A position
X2—A position
X3—A position
X4—A position
X5—A position
X6—B position

Step 3, Operation No. 2:

Engine E1: Backs into the siding connected to track
switch S5 and couples to car C1.
Selector switches:
In same position as Step 2.

Step 4, Operation No. 2:

Engine E1: Moves out of the siding pulling car C1, then
backs out to the outer loop via track
switches S1 and S2.
Selector switches:
In same position as Step 2.

43

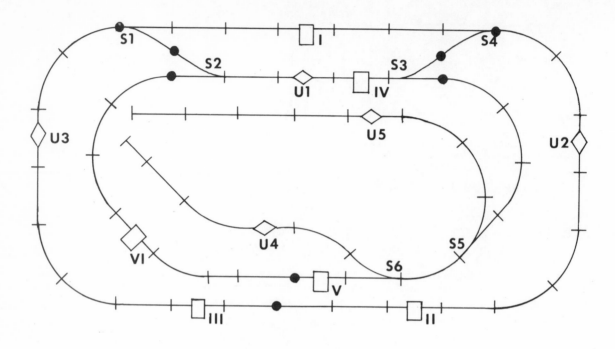

TRACK REQUIREMENTS:

24 straight sections

20 curved sections

2 half straight
sections

5 remote-control or
uncoupling sections

3 pr. switches

SCALE: 1/16″=1″

Note: Large dot signifies insulating pin in center rail.

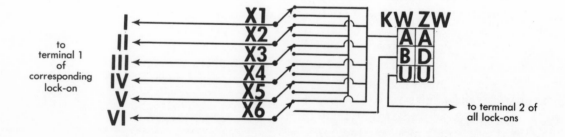

Figure 8
Track plan for a 4′ x 8′ space, O-27 track

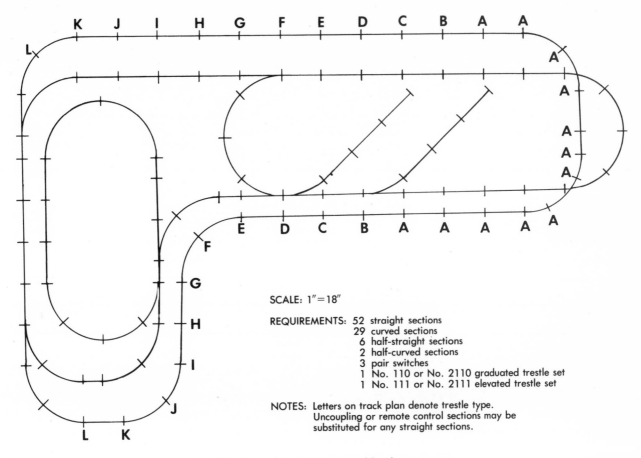

Figure 9

A track plan with certain desirable characteristics

SCALE: 1″=18″

REQUIREMENTS: 52 straight sections
29 curved sections
6 half-straight sections
2 half-curved sections
3 pair switches
1 No. 110 or No. 2110 graduated trestle set
1 No. 111 or No. 2111 elevated trestle set

NOTES: Letters on track plan denote trestle type.
Uncoupling or remote control sections may be
substituted for any straight sections.

Step 5, Operation No. 2:

Engine E1: Continues backing until C1 couples to the
rest of train 1.

Train 1: Proceeds around the outer loop with car C1
in the consist.

Train 2: Proceeds around the inner loop.

Selector switches:
X1—A position
X2—A position
X3—A position
X4—B position
X5—B position
X6—B position

Step 5, Operation No. 3:

Engine E1: Backs through block IV, then out to outer
loop via S3-S4 crossover. When car C1
passes over uncoupler U1 it is uncoupled
from engine E1.

Selector switches:
In same positions as Step 2.

Step 6, Operation No. 3:

Engine E1: Moves forward on the outer loop to block
III.

Selector switches:
In same positions as Step 2.

Step 7, Operation No. 3:

Engine E1: Backs in block IV via S1-S2 crossover,
couples to car C1, and pushes it back out to
the outer loop via the S3-S4 crossover.

Selector switches:
In same positions as Step 2.

Step 8, Operation No. 3:

Engine E1: Continues backing until C1 couples to the
rest of train 1.

Train 1: Proceeds in a counterclockwise direction
around the outer loop with car C1 in the
consist.

Train 2: Proceeds around the inner loop.

Selector switches:
X1—A position
X2—A position
X3—A position
X4—B position
X5—B position
X6—B position

An operation that can add a great deal of
interest to your sessions is the interchange of
cars between the two trains. On our 4′ × 8′ layout this can be accomplished easily, again
thanks to cab-control wiring.

45

Initial positions, Operation No. 4:

Train 1: Running clockwise on the outer loop.
Train 2: Running clockwise on the inner loop.
Car C1: Part of train 2, directly behind engine E2.
Selector switches:
    X1—A position
    X2—A position
    X3—A position
    X4—B position
    X5—B position
    X6—B position

Step 1, Operation No. 4:

Train 2: Backs into siding connected to track switch S5.
Car C1: Uncouples from train 2 at uncoupler U5 in the siding.
Engine E2: Moves forward to block IV pulling car C1.
Selector switches:
    In same positions as above.

Step 2, Operation No. 4:

Car C1: Uncouples from engine E1 at uncoupler U1 in block IV.
Engine E2: Continues to block V where it is stopped (transformer B off).
Engine E1: Uncouples from train 1 at uncoupler U3 and moves to block II.
Selector switches:
    In same positions as above.

Step 3, Operation No. 4:

Engine E1: Backs into block IV via the S3-S4 crossover, couples to car C1 and backs out to the outer loop via the S1-S2 crossover.
Selector switches:
    X1—A position
    X2—A position
    X3—A position
    X4—A position
    X5—B position
    X6—B position

Step 4, Operation No. 4:

Engine E1: Continues backing until car C1 couples to the rest of train 1.
Train 1: Proceeds around the outer loop with Car C1 in the consist.
Engine E2: Backs into the siding and couples to the rest of train 2.
Train 2: Moves out of the siding and proceeds around the inner loop.
Selector switches:
    X1—A position
    X2—A position
    X3—A position
    X4—B position
    X5—B position
    X6—B position

LAYING TRACKS

This section presents a track layout with certain desirable characteristics:

1) Only standard track sections are used—no track cutting is necessary.
2) All grades may be constructed with Lionel trestles and at least 1 full section of track is used between all upgrade and downgrade piers.
3) All tracks are sufficiently spaced to prevent sideswiping of trains.
4) Overpass trestles do not interfere with passage of trains on lower track.
5) All track around the perimeter is at a safe distance from the edge of the layout board.

In addition, this particular track plan was designed to fit on two 4' × 8' sheets of plywood or composition board, if O-27 track is used. As we've noted before, any O-27 layout may be made with O-gauge track, but it will require about 12½ percent more space.

It is customary to construct a simple framework to raise a layout above the floor. This framework can range from a simple 2 × 4 bracing to storage cabinets with shelves and doors, depending on your budget and carpentry experience. However, there are a few things to consider when you build framework.

First of all, how high do you want your layout? Most layouts are from 28 to 36 inches high, although some prefer eye-level pikes. Don't overlook a lower height, particularly if young children are going to be frequent spectators or helpers. Another thing to remember is that it's often necessary to climb onto a layout, so be sure to make a strong enough frame to support your weight. Finally, a "fence" should be attached to the edges of the board to prevent your equipment from falling to the floor. Wood is the least expensive material to use for this, but Plexiglas or Lucite will allow you to see all the trackside action.

SOUND DEADENING AND ACCESSORY PLACEMENT

One problem that must be faced when

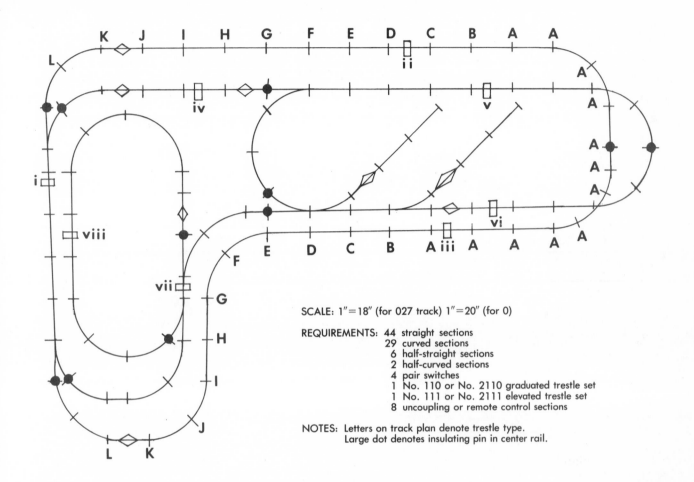

SCALE: 1″=18″ (for 027 track) 1″=20″ (for 0)

REQUIREMENTS: 44 straight sections
29 curved sections
6 half-straight sections
2 half-curved sections
4 pair switches
1 No. 110 or No. 2110 graduated trestle set
1 No. 111 or No. 2111 elevated trestle set
8 uncoupling or remote control sections

NOTES: Letters on track plan denote trestle type.
Large dot denotes insulating pin in center rail.

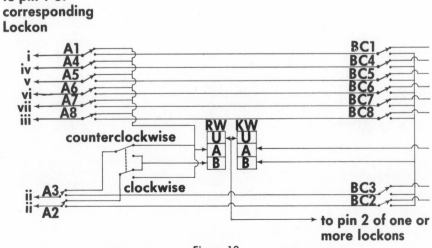

Figure 10
Track plan for wiring a remote cab layout

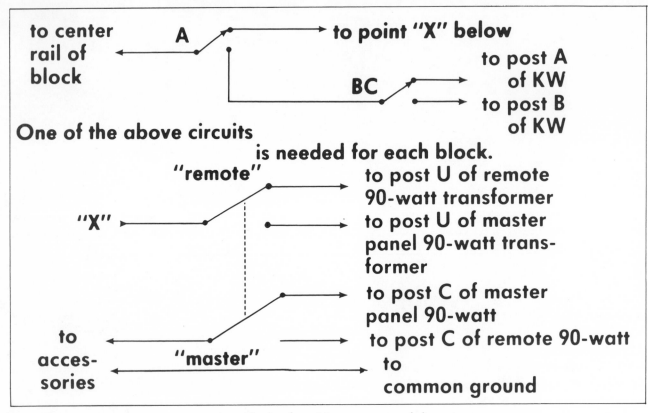

to center rail of block

A

to point "X" below

BC

to post A of KW

to post B of KW

One of the above circuits is needed for each block.

"remote"

"X"

to post U of remote 90-watt transformer

to post U of master panel 90-watt transformer

to post C of master panel 90-watt

to post C of remote 90-watt

to accessories

"master"

to common ground

Figure 11

A track plan for wiring a remote cab layout.

planning construction of a permanent layout is sound deadening. There are few things that detract from the total effect of a model railroad as much as locomotive gear noise. The problem is greater for tinplaters because of the sharp O and O-27 curves. Also, if you plan to run any of the new "Mighty Sound of Steam" locos on your pike, you certainly don't want anything interfering with the fine steam sound.

The first step toward a reasonably quiet layout is the design of framework that supports the layout board as solidly as possible. The more cross beams you have, the less the "sounding board" effect. Hard particle board will provide a more solid, less noisy layout foundation that will plywood. However, *do not* attach the track directly to the particle board. Instead glue sheets of insulation board over the hard layout board, using white glue or contact cement. There are many types of insulation board that are suitable for this use—Celotex, Homosote, Upson board, Fesco, etc. The main thing to keep in mind is that the material should be somewhat soft, yet firm enough to hold a wood screw.

You may find that insulation board lami-

nated to hard particle board will provide enough sound deadening to suit you. Try a small oval of track on such a foundation to see if it's adequate. Use short wood screws to mount the track to the insulation board *only*. If you use screws that are long enough to reach the particle board, you will partially defeat the purpose of the insulation board. Remember, you need not screw the track down tightly; the purpose of the screws is only to keep the track from shifting position.

If you feel that you need more sound deadening than the above method provides, try using roadbed under the track. There are many materials that can be used for roadbed, ranging from commercially fabricated cork strips to foam carpet padding. Carpet padding is quite inexpensive (considering the number of strips that can be cut from a sheet). You may even be able to get remnants from a carpet dealer for nothing or next to nothing. Of course, some method of camouflaging the padding (such as ballast) is absolutely necessary. You may, therefore, decide that prefabricated roadbed is worth the extra cost.

Another important consideration when planning a permanent layout is where the accessories should be placed. Of course, everyone has a different group of accessories to work with. However, the comments that follow should help you make good use of your particular equipment.

First of all, let's consider signals. Every signal on a model railroad should have a purpose, just as on prototype railroads. A signal can "protect" a section of track (considered as a mainline) from sidings and connecting tracks that "feed" into it. Such a signal would face a train approaching the mainline from a connecting track. The contactor that actuates the signal would be placed on the mainline near the point where the connecting track joins the mainline. In this configuration the signal will show a red indication whenever there is a train on the mainline. Thus, a train on the connecting track should be stopped. After the mainline train passes, the signal will return to green and the approaching train can proceed onto the mainline. If possible, signals should be placed everywhere on the layout that trains can move from a connecting track onto a mainline. On an L-shaped layout the three loops are considered mainlines, while the remaining track is mostly connecting track. Remember that signals should always face the right hand (engineer's) side of approaching trains.

Other accessories should be placed on the layout in groupings that make sense. For instance, a station area could be comprised of a No. 132 or No. 2133 station, a No. 128 newsstand, a No. 334 operating dispatching board, and a few lamp posts. An interchange area would be a good location to show off a No. 445 switch tower or a No. 192 railroad control tower. Manually operated accessories (such as the No. 460 piggyback transportation set) or accessories that require a considerable amount of manual intervention should be placed where they are easily reached. Planning should also be done for your operating cars. It's good practice to put any platforms, bins, etc. on sidings or connecting tracks, away from mainline trackage. The underpass track on the far right side of the L-shaped layout is a good place for tell-tale

poles for the No. 3424 operating brakeman car.

LIVE WIRES!

There are many ways to wire a large layout, depending on the transformers to be used and the type of operation desired. The following is a wiring plan for an L-shaped layout that is designed for cab-control operation. Power will be provided by a two-throttle KW (which will *normally* be used to operate trains on the two inner loops) and an RW (*normally* used to operate a train on the outer loop). The accessory load could be shared between the two transformers. Both transformers should be phased.

When applying cab-control wiring to a three train layout, a problem arises in the choice of selector switches. Ideally, single pole, *triple-throw* switches should be used, but such switches are rather expensive. Therefore, this wiring plan will make use of two SPDT switches for each block. (Apparently Atlas makes inexpensive panels containing four center-off SPDT slide switches.)

The use of the two switches is as follows: one block which it controls is connected to cab A (in this case, the RW), or to either of the other cabs. The second switch is in the circuit only if the first switch is *not* in the A position. This second switch is used to indicate whether the block is connected to cab B or Cab C (the two throttles of the KW). Therefore, we have the option of assigning any of our three cabs to any block on the layout. (For a discussion on operating a cab-control layout, see pages 40-46.)

The wiring diagram on the left shows all connections for the L-shaped layout. Note that because the layout has an upgrade-downgrade section and an RW has been chosen for one of the cabs, the automatic voltage control system that has been described can be used.

This system provides a higher voltage for the upgrade part than for the downgrade part. Note that this is true only when the RW is assigned to the outer loop blocks. A "clockwise-counterclockwise" switch is provided to change whichever side of this loop is considered the upgrade.

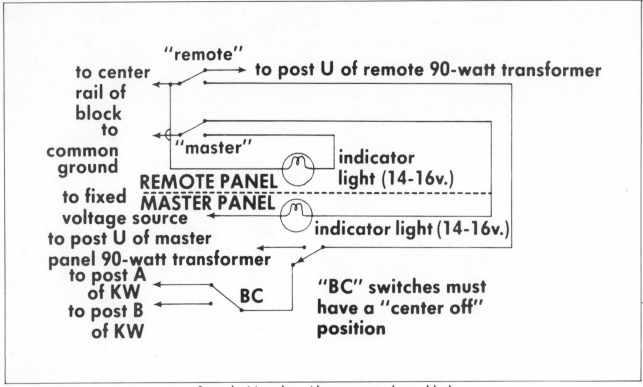

to center rail of block

to common ground

to fixed voltage source

to post U of master panel 90-watt transformer

to post A of KW

to post B of KW

"remote"

to post U of remote 90-watt transformer

"master"

indicator light (14-16v.)

REMOTE PANEL

MASTER PANEL

indicator light (14-16v.)

BC

"BC" switches must have a "center off" position

Figure 12   Second wiring plan with more control over blocks.

Note: Post A of each 90-watt transformer and post U of the KW are the common ground posts and should be connected together and to the outer track rails. Transformers should be phased.

Next, we will take a different approach to wiring this layout, featuring an optional remote cab for two-person operation.

REMOTE CAB WIRING

In the previous pages a basic cab control wiring plan for our L-shaped layout was presented. That plan was based on a central control panel containing all transformers and selector switches. Now we are going to look at two other approaches to wiring the same layout. The O/O-27 track plan may be found on page 47, while a Super "O" version of this L-shaped pike will be on page 52.

Operating a three train layout can become rather hectic for one person. Of course you can always enlist a visitor or family member to take over one of the cabs, but things will get a bit crowded around a single control panel. One solution is to provide a separate control panel containing one of the cabs at a location removed from the master control panel. When employing a remote cab, you should provide a means to operate the entire layout from the master control panel, for there will always be times when you will be the sole operator. In order to make full use of the extra transformer needed for the

master panel and to distribute the power load among all transformers, our wiring plan will have a switch to change connections to the remote and extra transformers. If the remote transformer is not being used to power a train, it will be used to power the accessories. Likewise, the accessories will be switched to the extra transformer on the master control panel when the remote transformer is being used to power a train.

There are many possible approaches to wiring a remote cab layout, depending on the degree of control that the remote operator will have. The simplest plan is one in which all control of the block/cab assignments (selector switches) remains with the master operator (who also controls two of the trains). The remote operator controls only the speed and direction of the remaining train. Such a wiring plan is shown in Figure 11. The choice of transformers is as follows: a 90 watt (1033/1044/4090) for the remote cab (R), another 90 watt for the extra cab on the master control panel (A), and a KW for the remaining cabs on the master panel (B and C). Note that there is a single DPDT switch which determines which small transformer is to be used to power the third train (either cab A on the master panel or the remote cab, R). This same switch will assign the accessories to the opposite 90-watt transformer.

A second wiring plan for the L-shaped layout gives more control over block selection to the remote cab operator. In this plan the remote cab panel contains an additional set of selector switches (one DPDT for each block). In addition a red indicator light is mounted next to each selector switch on the remote and master panels. These indicator lights let each operator know what the other is doing. The wiring for one of the blocks on the layout is shown in Figure 12. All blocks on the layout should be wired in similar fashion. If desired, a separate switch may be added to select which transformer powers the accessories.

When remote cab operation is desired, all "A" selector switches on the master panel should be in the position shown in Figure 2 (which removes transformer A from the circuit). The indicator lights work as follows: Each light on the master panel will light if its block is under control of the remote cab (R). Each light on the remote panel will light if its block is under control of either of the active master panel cabs (B or C) and that block is actually being used. A few simple rules must be followed for successful operation under this system. First, the remote cab operator may take control of a block only if its indicator light is off (meaning that the block is not being used by one of the other trains). Likewise, the master panel operator may not move either of his trains into a block if his red light for that block is on. It is important that the remote cab operator moves his selector switches for all blocks not actually being used by his train to the "master" position. Similarly, the master operator should move his "BC" switches for all blocks that his trains are not using to the "center off" position.

If it is desired to give more control to the remote cab operator, you may wire additional track switch controllers in "parallel" and mount them on the remote panel. This is particularly effective if 022 switches are used, as the controller lights will always indicate the true positions of the switches. To operate the entire layout from the master panel, *all* remote selector switches must be in the "master" position.

SUPER "O"

Lionel's Super "O" track was introduced in 1957 in an attempt to stave off the exodus to HO that was occurring at the time. The objective was to camouflage the long-standing sore spot of tinplate track: the center rail. The idea, though a good one, had only limited success.

The foundation for Super "O" track sections was a one-piece, brown plastic strip of simulated ties. The individual ties (16 per full straight or curved section) were connected together underneath the running rails. Instead of the normal flat shape, Super "O" ties were hump-shaped. The tie humps supported the "power blade," a strip of thin copper that took the place of the center rail. Running rails were more in keeping with tinplate tradition: plated sheet steel bent into hollow rail.

However, the Super "O" running rails had a realistic "T" shape and a lower profile. The flat surface of these rails made for greatly improved locomotive traction as well. Each full section of track had three metal "ties" mounted under the plastic tie strips. These served the same basic functions as the ties on conventional tinplate track: to hold the running rails in place, to provide a means of fastening the track to a layout surface, to electrically connect the running rails, and to complete the magnetic circuit for magnetraction locomotives. One of the unusual features of Super "O" track was the interlocking joints molded into the end ties of each section. These meant that the track pins were not responsible for physically joining the track sections, making track clips unnecessary for nonpermanent layouts.

Aside from appearance, Super "O" track differed from conventional tinplate track in that each curved section made up 30° of a circle. (O and O-27 curved sections make up 45° of a circle.) This meant that track plans for O and O-27 could not be "lifted" for Super "O" use. In many ways, the 30° curved track created more

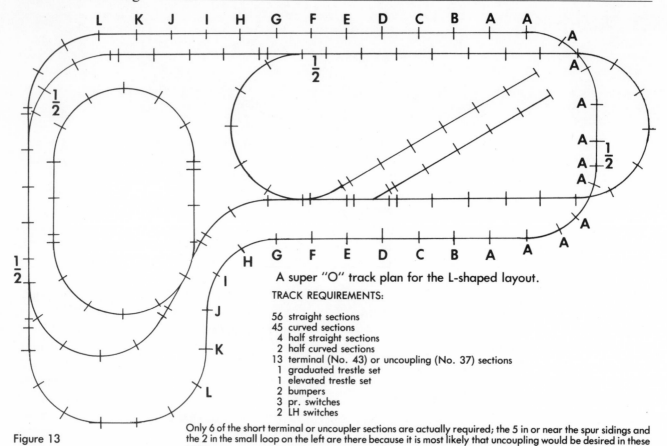

A super "O" track plan for the L-shaped layout.

TRACK REQUIREMENTS:

56 straight sections
45 curved sections
 4 half straight sections
 2 half curved sections
13 terminal (No. 43) or uncoupling (No. 37) sections
 1 graduated trestle set
 1 elevated trestle set
 2 bumpers
 3 pr. switches
 2 LH switches

Only 6 of the short terminal or uncoupler sections are actually required; the 5 in or near the spur sidings and the 2 in the small loop on the left are there because it is most likely that uncoupling would be desired in these areas.

Figure 13

interesting layout possibilities. Also, the wide radius curves offered better operation and appearance (radius to center: Super "O"–18", O–14½", O-27–12½").

Because Super "O" was such a radical departure from conventional tinplate track, provisions had to be made for many of the functions that had become part and parcel of Lionel railroading. For example, the time-honored method of connecting the transformer to the track via a CTC lock-on couldn't be used with Super "O," because there was no open space available to attach such a lock-on. The solution was separate lock-ons for the center rail and the outer rails. The "power" lock-on (No. 62) fit between any two plastic ties, while the "ground" lock-on (No. 61) could be attached to the outer rail. Later, a short terminal track section (No. 43) was introduced that had both center and outer rail connections.

Another common practice on Lionel layouts is the insulated rail method of actuating signals and automatic train control circuits. With conventional O and O-27 track, an insulated rail section can easily be made out of a regular section (see page 68). However, the outer rails cannot be removed easily from a Super "O" section. Therefore, Lionel sold special insulated rail straight (No. 48) and curved (No. 49) sections.

Operation of many accessories caused a problem because, again, there was no open space on the track for devices such as the power blades on the cattle car platform and the telltale poles for the operating brakeman car. Lionel solved this by offering a pair of short sections that had no plastic ties for a few inches (No. 38). When it came to the standard functions of a remote control track (uncoupling, actuating operating cars) Super "O" completely broke with tradition.

Instead of making a special remote control section, Lionel offered a set of blades (No. 36) that could be attached to any straight section for actuating operating cars and a short track section (No. 37) with an electromagnet for uncoupling. It's no wonder that many Lionel old-timers were bewildered when they saw the above items on the Super "O" pages of the late 50s Lionel catalogues!

All Lionel equipment may be operated successfully on Super "O" track except for "Scout"-type enclosed motor locos (including many of the plastic-bodied steamers made in the late 50s and early 60s). The contact rollers on these locos do not reach the center "power blade." Also, certain long locomotives (such as the No. 746) will strike the outside mounted switch box if the straight side of a switch is attached directly to a curved section. The solution is to put a short piece of straight track such as No. 37 or No. 43 between the switch and the curved track.

In Figure 13 is a Super "O" track plan for the L-shaped layout that has been discussed earlier in this chapter. This layout will fit on two 5' × 9' boards (admittedly, not the easiest size to find!). An effort has been made to use only track lengths that were produced by Lionel. However, if you decide to build this layout, you may not be able to find some of the shorter sections called for in the track plan. If necessary, Super "O" may be cut with a fine hacksaw in much the same manner as O or O-27 track.

If you are contemplating building a layout with Super "O" track, there are many factors that may affect your decision. First of all, it is relatively expensive compared to O or O-27 sectional track or Gargraves. However, it does give you better appearance and wider curves than sectional track, without the shaping required with Gargraves. At first, Super "O" track planning is a little perplexing (especially if you are used to O or O-27), but it ultimately offers more flexibility. Also, many track plans for sectional HO track are suitable for Super "O" without modification. Perhaps the most serious criticism leveled against it is that the thin copper "power blade" causes locomotive contact rollers to wear out much sooner than does the rounded center rail of O and O-27. Fortunately, most rollers are replaceable.

Below is a list of all Super "O" track components made by Lionel:

No. 31	Curved track, 9″ long.
No. 31-7	Power Blade connector, copper.
No. 31-15	Ground rail pin.
No. 32	Straight track, 9″ long.
No. 32-10	Insulating pin.
No. 32-20	Power blade insulator.
No. 33	Half curved track, 4½″ long.
No. 34	Half straight track, 5⅞″ long.
No. 36	Set of two 5½″ operating car blades.
No. 37	Uncoupling section, 1⅝″ long.
No. 38	Accessory adaptor track, 5⅜″ long.

No. 43	Terminal track, 1⅝″ long.
No. 48	Insulated straight track, 9″ long.
No. 49	Insulated curved track, 9″ long.
No. 61	Ground lock-on.
No. 62	Power lock-on.
No. 112	Remote control switches, non-derailing fixed voltage provision.
No. 120	90° crossing, 6⅛″ long each side.
No. 130	60° crossing, 8⅜″ long each side.
No. 142	Manual switches.

| No. 022-500 | O adaptor set |
| No. 1122-500 | O-27 adaptor set |

TRAIN LOCATION INDICATOR PANEL

One of the most important things a railroad dispatcher needs to know is where the trains are at any point in time. The same is true of a model railroad operator, who serves as dispatcher, engineer, and brakeman all in one. This section outlines the basic design for a train location indicator panel that follows general prototype practice. This panel can make a multiple-operator cab-control layout much easier to operate. It can also be a great aid to a single operator of a large layout.

The indicator panel consists of a number of lights strategically mounted on a piece of sheet metal or plywood on which a track diagram appears. This diagram must clearly show all blocks that the track is divided into. One light for each "cab," or transformer throttle, is placed adjacent to each block on the diagram. All lights for a given cab should be the same color.

The diagram in Figure 14 contains the track plan and wiring diagram for a small two cab layout with five blocks. Note that there is a good deal of insulated outer rail track, which is used to detect the occupation of a block. If you decide to build such an indicator panel for your layout, be sure to use as many contiguous insulated rail sections as possible in each block. You don't have to worry about your engines losing ground contact on these special sections, as the metal wheels of the passing train will keep the insulated rail grounded.

The cab selector switches shown in the diagram are the double pole, double throw (DPDT) type, unlike previous cab control wiring plans which employ SPDT switches. The extra pole is

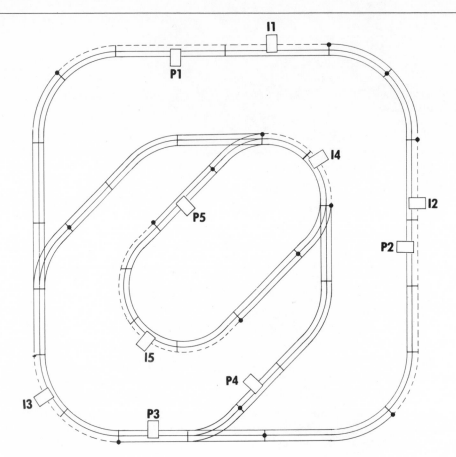

TRACK REQUIREMENTS:

  8 straight sections
16 curved sections
  2 half straight sections
  2 pr. switches

SCALE: 1" = 10" (for 027)
  Track is shown wider for clarity.

Dashed line indicates insulated rail.

Large dot indicates insulating pin. (Additional insulating pins that may be required for nonderailing switches are not shown.)

"I" lock-ons in each block must be attached to insulated rail side as shown.

One of these circuits is needed for each block on the layout. In addition, the "ground" posts of transformers A and B and the fixed voltage supply must be connected together (common ground). Pin 2 of at least one "P" lock-on must also be connected to the common ground.

This diagram is intended to illustrate the basic design of a train location indicator panel; it can be adapted for use on any three rail pike.

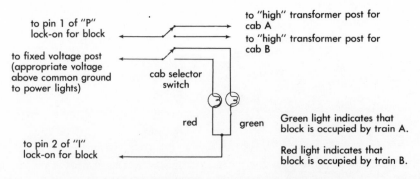

Figure 14
A track and wiring plan for a small 2-cab layout.

used to select which indicator panel light is in the circuit.

The panel works as follows: whenever a train is in a block, the indicator panel light for that train in that block is turned on. Therefore, the operator/s can tell at a glance which blocks are occupied *and* which train is in each block. This information is essential to the smooth operation of a large layout. Because the indicator panel is powered by a fixed voltage source, it functions whether or not the trains are moving.

The layout in Figure 15 provides for interesting operation using a yard engine (steam or diesel switcher, GP7 or 9) and road power (a steamer, a lashup of powered and dummy diesel units, or an electric). The nice part about this layout is that complex wiring and multiple transformers are not required. The layout consists of a triangular mainline loop connected to a small yard (tracks B, C, and D) and an engine service or storage track (A).

Basic operation is as follows: a train pulled by the road locomotive runs clockwise around the loop. Yard sidings B, C, and D are turned off via their SPST switches. These sidings contain additional rolling stock plus the switcher. At some point in time the road locomotive uncouples from the train at uncoupler UM and continues past track switch S1. This switch is now turned to the curved position, and the loco backs all the way into the engine storage/service track, A. Power to track A is turned off using its SPST switch. Similarly, power to tracks B, C, and D is turned on. The switcher now "comes to life" and moves out to the mainline. It breaks up the train on the mainline and moves cars from the sidings out onto the mainline. When a new train has been made up, the switcher returns to one of the three yard tracks, and power to these tracks is turned off. Finally, power to track A is turned on, and the road loco moves out and couples to the new train on the mainline.

Careful choice of accessories can enhance the illusion of real railroading on this layout. For example, the engine storage/service track could be covered by a No. 2785 engine house. If you have an operating water tower (No. 138) or a diesel fueling station (No. 415), these would be appropriate along track A instead of the engine house.

To enhance the "show" for visitors to the layout, have the road power take on water or fuel while the switcher is busy making up a new train. Track B has sufficient table space for accessories such as the No. 342 culvert loader, the No. 345 culvert unloader, the new No. 2788 coaling station, or the new No. 2175 Sandy Andy. As usual, signals would be appropriate to "protect" the 90° crossing. A station, loading accessory, or trackside structure could be placed near uncoupler US.

At a later date, this layout could be converted to cab-control operation by adding a second transformer, breaking the track into blocks, and providing block selector switches. If this is done, the switcher can be shuffling cars in the yard at the same time a train is running on the mainline.

The layout in Figure 16 makes use of the new No. 2317 motorized lift bridge to connect a small yard to the mainline track. Since this accessory replaces two sections of O-27 track, this track plan is suitable "as is" for O-27 use only. An O-gauge version would require a few pieces of short "fitter" track cut from straight sections.

Harold K. Moore has adapted a new lift bridge for O-gauge use in the following manner:

1. Using an ice pick, ream out the rail ends at each end of the bridge so the larger O track pins will fit.
2. On each track section that is to be fitted to the bridge ends, move the end cross tie back far enough so it does not rest on the bridge.
3. Recrimp these ties in their new locations.
4. You cannot use the plastic clips furnished with the bridge trestles as they will not fit O-gauge cross ties. The old metal clips are still available from many dealers, but *not* from the Lionel Service Department.

LIONEL'S 1957 CATALOGUE LAYOUT

The back cover of the 1957 Lionel catalogue was an artist's rendering of a finished basement family room (complete with Airex

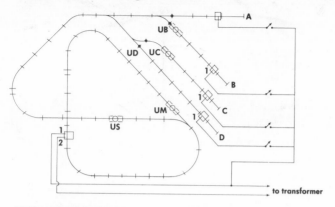

TRACK REQUIREMENTS:
- 33 straight sections
- 13 curved sections
- 2 half straight sections
- 5 uncoupling or remote control sections
- 2 pair switches
- 1 90° crossing
- 4 bumpers

SPACE REQUIREMENTS:
If 0-27 track is used, this layout will fit on a 6' x 8' surface with sufficient clearance on the edges. If 0 track is used, the layout surface should be at least 6 ⅔' x 9'.

NOTE: Large dot signifies an insulating pin in the center rail.

Figure 15

A track plan for operation of yard engine and road power.

fishing tackle on one wall!). In the picture father and son are descending the stairs, delighting over the room's magnificent centerpiece—a large, L-shaped Lionel layout equipped with virtually every accessory that was offered that year!! Small print in one corner of the page directed the drooling reader to pages 50–51 "for a working diagram of this layout." However, pages 50–51 contain only a rough sketch of the layout that describes accessory placement, along with a lot of advertising copy promoting Lionel accessories. We had always wished for a track plan of the layout, partly because we wondered if it could actually be built! The artist who drew the back cover took great liberties: straight sections of track were lengthened or shortened at will. In one section, a trestle is drawn squarely in the center of an underpass track!!

A few hours with a compass, protractor, and straightedge convinced us that the 1957 Lionel catalogue layout could be built quite easily—if O-gauge track were used. Super "O" has a completely different geometry than O and therefore is not a practical choice for this particular layout. While O-27 shares the same geometry as O-gauge, the 10% size reduction of O-27 causes some problems. Accessories do *not* shrink when used on an O-27 layout! Therefore, if you want to build the exact layout pictured on the catalogue—accessories and all—O-gauge track must be used.

Assumptions that we made when drawing the track plan were as follows: (1) only standard Lionel track components were to be used, (2) all overpasses were to be made at size "A" trestles, (3) all accessories in the catalogue picture were to be placed on the layout in the same positions where possible, (4) the layout could be built on two 5' × 9' boards as indicated in the catalogue. (We have no idea where you can buy 5' × 9' sheets of plywood!) The one major problem was the placement of the No. 464 lumber mill. The catalogue picture shows this accessory on the same siding as the No. 364 lumber conveyor. There is no way this could be done except to have the No. 464 on the opposite side of the track across from the No. 364. However, this placement would hide the action of the No. 464 lumber mill, so we moved it out to a relatively uncrowded secondary mainline. The catalogue picture shows the No. 3462P milk car platform in this place, so we put this platform on the siding with the No. 362 barrel loader. Otherwise, all accessories are placed correctly.

The layout appears to be designed for two train operation with one train running around the graded outer loop, the other running around the inner loop that surrounds the "culvert twins" and the station area. A third train could be added if the layout were wired for "cab-control" operation. Two motorized units are necessary to take full advantage of this track plan. The first is a No. 60 trolley which would run back and forth on the track behind the station. The other is one of the small Army or Navy type switchers (No. 41, No. 51, No. 56, etc.) which would be stationed on the tracks connected by the No. 350 transfer table. This is necessary because these small switchers are the only locos that would fit on the transfer table while coupled to a gondola (for the No. 282 gantry crane).

Legend for 1957 Lionel Catalogue Layout Diagram

Scale of drawing: 1" = 20"
Space requirements: Two 5' × 9' boards in an
                                  L configuration
Track requirements:
    79 OS O-gauge straight sections

The 2350 New Haven electric shown in a dramatic closeup.

The all-time favorite Lionel 2360 GG1 with two motors.

following page

A handsome display of Lionel 6464 series box cars.

The standard-gauge Lionel 9E locomotive as remanufactured by Williams Electric Trains.

The top of the line Lionel standard-gauge 408E with
twin motors as remanufactured by Williams Electric
Trains.

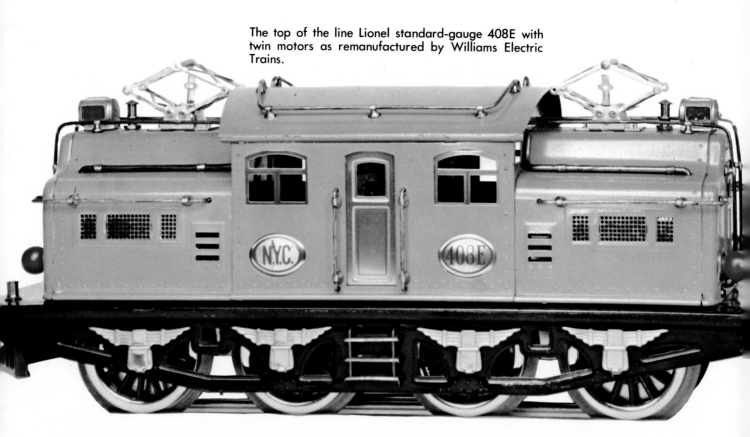

The firemen rush to the burning house on George Stanton's layout.

A diesel engine emerging from a tunnel and a portion of the Stanton oil field.

An overview of half of the Stanton layout.

Yard scene from the Stanton layout featuring the gantry crane and culvert loader.

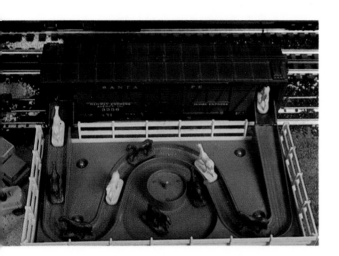

The Lionel horse corral in operation.

The highly desirable American Flyer lumber mill, which converts timber to lumber.

A busy triple portal tunnel on the Stanton layout.

The magnificent Lionel 381 and two "State" cars in standard gauge from the early 1930s. Today this is one of the most valuable train sets ever made.

The General being attacked by the Indians!

A bad man being hanged!

A busy industrial scene along the railroad

Town center in Stantonville.

The most famous of American eateries.

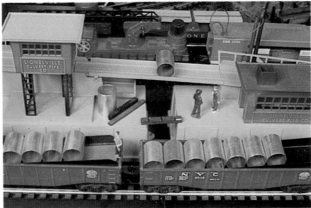

The Lionel culvert unloader, and a partial view of the culbert loader.

An active volunteer fire department protects the town.

A selection of Lionel Alco-type diesels: 205 Missouri Pacific, 208 Santa Fe, 209 New Haven, 210 Texas Special, 226 Boston & Maine, 218 Santa Fe, 227 Canadian National and 221 Santa Fe.

Four highly desired Lionel F3 diesels: the 2363 Illinois Central, 2240 Wabash, 2345 Western Pacific, and 2356 Southern.

A heavily loaded freight emerging from the tunnel.

Multiple grades on Neville Long's layout. (Photo by Neville Long)

A Lionel watertower refilling a thirsty tender on Neville Long's layout. (Photo by Neville Long)

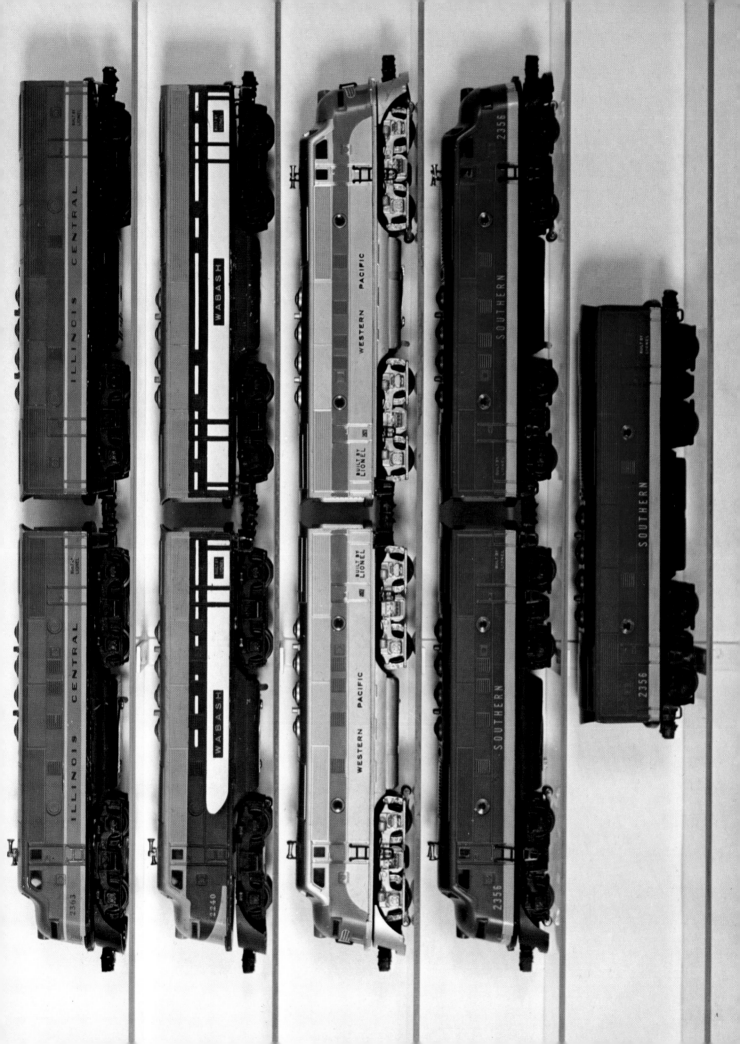

The scarce Canadian Pacific coach.

Multiple levels on Neville Long's handsome layout.

Some handsome scenery and trains on Neville Long's layout.

A Virginian FM against the magnificent scenery on the Neville Long layout.

Passenger cars waiting at the station for a rush of commuters. (Photo by Neville Long)

following page

Five Lionel diesels: 2365 Chesapeake & Ohio GP 7, 2337 Wabash GP-7, 2328 Burlington GP-7, 2338 Milwaukee Road GP-7 and the 2359 Boston and Maine GP-9.

Two CN diesels pull an enormous load. (Photo by
Neville Long)

A Santa Fe caboose against a beautiful background on
the Neville Long layout.

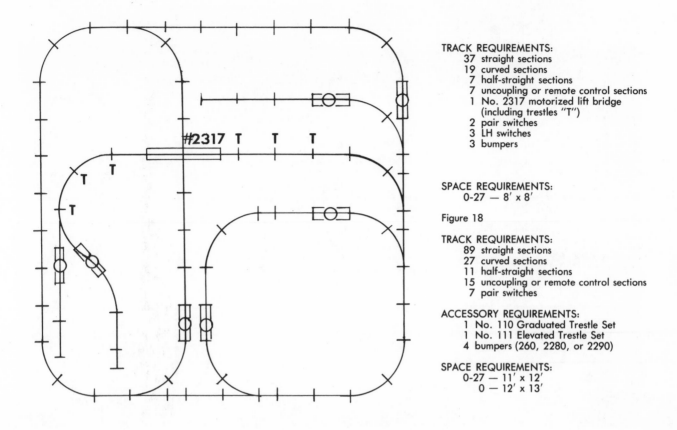

TRACK REQUIREMENTS:
37 straight sections
19 curved sections
7 half-straight sections
7 uncoupling or remote control sections
1 No. 2317 motorized lift bridge
(including trestles "T")
2 pair switches
3 LH switches
3 bumpers

SPACE REQUIREMENTS:
0-27 — 8' x 8'

Figure 18

TRACK REQUIREMENTS:
89 straight sections
27 curved sections
11 half-straight sections
15 uncoupling or remote control sections
7 pair switches

ACCESSORY REQUIREMENTS:
1 No. 110 Graduated Trestle Set
1 No. 111 Elevated Trestle Set
4 bumpers (260, 2280, or 2290)

SPACE REQUIREMENTS:
0-27 — 11' x 12'
0 — 12' x 13'

Figure 16   A track plan using the No. 2317 motorized lift bridge.

26 OC O-gauge curved sections
9 ½OS O-gauge "half-section" straight sections
9 ½OC O-gauge "half-section" curved sections
9 UCS O-gauge remote control sections
3 022LH Left hand O-gauge switches
5 022RH Right hand O-gauge switches
Accessory requirements:
1 No. 110 Graduated Trestle Set
1 No. 111 Elevated Trestle Set
(Note: Trestle size and placement is designated by the letters "A"-"L" on the layout diagram.)
1 No. 350 Transfer Table
8 No. 260 Illuminated Bumpers
Other accessories shown on the layout:
No. 71   Lamp Post (2)
No. 114   Newsstand with Horn
or
No. 118   Newsstand with Whistle
No. 128   Animated Newsstand
No. 133   Illuminated Passenger Station
No. 138   Water Tank
No. 140   Banjo Signal
No. 145   Automatic Gateman

No. 151   Automatic Semaphore
No. 155   Ringing Highway Signal
No. 195   Eight-Bulb Floodlight Tower
No. 197   Rotating Radar Tower
No. 214   Girder Bridge
No. 252   Automatic Crossing Gate
No. 253   Automatic Block Control Signal
No. 282   Operating Gantry Crane
No. 310   Billboard
No. 342   Culvert Loader
No. 345   Culvert Unloading Station
No. 352   Icing Station
No. 362   Operating Barrel Loader
No. 364   Operating Lumber Conveyor
No. 397   Operating Coal Loader
No. 410   Billboard Blinker
No. 415   Diesel Fueling Station
No. 445   Automatic Switch Tower
No. 450   Operating Signal Bridge
No. 464   Operating Lumber Mill
No. 465   Sound Dispatching Station
No. 497   Operating Coaling Station
No. 3356-100 Horse Car Corral
No. 3424-100 Tell-Tale Poles for Operating
             Brakeman Car (designated
             "T" on the layout diagram)
No. 3462P   Milk Car Platform

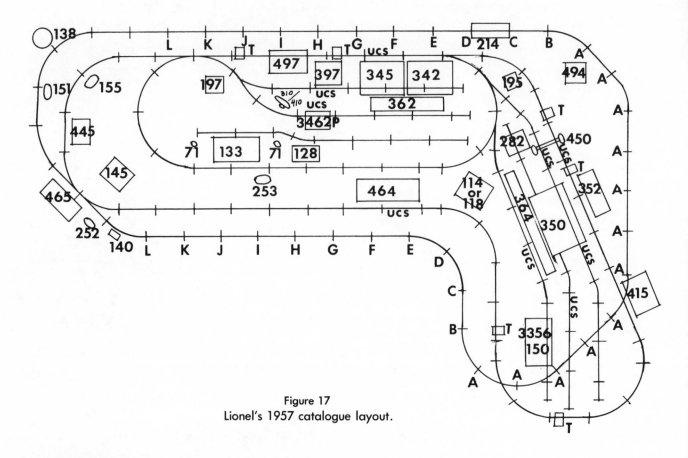

Figure 17
Lionel's 1957 catalogue layout.

A LAYOUT DESIGNED FOR OPERATION

If you have 140 or so square feet of space plus a box full of Lionel sectional track, why not build the layout shown in Figure 18? This layout avoids the crowded look of many large tinplate pikes, leaving a good deal of open space for accessories and scenic effects. This track plan was designed specifically for versatile railroad operation. It includes three track configurations that are the basic building blocks of model railroad layouts: the reversing loop, the "wye," and the passing siding.

Of course the main continuous running loop is in the center of the layout. This loop is elevated over the "wye" via a No. 110 graduated trestle set and a No. 111 elevated trestle set. Inside this main oval is a reversing loop, so called because a clockwise running train that enters this loop will emerge running counterclockwise. A complementary reversing loop is located in the lower left hand corner of the layout. This can be used to return a counterclockwise running train to the clockwise direction.

By far the most versatile feature of this layout is the "wye" at the bottom. This "wye" is situated between two yards: a classification yard consisting of passing sidings on the left and a yard consisting of spur (single-ended) sidings on the right. (Note that part of the "wye" trackage is used in one of the reversing loops.) Use of the "wye" makes the process of making and breaking up trains easier and more interesting. Typically, a double-ended locomotive (switcher, GP, U-Boat) is used to work these yards. The process of transferring a car from one yard to another via the "wye" is as follows: a switching loco pulls the car to be transferred from left to right across the top of the "wye." The loco uncouples from the car at point X and continues to point Y. The loco then backs down one leg of the "wye" to point Z. Now the loco moves forward up the other leg of the "wye" to point W. Finally,

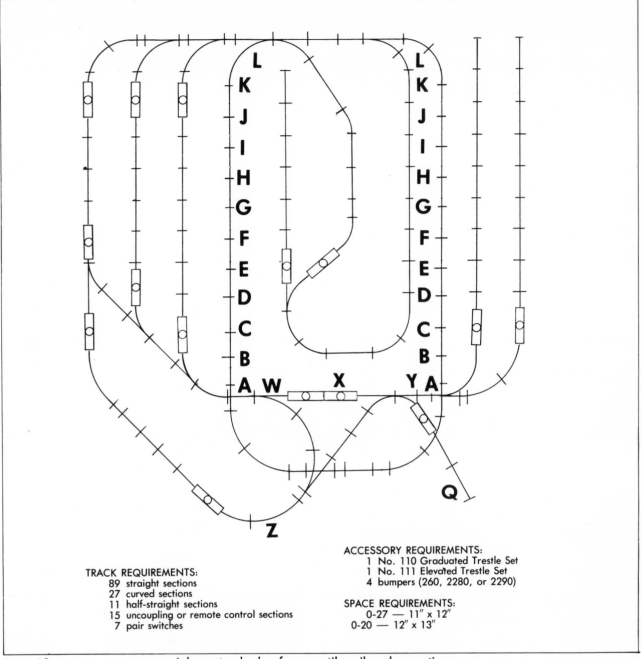

TRACK REQUIREMENTS:
89 straight sections
27 curved sections
11 half-straight sections
15 uncoupling or remote control sections
7 pair switches

ACCESSORY REQUIREMENTS:
1 No. 110 Graduated Trestle Set
1 No. 111 Elevated Trestle Set
4 bumpers (260, 2280, or 2290)

SPACE REQUIREMENTS:
0-27 — 11" x 12"
0-20 — 12" x 13"

Figure 18   A large track plan for versatile railroad operations.

the loco backs into the car at point X and pushes it into the spur siding yard on the right side of the layout. This process is reversed when transferring a car from the right side yard to the left side yard.

The classification yard on the left side of the layout contains a number of passing sidings that allow a loco to separate from and move around its own train. This configuration also allows a switcher to add or subtract cars from either side of a siding. Track Q, which runs diagonally at the bottom of the layout, makes an ideal locomotive storage/service track, if you have track Q lead into a turn-

table with a roundhouse to shelter your railroad's motive power.

Even though this layout has only one conventional continuous running loop, there could be three separate concurrent activities: a train running on the mainline loop, a second train running between the two reversing loops, and a switcher working the two yards. Naturally, cab-control wiring and, possibly, automatic-control wiring should be used to manage all three activities. Also, a good signaling system is advisable—particularly if you plan to have more than one operator running the layout.

PLATFORM OR TABLE CONSTRUCTION

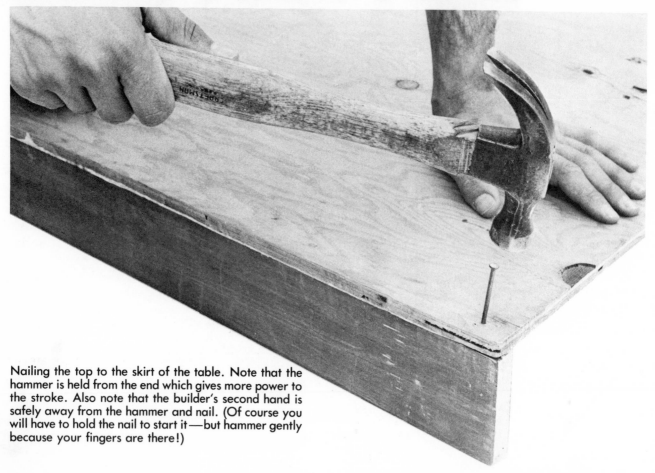

Nailing the top to the skirt of the table. Note that the hammer is held from the end which gives more power to the stroke. Also note that the builder's second hand is safely away from the hammer and nail. (Of course you will have to hold the nail to start it—but hammer gently because your fingers are there!)

Your model railroad layout literally will stand or fall on your early decisions regarding table design.

The instincts of most novice toy train operators are to build the closed-top train table, usually a 4′ × 8′ sheet of plywood standing on legs of 30 inches to 40 inches. It appears to be easier and quicker to build. The other option, of course, is the open-top table, commonly consisting of a frame with "joists" at regular intervals across an open area.

Although the short-run appeal of easier construction and earlier train operation are significant, in the long run an open-top design will have more possibilities and provide more satisfaction. The open-top looks more difficult, but it is only moderately so. It does offer a much greater variety in layout design and operation. With an open-top table, it is possible to have

valleys and lakes below the grade of the table top. Of equal importance, it is possible to have one track go down while the other track rises. The maximum grade with most O-gauge trains is a ½-inch rise or fall per foot of track, and you will need approximately five inches of clearance for one train over another. At least 10 feet of track length will be required on a closed-top table; the bottom track must lie flat on the table while the top track requires 10 feet of length to rise five inches above the lower track.

But with an open-top table, only five feet of track length are needed, since the bottom track can fall 2½ inches while the top track rises 2½ inches—both within five feet. This provides an added advantage, since slopes on curves should be avoided because they increase the likelihood of derailments. If you have a 4′ × 8′ area in which to build your layout, it is possible to have

One track crossing above another on a closed-top table.

the tracks pass over each other with all the slope on the straight track—if you use the open-top design. One great aid to elevating (and to depressing) track is the trestle, such as the Lionel No. 110 trestle, which is common and inexpensive.

PERIMETER TABLES

The perimeter layout is an important alternative to the 4' × 8' open-top or closed-top design. The perimeter layout provides long running distances for your engines and is easier to landscape, since the linear expanses accommodate track sidings and factories along the right-of-way.

The perimeter design also makes use of space which otherwise could not be used for a train layout. For example, in many basements the necessary space for a 4' × 8' layout can be spared, but not much more. That's 32 square feet, which does not favorably compare with the scores of square feet which can be secured by constructing a relatively narrow table along the basement walls. With some forethought and through negotiations with other family users of the basement, long and imaginative train journeys can be developed. These long runs also provide great opportunities for multiple elevations while reducing the risk of derailments.

There are two main variants of the perimeter table. One involves the track going entirely around the basement (or attic), with a widening of the layout at various locations to accommodate accessories and scenery. The other involves a perimeter layout with substantially widened areas to provide a "turnaround" area for train operation.

Most beginners overbuild. They use lumber that is needlessly heavy (and expen-

sive). The use of lighter lumber means easier sawing, easier nailing, easier hauling, and less strain on the budget. Lumber known as 2 by 2 is sufficient for the support legs for model railroad layout tables. The term 2 by 2 means that before drying and dressing, the lumber measured 2″ × 2″ square; at the lumber yard a 2 by 2 measures approximately 1⅝″ × 1⅝″. The horizontal members of the train table generally should be 1 by 4 strips. On an open-top table, 1 by 3's are used to run a single track line, while a 1 by 6 (or two 1 by 3's) will easily support a double track.

If you wish to construct a 4' by 8' closed-top table, you will need the following materials:
- 5 pieces, 1 by 4, 8 feet long.
- 3 pieces, 2 by 2, 7 feet long (for tall legs) or 2 pieces, 2 by 2, 8 feet long for shorter legs.
- 1 lb., 6d common nails.
- 1 sheet plywood interior grade, 4' × 8'.

The legs should be prepared first. The 7-foot lengths of 2 by 2, when cut in half, will provide six legs of up to 42 inches each. If you wish to build shorter table legs, use the 8-foot sections, cutting three legs from each. Some people prefer lower tables so that children can easily see trains being operated—30 inches high, for example, the height of a kitchen table. Others prefer higher tables for their layouts so that wiring and other work beneath the table surface can be more easily accomplished. A higher table also affords more storage space.

Lumber can be purchased in several grades. There are top grades, usually for staining and varnishing, medium grades, and very coarse grades, which are irregular and rough. Middle grades of pine or fir, whichever are less expensive, are recommended. Make sure you select the individual pieces yourself rather than permitting them to be selected by a clerk or store staffer; you will want the straightest pieces possible. Warped lumber has no place in model railroading.

The skirt for the table top should be made from the 1 by 4 strips, which should be ready to nail onto the side of the plywood sheet. (These pieces must be straight, especially if they are to be used in open-top construction.) Nail one of

Nailing the top to one of the short side pieces of the skirt. To make a stronger table, thinly coat the contacting surfaces of skirt and table with wood glue before nailing.

Nailing the long piece of the table skirt into the shorter piece substantially strengthens the table. However, wood splitting is a potential problem at this point. Hence, drilling a starter hole through the long skirt piece is recommended. Gluing before nailing is also recommended.

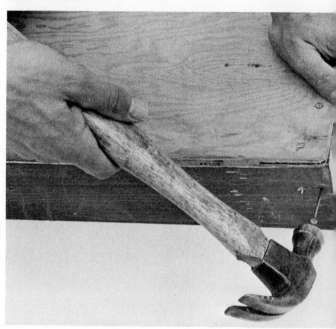

the 8-foot sections to the edge of the plywood sheet, after you have placed the sheet on one of the upright strips (as pictured in top right. Support the plywood on the other side with wood or books. Start at one end, nailing the sheet to the strip by working the skirt so that it conforms to the edge of the plywood; 1 by 4 stripping is bendable and will conform. For added strength, apply some reliable wood glue to the top side of the 1 by 4 strips and to the matching surface of the plywood before nailing.

The short side pieces are 46½ inches in length. These are cut from the 8-foot sections to fit inside the long side pieces. The latter are to be positioned under the appropriate ends of the plywood and nailed into it (using the 6d nails). For added strength, apply glue as outlined above. Finally, nail the ends of the long side pieces into the shorter side pieces.

TABLE LEGS

The six legs of your table should be made from 2 by 2 lumber at a height of your own choosing. The table surface should be turned upside down and each leg fastened individually. Each leg is to be fastened into each corner (at the juncture of the end and side skirts). The legs should be screwed into the skirts with lag screws (¼ inch in diameter and 2½ inches in length). Use two screws for each leg, and stag-

ger them when fastening. To prevent the lag screws from splitting the skirt, drill starter holes of approximately $3/16$ inch in diameter for each screw. For aesthetic and functional reasons, it is best to countersink the screw heads before fastening so that they will be flush with the table edge. Countersinking is a process by which a hole is made for the head of the screw to be recessed within the table edge. Take a wood or metal bit with at least a ⅝-inch diameter cutting surface and drill into the starter hole for ¼ inch.

The 2 by 2 legs will have to be reinforced, since a mere two screws at one end of a 30-inch or 40-inch thin leg will result in an unacceptable degree of wobble. The easiest method is to cut 23½-inch braces from the 1 by 4 stripping (for 30-inch legs; longer legs will require longer braces). Four braces can be cut from one 8-foot section of 1 by 4. By applying Figure 12 with care, only five cuts should be required to fashion the four braces from the 8-foot strip. The use of a miter-box is recommended to cut the 45-degree angles satisfactorily. (A miter box is little more than a simple box open at the short ends, with slots cut through at several angles, usually 30, 45, and 90 degrees.)

The reinforcing brace should be fastened to each leg either with the 6d nails or shorter ¼-inch diameter screws. If you wish to fasten the brace to the skirt you will have to build out

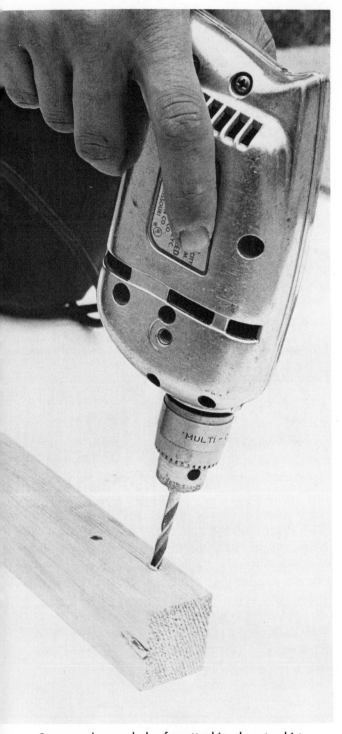

Staggered screw holes for attaching legs to skirt.

Your closed-top table now should be complete, unless you wish to add a small section to accommodate your transformer and other controls. To make this section, use a smaller sheet of plywood (perhaps 2′ × 4′) and build a skirt of 1″ × 4″ stripping around its perimeter, as you did for the train table. Then make two legs the same length as the table legs and attach them to the front edge of your control panel. Then nail or screw the long rear edge of the panel to the train table skirt.

BUILDING AN OPEN-TOP TABLE

The strength of the open-top design stems from the interconnection of the structural members, similar to a wooden or steel girder bridge. The open-top table does not rely on a flat sheet of plywood for its strength or stability. The basic 4′ × 8′ open-top table consists of four parallel joists (of 1″ × 4″ stripping) each 8 feet long, and several reinforcing pieces between the joists. Your basic list of materials will include:

- Four 1″ × 4″ strips, 8′ in length.
- Four 1″ × 4″ strips, each 10¾″ in length.
- Four 1″ × 4″ strips, each 17⅜″ in length.
- Two 1″ × 4″ strips, each 4′ in length.
- Eight 2″ × 2″ legs, each 30″ (or preferred) length.

Start to make your open-top table by forming a box with the inside joists A and B (see page 65) and the shorter reinforcing pieces C and D. Apply a high-quality wood glue to the joining edges, and nail joist A into reinforcing piece D. Then nail joist B into reinforcing piece D. Add short reinforcing pieces G and H and nail after glueing. Glue and nail end-piece E to pieces C, A, and B; also glue and nail end-piece F to pieces C, A, and B.

The next step is to glue and nail the long skirt M to pieces E and F. Follow this by attaching supports I and J (without glue—you may wish to remove them later), offset from pieces G and H to facilitate nailing. Then glue and nail skirt N to pieces E and F. Follow with supports K and L (also offset from pieces G and H), but omit glueing them.

the skirt so that the brace will be parallel to the skirt side. Small pieces of scrap wood should be used to make the skirt wide enough to equal the width of each leg. If you have some 2 by 2 scrap, you can nail this to the inside of the skirt. Then the brace should be nailed (or screwed) to the scrap block on the inside of the skirt. Obviously, on a 4′ × 8′ table it will be necessary to have braces on all four corner legs; the braces for the center legs are optional.

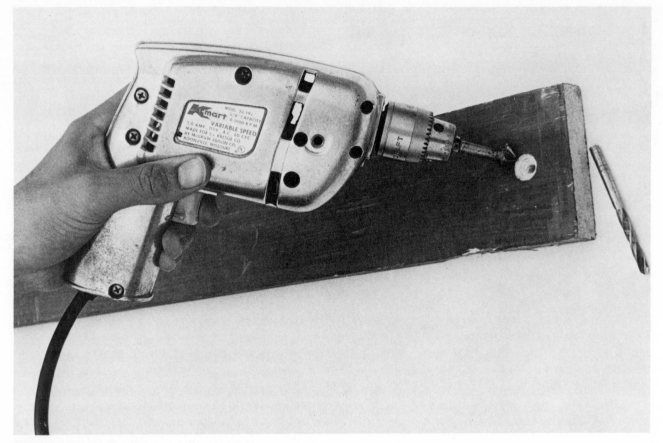

Using a power drill with special countersink bit to countersink a hole on a table leg. Countersinking is easily done and does much to give a professional appearance to your table.

Your open-top table is now ready for its legs. Cut the eight legs to the desired length. Glue and screw the legs to the skirt with No. 10 Phillips head screws (1½ inches long) or ¼-inch lag screws (1½ inches to 2 inches long). Drill starter holes for the screws to make insertion easier and to reduce the possibility of wood splits. (A variable-speed power drill can be enormously helpful in the laborious task of applying screws to a model train layout; seriously consider investing in one.) Your table legs also will need braces; use the instructions that refer to the erecting of the closed-top table.

Having completed the open-top table supporting structure, it is appropriate to consider laying track. Since the appeal of the open-top table is its ready compatibility with track grades, you should design your track layout to descend on one side of the table and to ascend on the other side. Let us assume that you have built a 4′ × 12′ open-top structure and that your joists are on one-foot centers (the center of one joist is about 12 inches from the center from the joists on either side of it).[1]

You will need spanners (pieces of wood) between the parallel joists to support your 1″ × 4″ roadbed. Let's assume that you are starting the decline just after the track straightens from the curve at the corner (or one foot from the table end). Cut a piece of 2 by 2 (or 1 by 4) approximately 11⅜ inches long to fill the gap between the joists (your actual measurements may differ somewhat). Your first spanning piece should be lightly fastened, by nails only, so that when the 1 by 4 roadbed is laid on top of it, the roadbed will be flush with the existing surface of the open-top table at the end of the curve.

If this is your first open-top table, it is recommended that the curved-track ends of the table be level (no grades) and mounted on plywood. After you have developed more skills in working on open-top tables, then experiment with elevating and descending curves. These

[1] Our plans provide measurements for constructing a 4′ × 8′ open-top table. To build a 4′ × 12′ table, simply build two 4′ × 6′ tables and position them together to share a common middle point.

4 × 8 open top table

A, B, M, N   1 × 4—8'

C, D, G, H   1 × 4—10¾"

I, J, K, L   1 × 4—17⅜"

E, F   1 × 4—4'

O, P, Q, R, S, T,   2 × 2—30"
    U, V

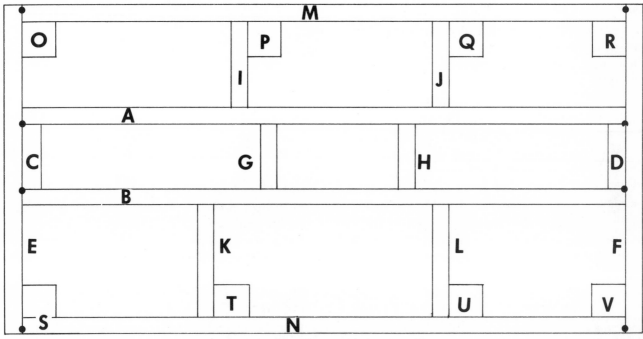

A basic plan for a 4' x 8' open-top table.

curves can be mounted on plywood cut to the track shape with a saber saw.

Assuming that you are using a piece of 1 by 4 that is five feet in length, you are allowed a drop of only 2½ inches over its length. Thus, at the end of the 1 by 4, locate another spanning piece between the joists so that the top of the piece is 2½ inches lower than the top of the first ing piece. Position this second piece so that it can support the start of the second piece of roadbed as well as the end of the first piece. Position your second 5-foot strip of roadbed on top of the second spanner and let it drop another 2½ inches over its length.

Let us also assume that you want to have a second track, running parallel to the first track. Starting at the other end of the train layout, you will want your roadbed to *rise* at the rate of ½ inch per foot of length. Thus, the first spanner

should be placed between the joists where the last piece of curving track is located. The next spanner for the rising track should be about 5 feet further on, fastened lightly so that its top is 2½ inches higher than that of the first spanner. The third spanner would be another 5 feet along the line, rising another 2½ inches (for a total of 5 inches above the top of the joists). At this point, you have reached the maximum required track clearance for any track below it at surface level. For example, your outside track could have a spur that goes beneath the inside track. For this spur you will need a switch, which will need support from beneath. To support the switch, place several additional joist spanners in appropriate locations beneath the switch itself.

Since your inside track is entering the curve 5 inches above the outside track, you will want to make provision for a piece of plywood to support your curve track. At the end of the layout you should use two pieces of plywood, each 18 inches wide and 4 feet long; one piece will support the upper curve, and the other will support the lower curve. The lower piece should sit directly on the joists; the upper piece should be elevated by pieces of 1 by 4 tacked to the inside of the table skirt. Notches should be cut in the four corners of the lower piece for clearance of the 1 by 4 supports. (Each notch should be about ⅝ inch.)

At the other end of the layout, the procedure should be comparable. The inner track is now the level track, sitting on a piece of ½-inch plywood that is supported only by the joists. A lower level is suspended underneath this plywood. It consists of ½-inch plywood suspended from 1 by 4 strips nailed into the inside of the table skirts. The top of the strips are flush with the joists and at their bottom, they are flush with the top surface of the lower-level plywood. The plywood is to be screwed and glued into these supports.

However, you will soon notice that the three inner joists are in the way of the lower-level roadbed. It will be necessary to cut through the joists and "box" them so that they will still provide support even after they have been cut. Before you cut off one foot from each of the three joists, it is necessary to find some temporary method of support without destroying the cohesion of the table.

The easiest method is to attach a supplemental leg, composed of either 1 by 4 or 2 by 2 lumber and attached to each joist at the point where it is to be cut. Now you may cut off the three inner joists 18 inches from the end of the table. A new end-piece should be nailed across the three shortened joists to provide more support.

For a more precise determination of where to cut the joists, take the lower-level plywood piece and use a bright marking pen to trace the exact location of the roadbed to be mounted on it. Then temporarily fasten this plywood to the joist bottoms. Note where the track intersects each of the three joists, and mark the areas of

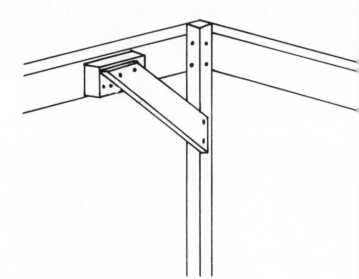

A basic plan for angular table bracing.

the joists to be removed to provide for train clearance. Before cutting the joists, make sure you provide temporary support of the joists by using another 1 by 4 and a "C" clamp on each joist. These supports will prevent the joists from coming loose when trimmed. Place the supports far enough back so that the plywood can be fastened after the joists are cut. (You may wish to leave these supports in place even after the plywood is fastened.)

To provide for the elevated sections use 2 pieces of ½" plywood, 18" × 4', one at each end. To facilitate laying track on the lower level in the joist plane—use two pieces of plywood, 18" × 4", one for each end. (See example on page 61.) The upper level plywood is supported by small pieces of wood tacked between it and the lower level plywood.

Our plans call for two parallel tracks. Start the outer track from the left side upper deck. The track will fall 4½" to the lower level. (The inner track starts on the upper level on the right side and falls 4½" to the lower level on the left.) It is supported by a 1 × 3 nine feet long (or 1 × 4) descending to the right. (Of course you can use shorter pieces as available.)

The 1 × 3 descends 4½" in the 9 feet. It is supported by two 1 × 4's or other small pieces tacked on to the joists. Note that you can use shorter pieces by moving the supports as necessary.

TRACK WORK

The quality of your track work is crucial to the operating success of your toy train layout. Fortunately, it is not particularly hard to achieve high quality track work; basically, all you have to do is follow simple and straightforward procedures.

If you are using section O-gauge (or O-27 or S-gauge) track, the first procedure is to make sure that the track is clean and free of oil and rust. Discoloration of the track will not adversely affect train performance. A number of cleaning fluids are commercially available for cleaning track; *be certain to follow the cautionary instructions on the bottle* even though most track cleaning fluids claim to be nontoxic and nonflammable. If your track is afflicted with heavy rusting (which you can feel with your fingertips) then you have some real work ahead of you. While steel wool commonly is an appropriate substance for removing rust, it creates problems for toy trains. Steel wool breaks down into small fibers which inevitably find their way into your locomotive motors (which attract small pieces of iron and steel because of their electromagnetic fields). These fibers can cause a short circuit, and in extreme cases can cause fire, destroying your little treasure. So don't use steel wool; instead, use emery paper. The fine grades cut rust readily and leave a smoothly finished surface.

If your track is scaly with rust, you should first use a wire brush made of steel. The best type is a wire brush mounted at the end of an electric grinder (with the grinder firmly mounted on a workbench). Such an arrangement allows you to hold the track with two hands, which is advisable during such cleaning. Remember to wear protective goggles. Less desirable is the ¼ inch power drill with a small wire brush unit, since it allows you only one free hand to hold the track; again, goggles are a must here. A safer method, albeit slower, is to brush the rust from the track by hand.

CLEANING AND TIGHTENING

The track rails are not the only part of the track which must be meticulously cleaned. Of utmost importance is the cleaning of the track pins (or any other connectors which join the sections of track). The reason for this is simple: if track pins are corroded then the electric current will not flow well to the next section. Thus the current may only reach that section by traveling entirely the other way around the layout, resulting in a voltage drop and poor train performance.

If several track pins are corroded or loose, the voltage will drop to below operating level in a whole section of a train layout. The idea is to make your track pins not only clean and shiny, but to keep them tightly secured. If they are loose, it is because the rail is not tight enough around the pins. If you take an ordinary pair of pliers and try to squeeze the rail more tightly around the pin, the rail usually expands and you make no progress. That's why the use of needlenose pliers is suggested.

If this technique does not succeed, you may have to extract the pin, crimp the pinless rail nearly shut, and push the pin back into place; this will be more difficult, however. When using this technique, use a different set of pliers (called lineman's pliers) which will grip each pin more securely. Sometimes the pins are missing from tracks; at your earliest opportunity, acquire a sizable quantity of original track pins for the gauge in which you are operating. Track pins definitely are preferable to nails. Lionel pins, for example, have secondary grooves near each end of each pin, which help secure the pin within the rail. Track pins are inexpensive and currently are available from Lionel or at your hobby store. (If necessary, you can use nails which have been decapitated by a bolt cutter, hacksaw, or nippers.)

FASTENING THE TRACK

Fastening the track to the table top or to the flat 1 by 4 wood strips of an open-top design is an important step in your railroad construction. For O-gauge and Standard-gauge track it's best to use ½-inch-long No. 4 or No. 5 wood screws; O-27 gauge track requires ⅜-inch-long No. 3

screws. Screw holes should first be "started" by tapping a 4d nail into the desired spot or by drilling a hole with a $^1/_{16}$ inch bit; these small drill bits, however, break quite easily—a flaw which can quickly become expensive.

You should not overtighten these wood screws, as this will strip a hole in the wood and ruin the hold of the screw. If you are doing a great deal of track fastening, the screwdriver eventually will cause a blister in your hand (especially if your hands are not work-toughened). This can be prevented by the use of a "ratchet-type" screwdriver, in which down pressure on the tool is concerted into a rotary motion to tighten the screw. Such a ratchet screwdriver generally costs $5 or less. If you have a variable-speed power drill, you can purchase a screwdriver blade attachment or fashion one from an old screwdriver.

Before fastening the track, you might consider using wooden ties to better simulate the ties (or "sleepers") found in real railroads. Such ties are commercially available and occasionally advertised in *Model Railroader*. However, it is relatively easy to make your own ties. Buy some wood approximately ½ inch thick for O-gauge ties (⅜ inch for O-27) and with a table saw cut the wood into strips which are 1½ inches wide. Then, sawing in the other direction, cut individual ½-inch ties from the larger strips.

After cutting your ties, you will want to stain them to resemble prototype ties which have been soaked in creosote. Buy a gallon of dark wood stain (preferably walnut) and pour a pint of it into a bucket. Toss in your ties and stir them around. Remove the ties with tweezers. Generally, a short bath will be sufficient if the wood is porous. Do not leave the stain exposed in the bucket longer than necessary, as it will evaporate quickly.

The ties can be individually fastened to the layout surface by using very fine finishing nails or brads. You might prefer to use the track itself to hold the ties in place if the ties are slightly higher than the model track ties.

INSULATED TRACK SECTIONS

Before fastening your track to the table, you may want to consider creating specially insulated outside rails for the control of accessories (and even to permit the operation of two separate trains on one track). Three-rail Lionel and Marx track has an insulated center rail, which is customarily known as the hot rail or the third rail. The two outer rails are grounded to each other through the metal ties. For controlling accessories or multiple train operations, it is necessary to insulate one of the outside rails on one or more sections of track. You may wish to use the switch devices made by Lionel and Marx to control their accessories. These devices—known as contactors—use the principle of pressure or weight to close (or open) the relevant circuit. Their problem is that weight adjustment is not entirely satisfactory; sometimes the contactor will produce the operation sequence that is desired, other times not. Another problem with the contactors is that several loose track sections are required for satisfactory operation. Operation with insulated track sections is much more reliable and provides longer operation sequences.

To create insulated track, you will need some track which can be dismantled for insulation purposes, as well as some insulation fiber. There are two alternative sources of this fiber: pieces of cardboard cut to the required size, or pieces of insulating fiber from existing pieces of track. Recycled pieces of fiber work best since the new cardboard tends to crack at the wrong spot when fitted into place.

Used track, especially track which is warped or rusted, is inexpensively available at train shows and is a prime source for track insulating fiber. Using a tack puller, carefully work loose the flanges which hold the center rail in place. Tack pullers have a tendency to slip when used to pry, so be careful to avoid gouged fingers. After you have loosened the flanges holding the center rail, slide or pull the rail from the flanges. Carefully remove the insulation from this rail and save it for later use.

Three different Lionel contactors: the 145C, 154C, and the 153C. The 145C is a simple on-off switch. The pressure of the train closes the air gap and completes the circuit turning the accessory on. The 154C is specially designed for the 154 highway flasher which has two red lights that alternately flash as the train goes by. The underside of the moveable rail contacting piece is insulated from the rail. The car wheels passing over this piece complete the circuit. As the car rolls over the first half of the contact it completes the circuit for the first bulb, as it rolls over the second half of the contact, it completes the circuit for the second bulb. 153C is the most elaborate of the three. When the train passes over it, it breaks (opens) one circuit and makes another.

A tack puller is a handy tool to loosen the track flange from the rail. Then the rail may be removed easily from the track and the insulation secured. Be careful that you do not apply to much pressure to the tack puller as it could slip and gouge your fingers.

Take a piece of track which needs to be equipped with an insulated outside rail, and, while the rail is still in place, remove the metal track pin. It is much easier to remove the track pin while the rail is still secure within the flanges on the ties. Hold the track securely in one hand and gradually work the pin out. You can help loosen the pin by wedging a screwdriver into the track beneath the pin so that the rail loosens around the pin (see next page). If the pin is difficult to extract, use lineman's pliers or locking pliers. Be careful not to distort the track while this operation is in progress.

After removing the track pin, loosen the flanges holding the rail in place and remove the nail. Then, with a pair of needle-nose pliers, bend the flanges so as to provide a slightly larger opening to accommodate the rail *plus* the newly installed insulation. Place the insulation on the rail in the proper locations; then carefully reinsert the rail within the flanges.

Next, arrange a little wooden block to fit under the track tie, and with a round punch gently tap the flanges back against the rail. Give the flange a slightly stronger tap to secure it against the rail. Repeat this process for the other ties. Then test the track to assure that neither

the center rail nor the new outside insulated rail is leaking any current. Turn your transformer to its maximum voltage. Apply one lead to the grounded outside rail. After that, gingerly apply the other transformer lead first to the insulated center rail and then to the insulated outer rail. If the rails are properly insulated, no spark should be visible.

You should acquire two *nylon* track pins for each piece of insulated track that is used (Lionel manufactures these pins). If the nylon track pins are not available, then toothpicks or small plastic knitting needles will suffice. Put nylon pins into each end of the newly insulated outside rail. When the "retooled" track is installed in the layout, it will be necessary to remove one steel pin from one of the adjoining track sections.

The purpose of insulating one outside rail from the flanges on its ties is to break the circuit from one section of rail to the next. Since a toy train accessory needs two wires, the insulated outside rail is used to complete the ground circuit, which is called U. The ground circuit is only completed when rolling stock passes over the specially prepared track. The wheels on the "live" ground side pick up the ground current and carry it through the axles to the wheels on the "dead" (or insulated) ground side. A lock-on is then affixed to this special section. A wire is

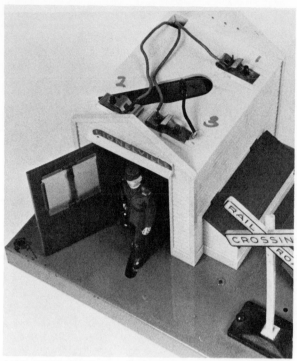

A No. 145 gateman with the roof removed to expose the wire connections. Post No. 2 may be used to provide a common hot line for both the bulb and the solenoid mechanism that moves the man. Post 3 provides a ground for the bulb, while post No. 1 provides a ground for the solenoid. Hook Post No. 2 to the CTC post that contacts the middle rail. Hook No. 3 to the CTC post that contacts the outside rail that is continually powered. Using a special piece of track with an insulated outside rail, hook No. 1 to the CTC post that contacts the outside rail that is only powered when a train passes.

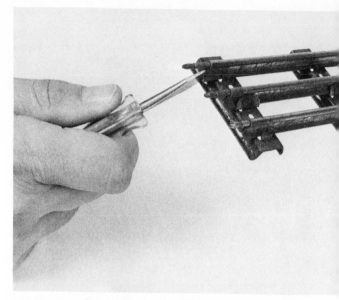

To remove a track pin from the rail it may be necessary to slightly spread the rail using a small screwdriver. Again, be careful about applying to much pressure—a slip may result and your fingers may suffer!

hooked to the lock-on post connecting the "dead" ground and the other end of the wire connected to the accessory. The second wire (known as the hot wire) is wired from the accessory to the transformer (or to a "bus bar" wire connected to the transformer).

Many different accessories can be connected to your special insulated track section. Initially, try the No. 252 Lionel gate and the No. 145 gateman. The No. 252 gate has two clip pressure-type connectors on its base. You should hook one of the clips (it doesn't matter which one) to the contact of the lock-on that is connected with the newly insulated outside rail. Hook the remaining clip to the other post of the lock-on that is connected to the center rail. When the train goes past, the gate will go down (using the track voltage). This action, however, may be too brisk for your taste. If so, then hook the wire that normally would go to the center rail to a transformer post which gives a 10–12 volt combination in conjunction with post U. (This assumes that you have hooked post U to

the outside rail and either post A, B, C, or D to the center rail.) This voltage will result in a more leisurely, and realistic, lowering of the warning gate.

The No. 145 gateman also can be hooked up using the insulated outside rail track section. Note that No. 145 has both a light and an electromagnet; the latter operates the door and the man. Generally, you would prefer to have the light continuously lighted so that your gateman can read or play cards or checkers while waiting for the trains. On the other hand, you only want the electromagnet energized when the train is going past. The No. 145 gateman has three spring-type connections to be found under the roof of the gatehouse. One is a common hot line for both the electromagnet and the bulb. The other two provide independent ground circuits for the bulb and the electromagnet.

You will want to use two lock-ons. One is to be put on one side of the track, so that it contacts the new outside insulated rail and the center rail; the other is to be put on the opposite side of the track. Here it will contact the regular outside ground rail and the center rail. You should hook the common hot line to the center rail using one of the two lock-ons. Hook the ground side of the light circuit to the continuously energized ground rail. Hook the electromagnet ground to the newly insulated outside rail via the lock-on. Now your No. 145 gateman will be continuously

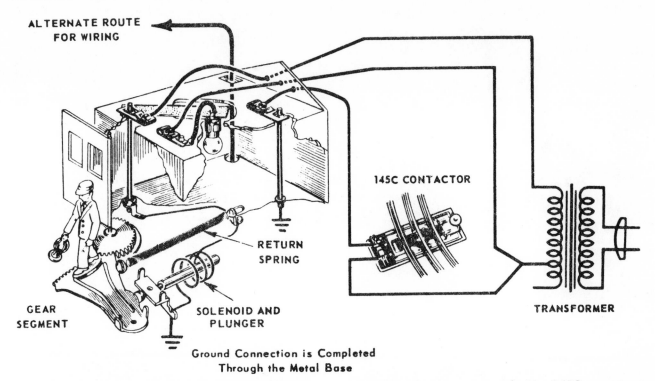

ALTERNATE ROUTE
FOR WIRING

145C CONTACTOR

RETURN
SPRING

GEAR
SEGMENT

SOLENOID AND
PLUNGER

TRANSFORMER

Ground Connection is Completed
Through the Metal Base

A wiring diagram for the No. 145 automatic gateman. So that the light remains burning between trains while the gateman rests.

Note that this diagram uses the No. 145C contactor to operate the gateman. This is a different approach than that detailed previously.

lighted as power is supplied to the track, but he will only come out of the shack when the train passes by.

SOLDERING TECHNIQUES AND TRACKWORK

Lionel made lock-ons for connecting the transformer to the track and for providing jumpers or leads to far-flung portions of toy train layouts. Lock-ons are inexpensive at train shows—good used ones can be found for only 25¢. But sometimes it is inconvenient to use lock-ons, or you discover that you have exhausted your supply. What to do? The solution is simple: solder the wire to the track.

Make sure that the tip of your soldering gun or iron is adequately tinned. This means that the tin should be clean, bright, and smooth. Once the tip has reached operating temperature and been touched to the solder, the solder should melt almost instantly and spread over the tip.

If you are using a pencil iron, you will need at least a 100-watt iron to solder copper bell wire to your track. Less than 100 watts will not heat the track enough to make the solder flow evenly; it will form into tiny balls and roll off onto your clothes or the floor. Most soldering guns are 100 watts or more. The 250-watt guns work better than the smaller ones, although they

are heavier to hold.

You also should buy a reel (or more) of a reliable lead-and-tin mix solder (either 50-50 mix or 60-40 lead-tin mix) which has a resin core. Do not buy acid-core solder; it will corrode your joints. Resin in the center of the solder strip serves as a flux and helps the solder adhere both to the copper wire and to the tin-plated track.

It is crucial that you clean the spot on the track where the solder is to be applied. Use very fine sandpaper to cut through the oxidation on the rail until the rail is shiny. Even new track should be sandpapered, since there may be a slight oxidation and/or some preservative that will inhibit solder adhesion.

Also, it is crucial that the soldering iron (or gun) be quite hot. Solder touched to the tip should melt instantly and flow evenly over the tip. Unless the iron is quite hot, all is in vain. Unfortunately, irons and guns develop pitted tips due to oxidation under heat. The pits prevent part of the tip surface from touching the track, resulting in inadequate transferal of heat. To remedy this, take a fine metal file and gently file the tip's flat contours to remove the pits. This can be done while the iron is hot, but requires great care. Don't get burned; if you must clean the tip while it is hot, get a friend to hold

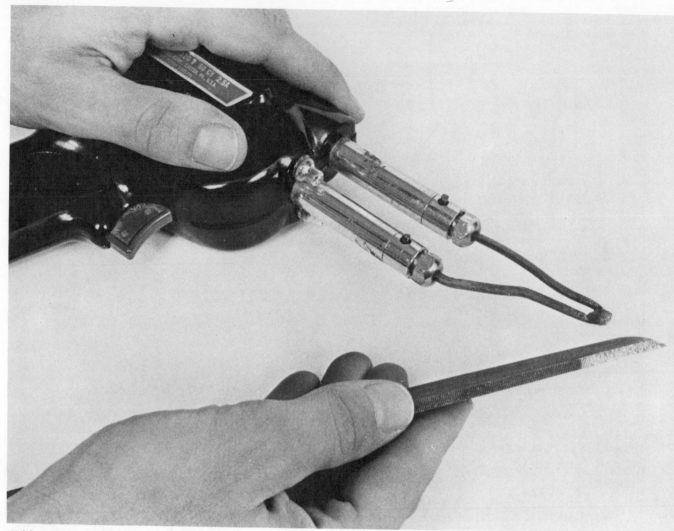

Soldering iron tips pit in use. Filing the tips carefully back to their original shape will dramatically increase the heat transmitted and the ease of soldering.

the soldering iron securely while you file.

Soldering gun tips can lose contact with their internal wiring; the extreme heat causes the steel inside the unit rapidly to oxidize. The contact point between the tip and the body of the iron becomes increasingly oxidized, impeding the flow of electricity. This is an insidious process, causing mounting frustration for the gun's user. Yet there is an easy solution: periodically loosen the nuts that tighten the protruding bars which grasp the tip. Practice loosening and tightening the tip while the iron is cold. The retaining nuts should be loosened only about a half-turn, and then retightened. Repeat the loosening and the tightening. This process will scrape away enough oxidation to make your soldering gun an effective tool again. In heavy soldering work, some guns need to be loosened

and tightened as often as every three or four joints.

Pencil irons, on the other hand, use several different means of fastening the tips to the body of the iron. Some use protruding plugs which extend from the tip and plug into the receiver body. Others use tips which screw into the body using threads much like those found on light bulbs and sockets. In both cases, removal and replacement of the tips several times should remove enough oxidation to put you back in business. If you choose to do this while the iron is still hot, be very careful that you don't get burned. Even though the iron is not hot enough to melt the solder, it will still be hot enough to melt any part of you it touches.

When soldering bell wire (No. 18 gauge) to the track, the process should be split into three

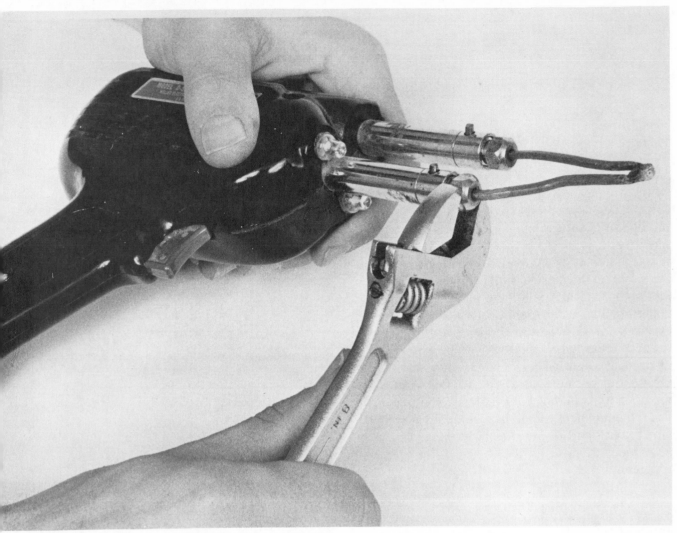

To keep your soldering iron efficient it is necessary to periodically lossen and retighten the retaining nuts. Loosen and tighten and loosen and tighten each nut. Be careful not to overtighten, as you can damage the gun.

stages. The first step is to tin the track; this means applying a thin coat of solder to a small area on the base of the track. The area must be free of all oxidation or preservatives so that the solder will flow evenly, instead of clumping and falling off. Next, bring your iron or gun to the area to be tinned, and hold it snugly against this area for several seconds. Apply solder to the track immediately above or adjacent to the iron. If the track is sufficiently heated, the solder will flow evenly over the area.

Then take your wire lead to be fastened to the track and strip the insulation from its end. Shine the bare wire with your fine sandpaper, if necessary. Touch your iron to the bare end of the wire for several seconds, and apply solder to the bare wire immediately along the soldering tip. The solder should flow evenly over the wire

on one side. Then take your needle-nose pliers and make a 90-degree end on the wire where the bare tip meets the insulated section. Place the tinned bare tip firmly against the tinned track section. Apply heat for several seconds until the solder on both pieces flows together. Remove your soldering iron, but hold the wire in place for another 8 to 10 seconds while the solder hardens.

THE BASICS ARE BEHIND YOU

Chapter 6 has provided detailed instructions for basic 4′ × 8′ open-top and closed-top toy train tables. No doubt, you will modify these to fit your room, your imagination, and your budget. Track laying was also considered. Not yet discussed is the building of scenery, which is intimately related to track placement. Sometimes people prefer to lay the track first and then build the scenery around the track; the main alternative is to integrate the laying of the track with the creation of the landscape. Read chapter 7 before laying your track, so that you keep open the option of integrating your landscaping and track work.

Chapter 6 also provided detailed instructions for that most useful skill in model railroading: soldering. You will have great success at soldering if you conscientiously provide clean surfaces and sufficient heat. Successful soldering accelerates what can otherwise be a process of drudgery and it adds dependability to your wiring. Furthermore, soldering will be useful in repairing and building your rolling stock. Older Lionel equipment often has soldered seams which may work loose. Properly applied, the techniques described will also help solve these problems.

When soldering wire to the track, it is also necessary to tin the wire. Strip the insulation from the wire end and then clean with emery paper. Heat the wire end and then bring the solder to the heated end. The solder should flow evenly over the bare end of the wire.

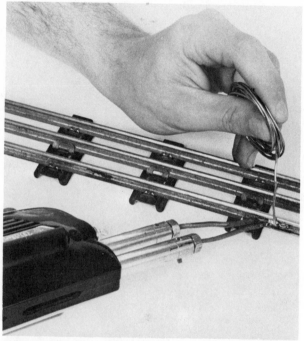

When soldering wire to track it is necessary to first tin the track. Heat the track and then bring your solder to the heated area. If the heat is adequate and the surface has been properly cleaned, the solder will flow evenly over the hot area. Otherwise the solder will bead and often fall off.

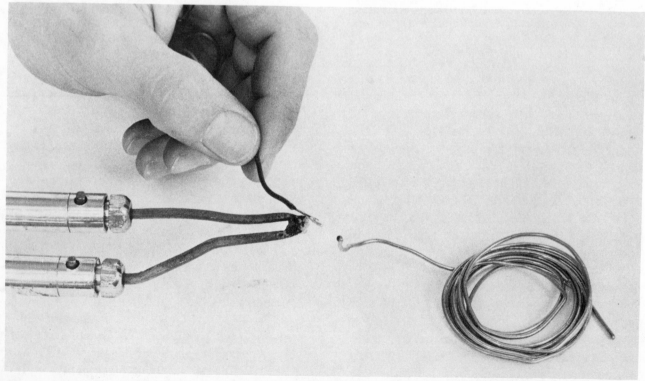

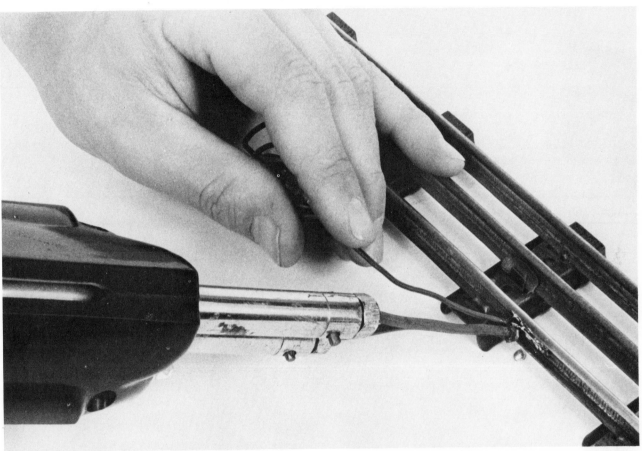

After both the wire and the track have been tinned, hold the tinned wire end against the tinned track section and apply heat. The solder should flow together. Hold the wire in place until the solder cools to a solid. Hint: wear a glove, because the wire end gets quite warm.

CONSTRUCTING SCENERY

A four-level section of Ralph Barger's magnificent layout. Open-top table designs greatly facilitate such interesting trackwork.

Illusion is at the heart of the model railroad. The illusion of scenery and the imaginations of you, your family, and friends continually pump the lifeblood of excitement into this creative hobby.

It is surprisingly easy to shift from the repressed, flat, monotonous layout of 4' × 8' plywood to the dynamic three-dimensional open-top layout. The first step is to be resolute: do not succumb to temptation by placing that sheet of plywood over your frame. Once you have nailed the sheet to the frame, you have severely limited the potential interest and impact of your layout. The open-top table, using roughly the same space, invites a creative approach toward motion and rolling landscapes.

As you have learned, the open-top table is easy to construct, low in cost, and ultimately more satisfying. In constructing your scenery and landscaping on an open-top table, there are two basic strategies: the use of screening or the use of a plasterlike substance known as Hydrocal. If you decide to go with screening, either steel or aluminum screening is available, often at no cost. Since relatively small pieces are required for landscaping, you may be able to salvage damaged window screens or front door screening.

It is best to start with the low hills and valleys; mountain building will come later. The gauge of screening will determine the degree of internal structural support required. Let's assume you've found some medium-weight screening which tends to hold its shape when you mold it. Put a section of this screening between two of the joists that cross the table. You can create a valley with gentle sloping sides or one with dramatic drop-offs. Your decision as to how you bend the screening will determine the geography. The screening should be crinkled so as to provide a surface which is not only more interesting but stronger.

When the screening is in the desired form, it is time to consider the papier-mâché flour mixtures that you will use to cover it. Of course, papier-mâché is just one of numerous materials you may use for landscaping; others include plaster of paris, wall-sizing, spackle, and patching plaster. These materials differ in cost and hardness of finish, as well as their ease of application.

Another source of landscaping material is the plaster-impregnated bandages which physicians use to set broken or sprained limbs. Although quite expensive, this material is a joy to apply and mold.

An old standby (and the least expensive material) is the basic flour and water mixture, to which a little vinegar should be added to retard spoilage and premature setting. To make a workable paste, *slowly* add the water to the flour, and not vice versa. Use very little water and form a thick paste similar to pancake batter; continue adding water, a little at a time, until the consistency is similar to thick paint. The reverse process does not work. Before wetting the flour, you may consider adding food coloring to either the flour or the water so that if chips occur after the landscaping has been done, the bare spots do not show up as a jarring white against your other landscaped colors. You can either add dry coloring material to the flour or you can add liquid food coloring to the water; it is also possible to use brown or olive latex paint as a coloring medium. It is recommended that you use a brownish dye for general paste coloring, possibly relieved with a little yellow or green.

Papier-mâché is not only fun to work with, but it is also very inexpensive. After you have mixed a flour-water combination, tear up pieces of newspaper into single-page strips of convenient size (perhaps 2″ × 8″) and put them into your pail of flour and water to soak. If you add a retardant (such as vinegar) you can let your mixture sit, and work on your landscaping over the course of a week or two. If you have added brown food coloring or latex paint to the papier-mâché, the material will have absorbed some characteristics of genuine earth.

After you have begun the process of laying the papier-mâché strips over the screening in your valley, let the first layer of papier-mâché dry overnight and next day take an inexpensive paintbrush and apply a layer of flour paste. Then cover the flour paste with another layer of papier-mâché. Alternatively, you may cover your papier-mâché layer with patching plaster or spackle (to which you've added food coloring). The plaster helps create irregular surfaces within your landscaping and hides the papier-mâché strips. When you apply the final plaster coat, make sure that it has an interesting and irregular texture; an ordinary table fork is often a handy tool to provide such texture. You may also want to sprinkle sand, gravel, or coffee grounds into the wet plaster to give it the feeling of roughness that you may desire.

After your landscape has dried overnight, you may wish to give it some more coloring of browns, golds, and greens. Since nature itself has so many various shades of brown, olive, tan, and green, you will want your own landscape to share these same variations. For example, assume that you have fashioned a gully; the bottom might be made "gravelly" with grays and tans. The sides would be darker green to indicate the presence of nutrients, vegetation, and water; the top of the gully would be brown and green. The best way to decide which colors to use is to go out and observe the actual topographical features you wish to recreate; you will probably see them as you've never seen them before. You can also study color photographs in books and magazines.

Your children will probably get even more satisfaction and enjoyment out of working with papier-mâché than you do. But a word of caution is necessary: since working with papier-mâché is a soggy operation, there will be considerable drippage onto the floors. A "carpet" of newspapers and/or drop cloths is strongly advised.

BE YOUR OWN MOUNTAIN MAN

The construction of valleys and low hills is relatively simple, since these need no underlying support system. Mountains, however, are another matter. The screening within your mountains will need support. This should not scare you off, since mountain building probably

Crumpled newspaper may serve as the underform for your low hills. Or it can be torn into strips, soaked in flour paste and used as papier mâché on screening to form mountains.

does more to convert a flat table design into an exciting multidimensional landscape than any other procedure. Mountains also provide the justification for model railroad tunnels, which will add interest and intrigue to your layout. Most modelers who decide to do landscaping also decide to construct mountains.

The open-top table design greatly facilitates erecting the supports which mountains require. These vertical supports should be made from 1″ × 2″ scraps or other thin strips of wood, which need only be thick enough to withstand small nails, tacks, or staples without splitting. Soft wood minimizes the risk of splitting and makes nailing easier. To further minimize the chance of splitting your supports, you should drill small holes through the supports for the nails or tacks.

Since the table joists are made from wobbly 1 by 4's, these also will need to be supported while you are tacking on your mountain supports. One approach is to persuade a friend or relative to bodily stabilize the joist while you are

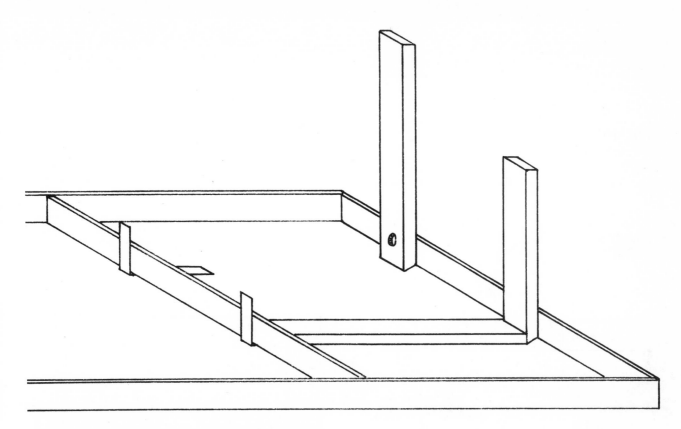

A diagram showing the vertical supports for a screen mountain process, with small holes drilled through supports for stability and 2" x 4" boards used to stabilize the joists. "C" clamps attach the Hydrocal supports to joists

tacking. A second approach is to wedge a 2 by 4 between the table skirt and the appropriate joist. Depending on the thickness of the supports, 4d or 6d finishing nails should be adequate.

After the supports have been readied, your screening should be molded and tacked or stapled to your supports. Care is needed here, since the supports are thin and light. If possible, hold a wooden block behind each mountain support when you tack or staple.

It goes without saying that mountains come in a wide variety of shapes and sizes. The pitch and roll of your mountains should reflect your own taste. You may desire to build old, weather-beaten mountains with their gentle, rounded slopes and peaks, such as the Appalachians in the East. Or you may prefer to fashion mountains of a more recent vintage (only five or ten million years old) which feature sharp peaks and enormous drop-offs, such as the Rockies or the Cascades of the West.

HYDROCAL

An alternative (or complement) to mountain building based on screening is mountain building using a combination of newspapers, ceiling tiles, paper toweling, and Hydrocal. Hydrocal dries much more quickly than plaster and to a harder finish. There are several advantages to this approach. First, it is much easier to mold interesting and irregular forms with these materials than with metal screening. The final product from the Hydrocal method is light and exceedingly strong, as well as nonflammable.

The first step in the Hydrocal method of building model mountains is to establish your desired height or major elevation. Once you know how tall and expansive your mountain(s) will be, you can start building the temporary supports that are required. These supports, usually 1 by 3's, should be fastened to the joists of your open-top table with the use of "C" clamps. (These should cost you less than $1 each, and can be reused repeatedly in the process of constructing and maintaining your model railroad.) "C" clamps are preferable to nails since they are installed faster, they will not split the support wood, and they can be readily removed.

After you have secured your mountain's upright supports, you will want to create a web of masking tape which will support your high elevations and large expanses of scenery. Masking tape is inexpensive, quickly applied, and strongly adheres to the vertical supports and to itself. The tape webbing should extend from the top of the supports down to the joists below, with plenty of lateral support between the supports. Through this process you are constructing the "skeleton" of your mountain.

After the tape webbing has been strung between the supports and connected to the joists, several sheets of newspaper should be laid flat over the webbing and attached with tape. You are now ready to start building the surface of your mountain with paper towels which have

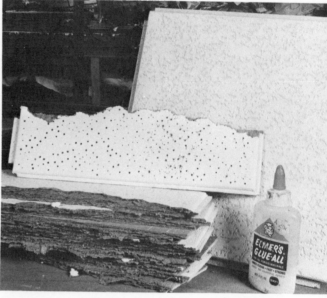

A small pile of ceiling tiles glued together to form part of a cliff. Any good general-purpose wood glue will do a fine job.

been soaked in Hydrocal.

To mix the proper Hydrocal solution, you will need a three-quart plastic container (a small plastic pail or, preferably, a rectangular dishpan). Start with a quart of water to which a few drops of dishwashing detergent have been added to help dissolve the Hydrocal powder. Add two quarts of powdered Hydrocal to the water and stir. Initially, the mixture will be very watery, but within five minutes the solution will acquire a uniform consistency similar to pancake batter. It is now ready for the paper toweling.

Soak each individual sheet of toweling briefly in the Hydrocal solution, making sure that both sides are soaked. Soaking should be accomplished within a few seconds. Then remove the sheet and drape it over the newspaper sheets atop the webbing. Hydrocal dries very hard very quickly; you will have only a minute or two at the most to shape the towel sheet into "mountain surface" after it has been soaked. You will have only about 10 minutes to use your entire panful.[1]

If you move the paper towel sheet after it has been setting for several minutes, the Hy-

Applying plaster to the edges of the broken ceiling tiles using a rough textured brush. This will create a more unified cliff but still retain rugged surfaces.

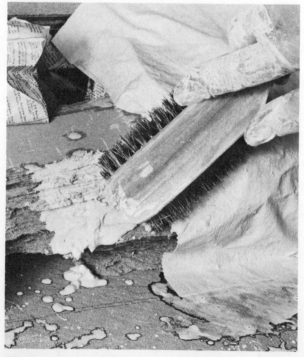

drocal has a strong tendency to crack and flake off into little pieces. Hydrocal adheres well both to plywood and to homosote, so you should have no problems in keeping the paper towels in place. Just make sure that you do not cause any movement in the toweling until the Hydrocal has had at least 12 hours to set. The primary advantage of Hydrocal over plaster of paris or spackling compound is that it has a much lower rate of shrinkage when it dries; this means less splitting, cracking, and flaking. Although these qualities make it ideal for model railroad landscaping, Hydrocal is not readily available in most hobby shops or hardware stores. One source of supply is J. R. Trains, 9176 Red Branch Road, Columbia, Maryland 21045.

Some model railroaders add a green or brown tone to the Hydrocal solution before using the paper towel sheets in order to minimize the effects of any chipping or flaking which does occur. A brown poster paint, such as "Tempera," or any other ready-mixed water color paint such as "Rich Art Moist Water Color," are recommended.

Hydrocal can be purchased in a variety of shades of white, although this is unimportant to most users, who color the solution before application. Hydrocal B-11 is recommended since it dries somewhat more slowly than other grades. After a session of making scenery with Hydrocal, it is important that the dishpan be thoroughly cleaned before the next batch is put into it; otherwise, small flakes will remain in the pan and detract from the appearance of further scenery projects. (As each batch becomes too hard for further use on paper towel sheets, the Hydrocal solution still may be molded to form rocks, boulders, and cliffs, or used as a texturizing agent by applying it with a stiff hairbrush to existing smooth surfaces of Hydrocal.)

CLIFFS AND PRECIPICES

Broken-up pieces of fiberboard ceiling tile are ideal for creating the face of cliffs. Often

these broken pieces can be obtained for free from a neighbor who is remodeling. (Asbestos ceiling tiles should be shunned, since asbestos is a known cause of several health problems, including cancer.) The ceiling tiles should be broken down into fiber pieces between 3 and 5 inches in width; then the pieces are glued onto each other so that a stack of the flat surfaces creates a jagged or craggy cliff face. To create a more unified cliff surface (or to improve upon the intentionally rough edges of the fiberboard pieces), spread molding plaster or patching plaster with a stiff brush across the rough edges; again, color the molding plaster before application. To control the setting rate of the molding plaster, use either vinegar or a compound known as retarder which is usually available at a nominal charge from the lumber yard or store where you bought the plaster.

The painting of the cliff surfaces is crucial to their realism. Since nature doesn't provide smooth uniform colors any more than it provides smooth regular surfaces, you must also provide a great deal of irregularity in shading. You should equip yourself with three or four shades of black, three or four shades each of gray and brown, if possible, and even several shades of white. These dark and light colors are used to create illusions. Undercuts and crevasses should be painted with the darker shades; the "exposed" surfaces should be lighter in color, and the top surfaces often should be shades of green or brown (to suggest vegetation). The toy train layout of Ralph Barger, of Columbia, Maryland, for example, has rocks and cliffs which are painted with shades of gray, with high-tones of light brown and rusty colors. Other layouts feature brown rocks in various shades, highlighted with yellows and greens. Since the Barger layout represents terrain from central Pennsylvania, he chose appropriately to feature the grays of the local granite.

(Barger also has used finely textured scale grass in five or six different colors to achieve a quite realistic appearance. This effect can most easily be accomplished by thinning Elmer's Glue, or a similar product, by 50 percent with

---

[1] As a beginner, you may end up with a rock-hard pan of Hydrocal. If this happens, do not despair. A few hammer blows to your plastic pan and a few pokes will cause the Hydrocal to fall out.

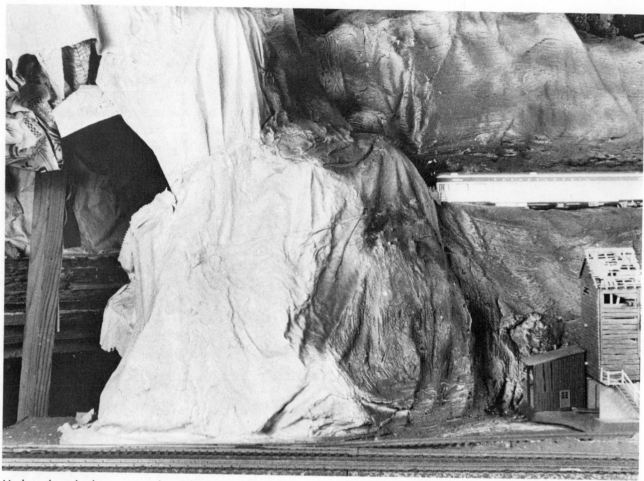

Hydrocal-soaked paper towels applied over newspaper to form part of a mountain. Note that some part has yet to be painted.

water and applying the glue solution with a paintbrush to the soon-to-be "grassy" area. Grass of several shades can be purchased in bulk at hobby stores. You should find an old saltshaker for each shade and sprinkle the grass onto the gluey surface as you would salt your steak and eggs.)

Unlike real mountains, your mountains do not have to be "complete" on all sides. Indeed, it is preferable to leave the unexposed sides open for access from the rear. Since you may wish to lay track in a tunnel through the mountains, access to the innards of the mountain will greatly facilitate the recovery of derailed trains; you will learn that trains have a habit of derailing inside mountains and other

less accessible spots. If you plan to run trains through your mountains, leave sufficient clearance laterally and overhead. Remember that the required lateral clearance on curved track is substantially greater than on straight track. And provide clearance for your largest and tallest rolling stock (such as boom-crane cars or the large aluminum passenger cars). If you must lay curved trackage within a mountain, make sure it is the widest curve possible, since sharper curves result in more derailments. And make sure that this trackwork is clean and solidly laid, to further minimize problems aggravated by inaccessibility.

Even model railroad mountains should show a "progression" of scenery and surface vegetation, just as do real mountains, with certain vegetation flourishing at certain heights, eventually capped by bare rock or snow. Mountains often may have streams which acquire some breadth toward the bottom of the mountain. You should be certain that you study real mountains (or photographs of them) before trying to reconstruct them; there is a mountain of work in such landscaping, and you should know what you want before you begin.

WATER ON THE LAYOUT

Model railroad newcomers should not use real water on their layouts, as it can be just too troublesome. There is a strong possibility of leakage, also of electric shocks from the current in nearby tracks, and the water tends to become scummy and/or evaporate quickly. For beginners, a transparent, clingy plastic sheeting such as Saran Wrap, normally used for wrapping food, is recommended. Crumpled Saran Wrap placed on top of a blue-painted surface results in a fine illusion of water.

If you insist on having real water on your layout, you can accomplish this perilous project if you are determined to use a lot of patience and care. First you must decide whether you will be constructing a river, a canal, a brook, or just a pond. Then select the appropriate container accordingly. This may be a large pan for a lake or pond, or a long metal container (like the ones grade school kids use to wet their paper before finger painting). A plastic window box normally intended for flowers and plants also may be appropriate.

If you have an open-top table, be prepared to do some work on the joists to adapt them to the water container. If you have a closed-top design, you will probably have to use a coping saw to cut a section from your table top to fit the container. A container with a lip around the rim will help prevent it from falling through the opening. After the container has been placed in the opening, use putty to seal the rim. The inside of the container should now be painted the desired colors (predominantly blue).[2]

Install a small aquarium air pump under the table (or hide it inside a nearby structure) and run plastic tubing into the container. The tubing should be run through the putty around the rim, over the edge, and then down into the water. Paint the tubing appropriate colors so that it blends with the landscaping and the inside surface of the container. Before you add the water, you may wish to install another larger container under the table directly under your "river" in case of a leak.

The top surface edges should be camouflaged with landscaping material (such as lichen) and the geometric shapes of the container can be disguised with aquarium rocks or "permascene." The water level should be kept about ½ inch below the table surface to prevent "siphoning" onto the table surface, and the water will have to be changed once every three or four months. The air pump should be kept operating 24 hours a day and also should be checked periodically for possible malfunctions. All electrical wiring should be kept well away from the area. If you want to run track over the water, use a girder bridge which has sidewalls or guards. Lionel locomotives do not operate properly when immersed in water.

COFFEE AS MOTHER EARTH

Coffee is exorbitantly priced today; you might as well get your maximum return from your pound of Maxwell House. After you have used the coffee grounds to brew your coffee, you can reuse them to help create the illusion of earth on your toy train layout.

Coffee grounds should be thoroughly dried by spreading them thinly over a sheet of newspaper. After they have dried, they can be sprinkled loosely onto the train table—but this is not particularly recommended, since they can too easily shift or get blown away. It is better to sprinkle the grounds onto the papier-mâché mixture of your mountains before it dries.

---

[2] The suggestions for including real water in a model train layout were provided by Harold K. Moore.

Landscaping cement such as that made by Lifelike will also hold down your coffee grounds, or you can sprinkle them onto any surface which has been freshly painted with dark green or greenish-brown. (Artificial earth can be purchased at hobby stores; it is expensive and generally considered an extravagance.)

Coffee grounds also can be useful when dried and mixed with sawdust which has been dyed green to be used for grass, although this is not always a rewarding approach. Store-bought grass mixtures are most reliable.

TREES AND WOODSY THINGS

Very fine miniature trees are available at moderate costs from a number of suppliers. Currently, from six to eight medium-sized trees can be purchased for $2.50. If you plan to have 100 trees on your layout, your investment would be close to $40. With a little nudging, you might be able to use such a volume purchase to obtain a significant discount.

There are, in addition, a number of methods for making your own trees and shrubs. One excellent source of materials for trees are the artificial ornamental wreaths used during the Christmas season; these can be purchased very inexpensively after the end of the season. If the wreaths happen to be a bit shopworn, this won't matter since your trees will come from dismembered wreaths. One single wreath should provide enough material for at least 100 shrubs and minor plants, or perhaps half that many trees.

To make trees from the wreath material, you will need some relatively rigid No. 14- or 16-gauge wire. With this wire, form a tree trunk and the main branches; onto this frame, press and glue the detached wreath material. The wreath material also can be tied to the main branches with a thinner wire (22 gauge). Lichen also may be used to form the tree frame's leafy covering. Lichen is available in bulk boxes in hobby stores for less than $6; a bulk box usually can provide "foliage" for at least 50 trees, and the lichen comes precolored, which is a significant convenience.

Another source of model railroad trees is someone else's train layout. If a train layout in your area becomes available for sale, check it out for usable landscaping. Or if you have a friend who regularly buys and sells used trains, let him know of your needs. Very often such persons consider the actual layout to be superfluous, since they usually have to cart it away for disposal. They may be glad to have you "loot" the layout for a variety of landscaping materials.

TRACK BALLAST

Even model railroads need some sort of ballast to minimize "erosion" effects on railroad track and keep the ties in place. There are a number of approaches to ballasting your track, if only to upgrade its appearance of authenticity. One attractive method has been developed by Ralph Barger of Columbia, Maryland, who suggests the use of rolled roofing material as basic ballasting beneath the track. The rolls usually are available for less than $10 for a 100 square foot roll, and come in numerous shades of black, gray, and other colors.

To apply this type of ballast, the roofing is laid directly on top of the plywood or homosote (or other insulating board) and fastened with the screws and nails which hold the track in place. To create a more realistic roadbed, it is suggested that you apply a very light "dusting" of flat black spray paint to the surface of the roofing material. If the track already has been laid, you may wish to mask the rails with tape before paint-dusting. Many model railroaders, however, wish their rails to look more realistic by allowing the overspray to coat the rails and the ties. If the paint is gently dusted onto the area, then it will be easy to remove from the top surface of the rail with an abrasive track cleaner. If you are using Super "O" track with shiny brown ties, the black spray paint dusting will substantially enhance its appearance. But use caution in the vicinity of switches and buildings; your spray can may too easily spread black paint to improper items.

The rolled roofing material is approximately 36 inches wide by 33 feet long. For straight or curved track in normal right-of-ways, strips of the roofing material are usually cut slightly wider than the track as ballast. In large areas in which there are numerous tracks, such as switching yards, you may wish to use the entire 36-inch width without cutting it into strips, or you may need even more than 36 inches. This would present you with "seam" problems, which are unsightly and amateurish. You should apply some Elmer's Glue to any such seams and sprinkle artificial scale coal on the glue while still wet. Not only will the seam disappear, but the coal will add more texture to your yard, giving the impression of a coal spill.

Although the roofing rolls are 36 inches wide, one of the edges has about a 2-inch space which contains no "grit" or rough surface (since it was intended to be tucked under the next layer on the roof). This 2-inch margin should be removed from the material by scoring it and bending it off. It is important to score this material only on the smooth side (or backside), otherwise the grit will severely damage your knife blade, rendering it dull and useless within a few strokes.

WORKING ON THE ROAD GANG

Depending on the type of world you wish to create, you probably will want to build some motor vehicle roads for the cars and trucks usually associated with twentieth century trains. You may want to build a six-lane divided highway (complete with cloverleafs) or you may be satisfied with narrow, winding country roads which narrow into one-lane bridges.

Most of your roads may be painted directly onto the flat surface of your closed-top table or onto strips of wood for your open-top design. If you are constructing a residential subdivision and the local zoning requires curbing, then strips of cardboard glued along the road edge will meet the local standards. Roads and streets, of course, attract traffic; you can purchase your vehicles at hobby stores and elsewhere (including train shows). You'll probably also wish to install stop signs, no-parking signs, and even billboards (if your community still permits

them). Most of these items can be fashioned from pieces of scrap cardboard and wood, painted with a steady hand. At one point in the mid-1950s many of these road sign attractions were available, preprinted, from small manufacturers. If you search diligently at train shows, you may be rewarded with inexpensive signs made to fit the scale of your railroad.

MASS-PRODUCED BUILDINGS

The model railroader is faced with a very large selection of manufactured buildings for the layout. Structures have been manufactured by Lionel, American Flyer, Marx, Ives, Skyline, Plasticville, Authenticast, and numerous other companies. The Plasticville structures are by far the most common. These buildings are manufactured to a scale which accommodates both Lionel and American Flyer trains. They assemble easily and do not deteriorate; even the older structures can be "bathed" into appearing new.

Plasticville and other plastic buildings often are available at train shows in used condition for modest sums. Sometimes, though they don't deteriorate exactly, they have been disassembled and reassembled so many times that they easily fall apart; in such cases, it's time to apply plastic cement. Even the structures missing sides or roofing can be repaired with cardboard, or positioned on your layout so their worst features are hidden.

Lionel made quite a number of buildings over the years, as well as some delightful metal houses in the 1930s. For more than 40 years, Lionel manufactured a long series of different train stations, some of them charming and quaint, others elegant and expensive. Some are architecturally suitable for a remote locale on a suburban commuter route; others are more appropriate for a larger city center site.

Today, Lionel offers a wide variety of handsome and realistic plastic kit buildings for train layouts. These include a grain elevator, a switch tower, a water tank, a "Rico" passenger station, a coaling station, an engine house, and a gravel loader. These are available in hobby stores and department stores, or at train shows

The Plasticville log cabin. This is one of several dozen buildings made by Bachmann under the Plasticville trademark. Plasticville buildings are often available at train shows for under $2.00.

and mail order houses at substantial discounts from list price.

Skyline, a competitor of Plasticville in the late 1940s and 1950s, manufactured buildings in metal, cardboard, and plastic. Its finely detailed cardboard buildings are reminiscent of the Lionel metal houses of an earlier period. These structures, sometimes in battered condition, are available at train shows at nominal cost. They are quite serviceable if you are willing to reinforce them internally with wood strips and glue.

Collectors often have accumulations both of cardboard and plastic buildings. You may attend train shows, however, in which there are almost no displays of buildings. This may be because the show exhibitors feel it is not worthwhile to haul these items around since they sell so inexpensively. In such cases, you should put up a small sign on a friend's table at the show, proclaiming your interest. Plastic and cardboard structures will come out of the woodwork. You may also wish to place a notice in your local train club newsletter.

Lionel, Plasticville, American Flyer, Marx, and Lifelike all have manufactured lamp posts of various sizes and shapes suitable for model train layouts. Some are elegant (Lionel's), some are novel (Marx's), some were designed for a railroad of the 1920s, others fit the 1950s best. Keep your eyes open for these at train shows; a little soldering can make them like new. (Bulbs will be difficult to replace in some of the older models; check to see if they work before purchasing.)

Two recent Lionel-Fundimension plastic kit buildings: the No. 2796 grain elevator and the No. 2789 water tower. These are very attractive, easily assembled, and very reasonably priced.

Three inexpensive accessories—a Marx crossing flasher with two lights, an American Flyer billboard with diesel horn, and a Marx crossing gate. The Marx flasher requires a special contactor. The gate may be controlled either by a contactor or an insulated third rail.

MAKING YOUR OWN MODEL RAILROAD STRUCTURES

For model railroaders seeking more challenge and personalization of their layouts, it is possible to build their own structures (and rolling stock, for that matter). There are numerous plans for such structures published regularly in the HO-gauge magazines; by enlarging the plans by 150 to 175 percent you can approximate the size for O-gauge layouts. If you can draw a straight line with a ruler and you are willing to spend from 10 to 20 or more hours on one structure, you should consider building your own.

At present, the selection of store-bought kits is rather limited and you often will need a structure for which no kit has been produced. Residential facades, storefronts and industrial plants are almost nonexistent in the ready-to-assemble kits. You may prefer to produce a model of your own hometown's main street.

Preprinted brick walls, stone walls, roof shingles, and tiles are available for the "scratch builder" at most resourceful hobby stores. While these products may be useful, they are not necessary. There is a variety of inexpensive and readily available materials for such work. First, you should acquire a supply of manila paper in a heavy stock (such as new or used file folders) and in lighter grades; the latter is suitable for building facades, while the former is ideal for roofs and foundations. You will also need several sheets of balsa wood in 1/16 inch and 1/8 inch thickness, which can be found at most hobby stores. Cardboard in several grades (including the grade used to back legal pads of paper) will be quite useful. Elmer's Glue should be your adhesive. You should need very few other materials, if any.

In addition to these few materials, you will need some drafting talent and some blocks of spare time, but you will not need drawing ability. If you can draw a straight line with a pencil and straightedge, and if you can scale down a picture or photograph to the appropriate measurements for your model railroad, and if you can cut a straight line with an Exacto knife . . . then read on.

Your first structure will probably take you longer than your subsequent efforts, because you must first learn the characteristic dimensions of doors, windows, and other items as well as the heights of various building styles. You must also begin to feel at ease in "framing" your structures; you will quickly realize how durable a lightweight paper structure can be if it is adequately braced.

OPERATING AND MAINTENANCE

Lionel's smoking engines are great fun to watch. The smoke unit is sychronized with the drivers.

Many men and women in America treasure fond memories of the toy trains of their childhood. A favorite recollection is the pitch darkness of the basement or attic where the train layout had been built, lighted only by the tiny rays of light from the small bulbs in the houses and the headlight of the locomotive.

The headlight would cast long shadows across the walls as it made its circuit around the layout. The flickering shadows would be accompanied by the pounding of the locomotive wheels. Suddenly, there would be the blaring of the engine whistle as the train reached the crossing.

Watching with eyes the level of the table top, you saw the train race around the curves with the caboose bobbing at the end of the train, its lights flickering on and off. In the daytime, more houses would be built so that there would be more small lights at night. A second train would be added on an adjoining track and the two trains would stream toward each other before passing in the night. It was very exciting.

You may also remember when you built your first major train layout as an adult. Your oldest child was then, perhaps, only two years old. He and you together, each in your own way, were completely preoccupied by the train as it sped around the circle. You imagined being the engineer in the cab, holding the throttle wide open while the fireman was vigorously shoveling coal into the firebox. You felt the searing heat from the firebox and you could hear the roar of the steam escaping and see the clouds of black and gray smoke belching from the smokestack. For you, the real magic of toy trains is in their operation and in the effect that operation has on the imagination.

When you first start operating your train, it will be a challenge for you merely to power the train around the loop of track without derailment. But later as you become more experienced, you will want to develop more complex operations.

For example, you may wish to develop a "timetable" to control the separate departures and arrivals of your trains. If you have four trains, the first one can be designated as a fast-unit freight train which must get to market quickly to deliver its load of perishable vegetables. You can have a slower mixed-freight train which delivers and acquires various boxcars at industries along the way. You can also have an express passenger line which carries affluent suburban dwellers into the center of the city for work, as well as a battered passenger service which limps along from the suburbs into the town.

If you have two main track lines, each of which has several sidings, you can put together a sophisticated schedule of operation. Your suburban passenger express service, for example, might be scheduled to leave the suburbs at 8:05 a.m. and arrive downtown at 8:42 a.m., while the normal passenger service train can shuffle along with an earlier departure at 7:49 a.m. and a later arrival of 8:45 a.m. The fast freight could leave Redlands at 7:30 a.m. on Wednesday and arrive at your freight terminal at 8:35 p.m. Thursday. Finally, your slow freight could start its wanderings at 7:35 a.m., stopping at nearly every siding along the way.

When you build your layout you will want to plan for the types of operations you wish to perform, usually with two loops and several sidings. Real-life occurrences and mishaps which reduce railroad efficiency can also happen on your model railroad. Your track work may result in occasional derailments—just like on Conrail and Amtrak—and your passenger service can be interrupted by mechanical breakdowns (especially on the older equipment). All of these activities can be monitored by you in your "control tower" as you direct the entry of the freight trains and passenger service into the downtown rail complexes.

You should consider developing a script, and perhaps encouraging your spouse and children to join in. Imagine a dispute flaring up between the porters' union and the stewards' union over jurisdiction for union organizing; the dispute disrupts passenger service for a period. Imagine the contents of your daily newspaper and how it would affect operations in your own toy train world. A coal strike, an oil embargo, severe winter weather, spring floods, railroad bankruptcy, and other regrettables and calamities can all become part of the evolving script.

Your train world also can be linked to high-fidelity recordings of actual train operation. A firm by the name of Semaphore Records produces fine recordings of various railroad sounds; these should be transferred to your tape cassette machine. The sounds of a steam engine leaving the loading platform can be coordinated with the actual movement of your toy locomotive from your station. There are many different sounds: sounds of rolling stock coupling in the switchyard, sounds of wheels slipping and skidding on the tracks, sounds of bells and whistles and steam. These recordings are expecially effective when played at high volume in a darkened room. You can keep the volume low as your locomotive leaves the mountain tunnel and heads toward you, the sound getting louder and louder until you and your visitors feel that a real Hudson locomotive is charging through your basement.

There are other city sounds you may wish to add to your collection of "noise" tapes. Tape the sounds of police cars and sirens rushing to break up a late night domestic quarrel at someone's residence, or the sounds of garbage trucks making their pickups, or the sound of the factory work whistle as the 4 o'clock shift gets out. You may wish to add aircraft noises which you can tape at your local airport. Practice coordinating your sounds with actual movements on the train table, such as the series of bangs from a freight train's couplers when it begins to move.

More than 30 years ago, Lionel developed simulated smoke for its locomotives. It is quite harmless and makes for effective simulation. A narrow beam light source set up so that it shoots light down a straight track section can dramatically highlight the smoke from the chugging engine.

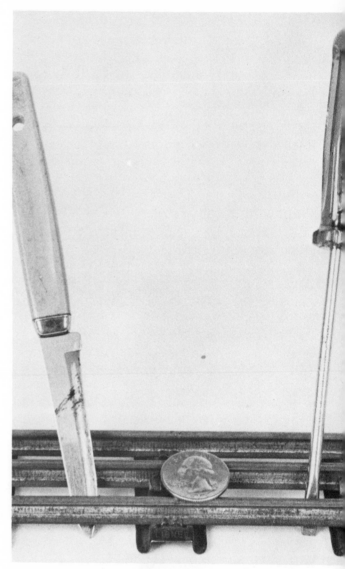

How to cause a short—either a coin or tool across the track.

BEGINNING OPERATION

There are several elementary procedures you should go through as you prepare to operate your trains. Check to be sure that the locomotive headlight turns on simultaneously with the transformer, and that the engine begins either to hum or to actually move. Are all the cars on the tracks properly? Does the transformer start to change its noise pitch or throb as you increase the track voltage? If there is a throbbing sound (or louder hum) then you probably have a short circuit; you should check the wires going from the transformer to the track. Are these wires properly insulated and the bare areas free of contact with each other? Disconnect the wires to the track lock-on and turn the transformer on. If there is no hum or throb, then you know the problem is in the track.

The most common source of short circuits is a derailed car or locomotive. You should check all the wheels on your engines and rolling stock. Other short sources include misplaced pieces of metal which are contacting the track: screw drivers, track pins, steel wool, track clips, or a piece of wire. (In a short circuit, usually a piece of metal is somehow linking together your ground line and your hot line, causing too much power to flow.)

REVERSING YOUR TRAIN

Lionel trains usually have a three-position reversing mechanism which is known as an E-unit. The basic design for this unit was developed by the Ives Toy Train Co. in 1924. Lionel acquired ownership of the design when it purchased Ives's assets after the latter's bankruptcy in the early 1930s. The three positions of the E-unit are forward, neutral, and reverse. When the train is in neutral, the light should be shining and the locomotive emitting a pleasant hum. This hum comes from the reversing unit, which is an electromagnetic coil of enameled, insulated wire, a metal shaft, and a pawl. The pawl rotates a small drum with copper sections mounted on its surface. When the track power is turned on, the coil becomes energized, pulling the shaft up into the coil; this, in turn, pulls the pawl up, which rotates the drum. When the track power is turned off, the coil no longer is energized and the shaft drops, as does the pawl. When the power goes on again, the pawl goes up and the drum rotates.

The copper sections of the drum come into contact with two sets of light copper springs (or "fingers"). The rotation of the drum changes

when fingers within each set are electrically in contact with each other through the copper sections of the drum. This alternating pattern of electrical contacts causes the locomotive to be either in neutral, forward, or reverse.

The E-unit has a switch which stops the drum from rotating by blocking the power to the electromagnet. Thus, the coil is locked out when the locomotive is running in the desired direction. When you open the circuit to the coil, the shaft drops, but does not cause the drum to rotate. The drum rotates only when the coil is reenergized.

There are several situations in which you might wish your loco to travel in only one direction, and not to sequence-reverse whenever a power interruption occurs. For example, sequence-reversing is undesirable with a multiple train operation using "blocks." (See *Multiple Train Operation*.) In such operations the blocks are established to prevent a faster train from catching a slower train. Through these blocks, current is blocked from reaching the section of track just behind the section in which a train is located. When a speedy train No. 1 enters the "dead" track section because the slower train No. 2 is directly ahead, then train No. 1's E-unit will automatically sequence into the neutral position (as a result of the power being removed). This is highly undesirable, as it confounds the directional sequence for all other trains running off your transformer.

Another situation in which you would want to disconnect the reversing mechanism involves sections of rough track in which small dead spots occur. Often it is not immediately practical to make the repairs on the track, yet you wish to avoid the annoyance of having to sequence every train whenever it passes over one of these spots and slips into neutral. You will also want to avoid sequencing in "cab-control" train operation in which a train is transferred from one power supply to another, or on model train layouts which have separate transformers

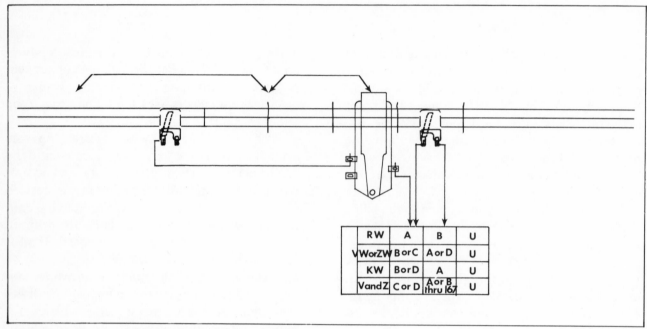

RW	A	B	U
V W or ZW	B or C	A or D	U
KW	B or D	A	U
V and Z	C or D	A or B thru 167	U

A block system using a 153C contactor as a switch to turn power off in the insulated block.

controlling individual segments of track. You also may wish to lock the reversing unit whenever the E-unit is not functioning properly and you are unable to make immediate repairs.

WHISTLE AND HORN UNITS

Over the years, Lionel has developed a series of different whistle and horn units for its locomotives. The remote control whistle was introduced by Lionel in the mid-1930s and was a major innovation in model railroading. This whistle unit used a clever but simple technique: inside the locomotive tender was a motor with a spiral-shaped whistle chamber. The motor turned a fan which blew air into the whistle chamber and created the distinctive tones. The motor drew its power from the track current, but was regulated by a relay so that it only functioned upon the operator's command.

Lionel's main innovation was to develop a DC relay mounted in the car which could be operated from the transformer. When activated,

the transformer would generate a small direct current (between 2 and 3 volts) which accompanied the normal output of from 9 to 18 volts of AC current. The transformer relay generated this small DC current by rectifying the AC current into DC through a small silicone disc. These discs, however, were easily destroyed by short circuits. Accordingly, if you know you have a short circuit on your layout do not operate the whistle controller until you have

SMOKE UNITS

Shortly after World War II, Lionel began to experiment with smoke units for its locomotives, which resulted in another remarkable advance for toy trains. These "smoking" engines (as well as the knuckle couplers and magnetraction) helped Lionel achieve an overwhelming dominance of the toy train market in the 1950s.

The original Lionel smoke unit consisted of an oversized light bulb with a depression in its top to hold a smoke tablet; such a tablet was

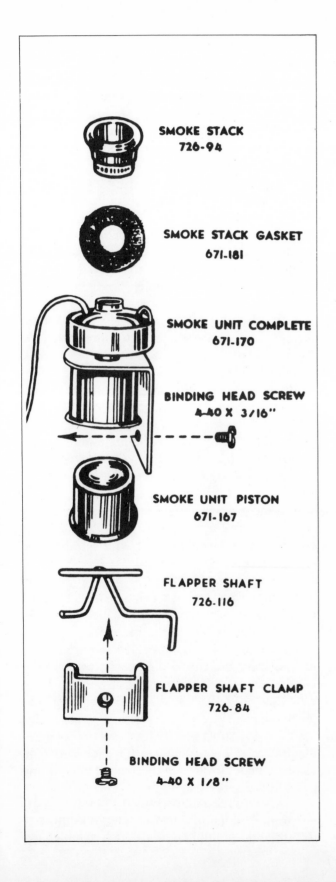

SMOKE STACK
726-94

SMOKE STACK GASKET
671-181

SMOKE UNIT COMPLETE
671-170

BINDING HEAD SCREW
4-40 X 3/16"

SMOKE UNIT PISTON
671-167

FLAPPER SHAFT
726-116

FLAPPER SHAFT CLAMP
726-84

BINDING HEAD SCREW
4-40 X 1/8"

placed on the bulb and the heat would eventually cause the tablet to smoke. But it was not a totally satisfactory arrangement, and in 1947 Lionel produced an improved smoke unit which used a small heating coil in a miniature ceramic bowl, complete with a small bellows system. The bellows was driven by a cam-type lever, activated by the main piston rod as it entered the pistons. This new smoke unit was quite successful, remaining basically unchanged for a decade.

Lionel claimed publicly that the smoke tablets were harmless, even if swallowed by the children. There is not available evidence to the contrary, but it is nevertheless advisable to keep these tablets out of reach of young children unless supervised. The proper tablets for the ceramic smoke unit are found in bottles marked "SP," which are no longer produced by Lionel. It is possible, however, to use liquid Lionel smoke instead of the tablets; place no more than one or two drops in the ceramic unit, otherwise the unit will become clogged and inoperative.

The tablet smoke units generally function well, as long as each tablet is fully consumed before a second one is placed in the ceramic unit. Premature placement of a second tablet results in clogging of the unit and reduced smoke. If your engine is not producing enough smoke, let it sit in neutral at the maximum voltage for a minute or so to heat up the coils; then sequence the engine from reverse to forward and run several loops at the maximum safe speed in order to clear out your smoke unit. It is strongly recommended that you *do not* under any circumstances stick a pointed object into the ceramic chamber and resistance wire; this creates considerable risk of severing the resistance wire.

A third type of Lionel smoke unit has a small chamber which holds liquid smoke, allowing it to drop onto a heated coil. This innovation was developed in the late 1950s, and liquid smoke is still being marketed by Lionel. The liquid smoke unit locomotives are readily identifiable by their small red plastic chambers to be seen inside the smokestacks.

Lionel's knuckle coupler that uses the plate lever mechanism is a very reliable mechanism. In the illustration the knuckle is being opened by gently pulling back the retaining pin.

Very few of the early smoke bulb locomotives survive with the original bulb intact. Because of their unsatisfactory operation, Lionel produced a conversion kit at modest cost for updating the equipment. However, collectors place high value on these original smoke-bulb locomotives, and, if you are lucky enough to find a functional one, you should try to preserve yours rather than convert it.

COUPLERS

Lionel made a number of different uncoupling units after World War II. However, before the war, Lionel achieved a major advance by developing a remote control uncoupler. The company adapted its latch-and-pin coupler with a box that caught the pin and replaced the latch. The box could be opened on a special piece of track through the activation of a solenoid. (A solenoid is another name for an electromagnet consisting of a hollow core with wire wrapped around it and a piece of iron or steel that is pulled up into the core by the magnetic force.)

The Lionel uncoupler of 1938 used a box which held the link pin. In the uncoupling process, the box is pushed up so that the link pin clears. To operate this uncoupler, Lionel initially used a metal contact shoe that was designed to operate only on a special remote control track. When the remote control button was pushed, additional control rails were energized and a circuit was completed for operating the electromagnet. The magnet pulled the steel shaft in the coupler toward the magnet, and by a lever arrangement the coupling box was pulled open. While this technically amounted to remote control uncoupling, the box did not resemble a prototype coupler, and thus lacked realism.

In 1945, Lionel substantially changed the design of its couplers to provide more authenticity, although they were still too large by scale standards. There also were some alterations made in the uncoupling track section, while the basic lever and electromagnet mechanism was retained. In 1948, Lionel redesigned the uncoupling system to operate with a plate-lever mechanism. The plate, mounted on the bottom of the truck, was designed to be pulled down by an electromagnet, activating a lever which released the pin which held the coupler fastened. At this point a coupler spring opened the coupler. The mechanism proved durable and trouble-free.

Lionel's first coupler was part of a system in which the uncoupling track provided a special power source which activated an electromagnet carried on each car. In the second version, introduced in 1948–49, the electromagnet was moved from the car to the special track and a completely mechanical device appeared on each car. The cost of manufacturing the mechanical device (the lever arrangement) for each car was substantially less than that of manufacturing an electromagnet for each car. One electromagnet located in the special uncoupling track could serve many cars.

In 1957, Lionel introduced the third major version of the coupler. This involved a further simplification of the equipment carried on each car. The plate was omitted and the retaining pin was released by a simple metal disc. This must have resulted in a substantial cost savings for Lionel, if not for its customers. Some of the discs, however, proved to be less than durable and required replacement. The uncoupling track section with the electromagnet featured a red plastic center with a metal button in the middle. These track sections work well and are compatible with both Type 2 and Type 3 uncoupling units.

UNCOUPLING PROBLEMS

If your cars are not uncoupling properly, you should first check to make sure that your electromagnet is functioning. This is easily accomplished with a screwdriver; hold the blade about half an inch over the electromagnet and press the uncoupler button. If the screwdriver is pulled toward the magnet, then it is working properly; if not, a likely possibility is a loose wire at the screw terminal, or a break in the wire from the uncoupling button to the track. There might be a loose connection within the uncoupling control unit, or a loose wire on the underside of the uncoupling track; but both of these developments are uncommon.

If you have determined that the electromagnet is functioning properly, you can use your finger to simulate the downward movement of the disc in the Type 3 coupling unit. When the disc is pulled down, the holding pin is released and the spring pushes out the knuckle. (If you have the plate-type coupling unit it is difficult to simulate the plate movement. You should watch, however, the electromagnet effect on the plate to determine if it is being pulled down. You can release the holding pin at the knuckle end and determine if there is sufficient spring tension to push out the knuckle. In the case of the early Type I units, you should also make sure that there is electric current in the control rails with which the sliding shoe makes contact.)

MULTIPLE TRAIN OPERATION
The simultaneous operation of several

trains on your layout can add considerable excitement and realism. Perhaps the most common example of multiple operation is on track laid in two separate loops and controlled by different transformers or by one transformer with multiple-speed controls. (It is usually cheaper to buy two smaller transformers such as Lionel No. 1032, 1033, or 1034 than to buy a single large transformer such as the KW which controls two trains simultaneously.[1] Due to the Consumer Products Safety Commission's ruling on power levels in transformers, Lionel no longer manufactures transformers capable of running two trains independently.)

Running two trains on one track is more demanding, but it has its appeal—especially if you can prevent the two trains from crashing into each other. The most efficient method for such operation is to build "blocks" along the right-of-way. A block consists of four or five pieces of track which are insulated from the adjoining four or five pieces. This insulation usually is accomplished by removing the metal pin from the center rail and replacing it with a plastic pin manufactured for this purpose (or a toothpick).

The power necessary to complete the circuit for the middle rail is then controlled by a switch which turns the current on in this block only when there is safe passage. A common design contains several of these blocks so that when one train is in one block, the block immediately following will automatically be without power; this prevents the second train from catching up with the first train. This is most readily accomplished by using a simple pressure-operated switch made by Lionel known as a 153-C contactor. This switch is placed under the track and when the engine and cars pass over the section containing the switch, the switch opens the circuit (breaks the circuit) supplying current to the block immediately *behind* the block in which the train is located.

---

[1] If two different transformers are used, it is necessary that they be in phase. See page 00 for a discussion of phasing.

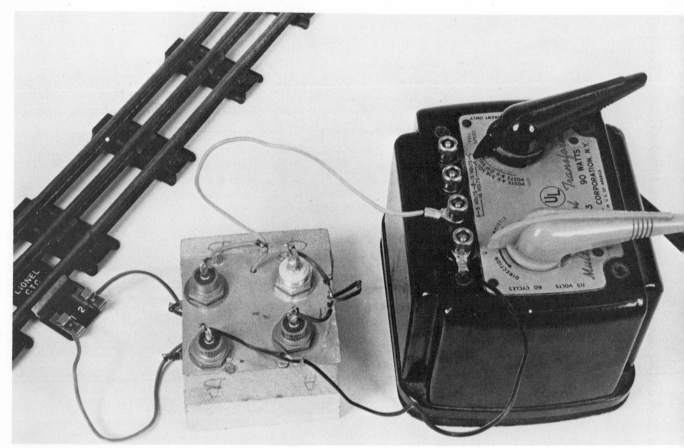

A Lionel transformer wired to a full wave bridge rectifier consisting of four diodes. This combination provides efficient and low cost DC current to the track.

TRAIN OPERATION AND WIRING

One appealing pair of options open to contemporary model railroaders is whether to operate a train on alternating current (AC) or direct current (DC). Most toy trains, and nearly all Lionel trains, have universal motors which can run on either AC or DC. These motors actually function more efficiently on DC in that for any given voltage the trains will run faster and build up less heat. Furthermore, DC operation provides a trouble-free reversing mechanism so that E-units (which are trouble-prone) need not be used. And many relays which are useful in multiple train operation are most readily available for DC operation. However, most Lionel, American Flyer, and Marx train sets have been equipped for AC operation. A typical train set

includes a transformer which takes the usual 110–120 volt AC delivered by your power company and reduces it to between 5 and 20 volts; the current retains its alternating characteristics. In recent years, however, the availability of inexpensive and reliable diodes for converting AC to DC gives train operators another option.

It must be observed at this point that nearly 99 percent of all train set transformers are made to be powered by 110–120 volt *alternating* current. If you do not have this current in your home, do not plug your transformer into the wall; seek additional advice from your local hobby shop.

If you wish to obtain direct current, proceed with plugging your transformer into the

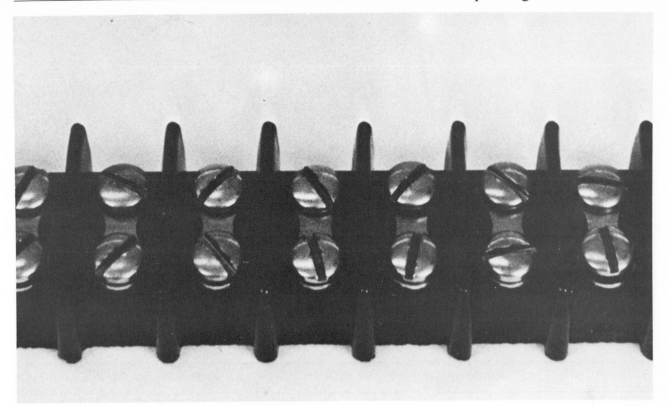

A bus bar with many screw terminals for wiring a layout. This device helps control the maze of wiring that rapidly develops under even small layouts.

wall receptacle; however, between the transformer and the track, diodes will be installed to convert the alternating current into direct current. Four diodes will be required; they should be mounted on a piece of aluminum stock (or tin stock made from a tin can) with the wires arranged as shown at top left. The aluminum or tin serves as a heat sink, a means of dispersing heat from the rectifying process. This set of four diodes is termed a full-wave bridge rectifier. Additionally, two diodes which form a half-wave bridge rectifier must be placed in the

Current reversed by STDP switch.

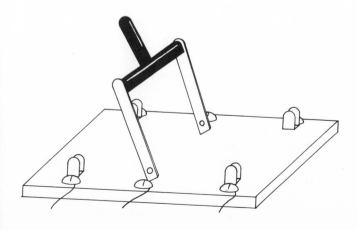

locomotive between the pickup shoe and one brush, or between the brush and the armature. It is recommended that diodes with at least a 10-amp capacity be used for the full-wave bridge rectifier linking the transformer to the track.

After you have wired your track and locomotive as indicated, you may remove the entire E-unit (the reversing mechanism) from the circuit. This can be accomplished by locking the E-unit in either the forward position or the reverse position. When you wish to reverse the locomotive, it will be necessary to reverse the current. There is a very simple switch known as a single-throw double-pole switch which will permit you to reverse the current (as diagrammed in at the left). Normally, direct current flows in one direction. If you reverse the wires to the track by the use of this switch, the train will reverse directions. (One limitation of this procedure is that you lose the neutral position in your locomotive. With DC reversing, there are only two motor positions. Another consideration is that Lionel horns and whistles cannot be operated by remote control unless AC is used. These whistles and horns are activated by low-voltage DC and thus would be constantly blaring. DC users thus should disconnect the horn and whistle units.

Using a crimping tool to fasten a solderless connector to a piece of 20-gauge wire. The insulation on the end of the wire has already been removed.

There are three major reasons for converting to DC use with your model railroad. As mentioned, the engines run cooler and with more power. Secondly, the E-units with their high rate of failure can be disconnected. And thirdly, the DC relay switches, which are so useful in multiple train operation, are more widely available than the AC relay switches.

It is possible to operate nonconverted engines on your DC track and retain the reversing unit capabilities. But this should be done only with engines which operate correctly and whose reversing units are intact.

MORE WIRING

Even a semisophisticated model railroad layout will have a great deal of wiring assembled beneath the table top surface. It's crucial that you position your wires according to a proper plan.

To begin with, it will not be enough to simply plug in your transformer and hook it to the track with a single lock-on. The plated steel train track is not a particularly good conductor of electricity (compared to copper or alumi-

num). Thus from the onset you should plan to have a number of supplemental leads connected to the track, particularly for the center rail (which has only half as much capacity for current as the two outer rails).

The recommended procedure is to run two 20-gauge copper bell wires completely around your layout perimeter; these wires are called a bus bar. To fashion your track leads, take short pieces of insulated copper wire and strip the insulation from both ends. Drill a small hole through the board beneath your roadbed and track and run the wire up through the hole. This wire should be connected to the center rail either by a lock-on or, preferably, by soldering and tinning.

It will also be wise to color code your wiring beneath your train table. Use red wire for carry-

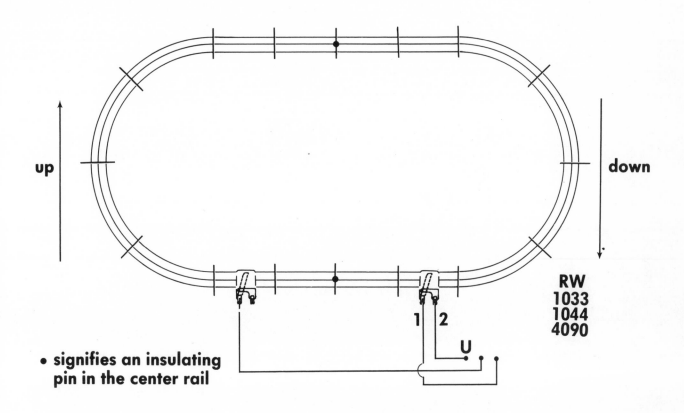

up

down

RW
1033
1044
4090

1 2

U

• signifies an insulating
pin in the center rail

A diagram for layout with upgrade and downgrade.

ing the "hot" side of the main track wiring. Adopt white as the universal ground color for all track wiring and accessories. Be sure that you have enough red and white wiring for your purposes, since the red and white wiring both will need to stretch entirely around your train table.

You should also adopt one set of colored wiring for each transformer. Transformer No. 1 might be color coded red, white, and blue, while Transformer No. 2 would use yellow, orange, and green. Record your color schemes inside the cover of this book. Most Lionel transformers use letter codes A, B, and C (and sometimes D) to indicate the separate terminals, and nearly all of them also have a U post which serves as a common ground post. Since the U post is the common ground for the other posts, you will need only one ground bus wire around the circumference of your train table; this substantially reduces the wiring required.

In addition, most transformers have combinations of posts that produce different *fixed* voltages; other post combinations will give you *variable* voltages. (See page 100 for chart.) Normally, the fixed voltage posts are used to operate accessories and the variable posts to operate the trains. In wiring accessories, several different fixed voltage levels may be used. A lower voltage circuit is often used for the illumination of buildings. (If you use between 10 and 12 volts and furnish the structure with 18-volt bulbs, these bulbs will last a very long time and provide soft, pleasant illumination.)

Accessories such as the No. 152 crossing and 15 volts. If a level of 18 volts is used, the gate action is too brisk and unauthentic; the gate should descend smoothly and without hesitation, but it should not bounce. This is also true with the operating gatemen (either No. 145 or

Transformer	Common Ground Post	Fixed Voltage Posts	Variable Voltage Posts
1032 1033	A	B: 5 V. C: 16 V.	U: 5-16 V.
1044 4090	B	C: 11 V.	U: 0-11 V.
	C	A: 16 V. B: 11 V.	none
	U	none	A: 5-16 V. B: 0-11 V.
LW	A	B: 18 V. C: 14 V.	U: 6-20 V.
RW	A	C: 9 V. D: 19 V.	U: 9-19 V.
	B	C: 6 V. D: 16 V.	U: 6-16 V.
	D	A: 19 V. B: 16 V. C: 10 V.	none
	U	none	A: 9-19 V. B: 6-16 V.
TW	A	B: 7 V. C: 18 V. D: 14 V.	U: 7-18 V.
	B	A: 7 V.	U: 0-11 V.
		see text on use of posts E and F	
KW	U	C: 6 V. D: 20 V.	A: 6-20 V.* B: 6-20 V.*
	C	D: 14 V. U: 6 V.	A: 0-14 V.* B: 0-14 V.*
VW ZW	U	none	A: 6-20 V.* B: 6-20 V.* C: 6-20 V.* D: 6-20 V.*
V Z	U	none	A: 6-25 V.* B: 6-25 V.* C: 6-25 V.* D: 6-25 V.*
R	A	B: 8V. D: 14 V.	C: 14-24 V.* F: 14-24 V.*
	B	A: 8 V. E: 16 V.	C: 6-16 V.* F: 6-16 V.*
	D	A: 14 V. E: 10 V.	none
A Q	A	B: 8 V. C: 14 V.	U: 14-24 V.
	B	A: 8 V. C: 6 V.	U: 6-16 V.
	U	none	A: 14-24 V. B: 6-16 V.
S	A	B: 5 V. C: 19 V.	U: 10-19 V.
	B	C: 14 V.	U: 5-14 V.
	C	A: 19 V. B: 14 V.	none
	U	none	A: 10-19 V. B: 5-14 V.

*Note: Multiple variable voltages marked with *'s ure controlled by independent throttles.*

45). With the vibrating accessories (which use an interrupting coil) you should experiment between 12 and 18 volts until you get the desired effect.

Soldering under a model railroad table is moderately difficult, especially for less nimble enthusiasts. It is advisable that you remember to "tin" all surfaces to be joined, before you actually try to solder them together; after tinning, only a moderate amount of heat (and a brief deep knee-bend) will be needed to join two tinned wires.

There are, however, several alternatives to soldering these lead wires to the bus bar beneath the train table. First, you can splice the lead around the bus bar, and then press it tightly to the bus bar with a pair of pliers. Regrettably, there is a tendency for these joints to work loose. A second approach is to solder the leads to the bus bars *before* mounting the bus bars to the underside of the train table. Lay the bus bar wires on the floor approximately in their ultimate positions. Solder 6-inch wire leads to the bus bars about every 18 inches, and then drill holes through the roadbed from beneath the table for the wire leads to the track.

In addition to soldering and splicing, you may consider using the cone-shaped plastic connectors commonly used in domestic light switches. The wires to be joined are stripped only to the depth of the cone; the wires are then twisted together and the plastic cone is screwed onto the twisted wires. Be certain that you do not overscrew (and break the wires) or underscrew (and induce a loose connection). A little practice will improve all of the above skills.

Solderless terminals are another valid alternative. These connectors come in the form of rings, hooks, plugs, butt splices, and blade-receptacle combinations. The wiring ends are stripped only far enough to fit into the hollow tube on each connector, and then the tube is crimped around the wire with pliers. (These connectors come in various sizes; buy the proper tube diameter to fit No. 18- or 20-gauge wire. For ring connectors, the Lionel transformer posts are usually No. 8 stud size.)

USING TRANSFORMERS

Here is a useful guide to using Lionel transformers in common ground applications. (The guide generally applies to Marx and American Flyer transformers as well.) There are many advantages to using a common ground wiring system on your layout: signal and accessory wiring, cab control wiring, fixed voltage switches, remote control track operation, and automatic layouts are all made easier if such a system is employed. Although all the necessary power for your layout may be obtained from a single transformer, it is possible (and often desirable) to use multiple transformers.

All of the Lionel transformers that have a variety of fixed and variable voltages can be used to supply power to a common ground layout. Each transformer can be connected in many different ways to obtain the various voltages that may be desired. The chart in the next column lists the voltages available from most of the transformers made in the past 35 years.

As you can see from the chart, each transformer has its own characteristics. Perhaps the most flexible of all are the ZW, VW, V, and Z models which offer four independently variable voltages. However, several of the smaller transformers can be used in interesting applications that are not possible with the ZW type. For example, consider a layout that has an upgrade and downgrade. If you have ever operated such a layout you know that it requires constant adjustment of the throttle to give the train enough power to climb the grade and to prevent derailment when the train comes back down. Page 99 shows the wiring for such a layout that takes advantage of the voltages available from several small Lionel transformers.

This type of wiring keeps the train under control of some throttle, whistle, and direction controls, but provides a lower voltage when the train is on the downgrade. Therefore, the throttle could be left at one setting and the danger of a derailment would be greatly reduced. This is particularly useful on a large multiple train layout operated by one person. The same effect could be achieved using a KW transformer.

In both of the circuits in the chart, a DPDT[2] switch could be added to reverse the connections when the train is operating counterclockwise.

In addition to the chart on the left, some comments should be made about the KW and TW transformers:

KW If U is chosen to be the common ground post there are no fixed voltage posts available to power most accessories (12–16 volts). Therefore, it is quite common to use posts C and D to obtain 14 volts and not employ common ground wiring for the accessories. Perhaps the best thing to do in this case is to use a separate accessory transformer that shares the common ground as will be described behow. Note: if U is the common ground post, post D makes an excellent choice for powering 022 switches.

TW In addition to the posts listed in the chart, there are two additional posts, E and F, that supply 14 volts from an independent secondary accessory transformer. Again, if accessories are powered from these posts, they cannot employ common ground wiring. Since there are other fixed voltage posts available, you can power most accessories from E and F and use common ground wiring for only those accessories that require it (such as insulated rail actuated signals). Note: If A is the common ground post, use post C for powering 022 switches.

Remember that regardless of the number of fixed or variable voltages only a finite amount of power can be drawn from a transformer. Since all of the voltages come from the same secondary winding (except for posts E and F of a TW), a heavy load on one circuit will cause voltage drops in the other circuits. For this reason and for added flexibility it is often desirable to use more than one transformer to power a large layout. In this way the total power load is distributed over all of the transformers, and you can take advantage of the particular characteristics of several different models.

Phasing of multiple transformers is necessary to insure that the peaks of the alternating current from each coincide. This can easily be done as follows: connect the common ground posts of each transformer together. Then, set the throttles of each to produce approximately the same voltage. Next, touch a wire between the output voltage posts of the transformers. If a large spark is produced, reverse the plug of one transformer and try again. Once you have phased the transformers, mark their plugs in some fashion so that you won't have to go through the phasing process again. One of the handiest things you can have on a permanent, multiple transformer layout is an outlet box with switches for each outlet. Once the transformers are phased, their plugs need never be removed from the outlet box.

---

[2] Double-pole double-throw.

REPAIR TECHNIQUES

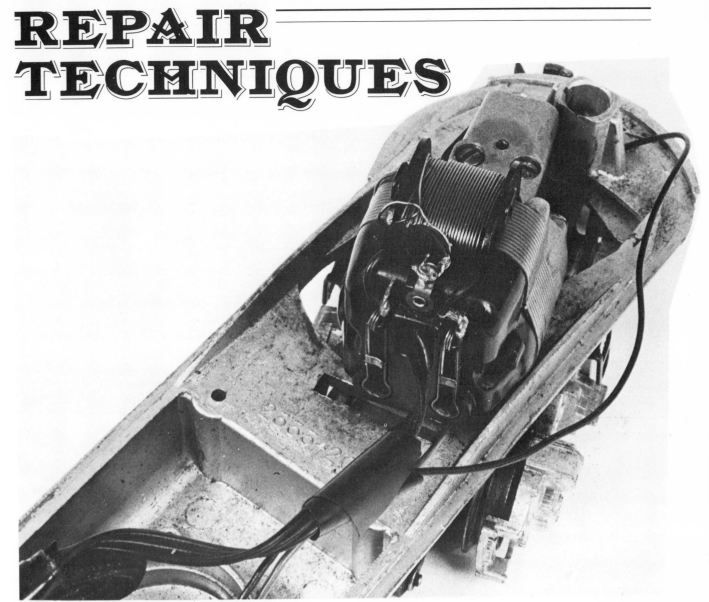

A motor from a Lionel Santa Fe, circa 1952. The motor consists of field laminations and a field coil, an armature (which is hidden by the brush holder), two brushes and the brush holder with springs to retain tension on the brushes.

Face it: you are going to have to make repairs on your model railroad. Repairs and repairs and more repairs. Mankind, Mother Nature, and the planned obsolescence of modern materials have all conspired against you and you can't beat them. You are going to have to learn how to troubleshoot your problems yourself.

In many cases, *diagnosing* the problem is the biggest part of your work. Once you have figured out *why* your locomotive just sits there and hums or why your favorite caboose won't light up inside, the corrective actions can be quite easy.

Basically, you should conceive of your model railroad equipment as the sum of many parts of an electrical circuit consisting of a hot wire and a ground wire. At first, you may wish to diagram this circuit on a sheet of paper, but soon you will do it easily and almost automatically in your mind. Let's imagine a common model railroad electrical problem and walk it through the circuit concept.

It is not at all unusual for the interior lighting in the O-gauge passenger cars not to function. Here you have this gorgeous, streamlined string of silver and red Santa Fe cars, each of them looking as great as they are expensive, except for the dud near the end which is dark inside. You know that the problem is lurking somewhere between your fingertips and that darkened car.

Actually, you can narrow down the scope of the problem ever further: it lies somewhere between the transformer and the dark light bulb inside the passenger car. You can see that the light in your locomotive is functioning properly, as are all the lights in the other cars. So you have two choices: to start hunting from the operating end (the dark bulb) or from the power end (the transformer). Since the other train lights are working fine, it makes more sense to start troubleshooting from the dark bulb end.

It's helpful to know that the most frequent cause of bulb malfunction is not a burned-out bulb; rather, it is a loose bulb in the socket. Bulbs lead the list of all model train hardware which malfunction due to the vibrations of normal operation; this is because the bulb socket threads were designed to allow you to remove the bulb easily. (The style of bulb-and-socket known as bayonet, however, provides easy removal without frequent loosening problems. Small springs in these sockets keep the bottom of the socket in contact with the bulb, usually preventing bulb rotation by vibration.) But when you check your bulb for looseness inside the Santa Fe passenger car, you determine that it is secure and that looseness is not the problem. Next, you should try the "burned-out" hypothesis.

A burned-out bulb amounts to a broken circuit. Inside these bulbs, the hot line comes through the base of the bulb and meets the ground line flowing through the threads on the side of the bulb. These two lines form a circuit within the resistance wire in the bulb, which glows with the force of the electrical current. This resistance wire becomes quite hot and very gradually oxidizes until part of it oxidizes into nothingness. The wire snaps and the circuit is broken. The light disappears and the bulb is officially "burned-out."

If it is not evident that the bulb is burned-out, then try exchanging it with a new bulb or one you know is functional. If the replacement bulb does not function in the socket, then the problem obviously lies in the circuit leading to the bulb. If the replacement bulb does light up, then either the old bulb is burned-out or the oxidation must be removed from the bottom

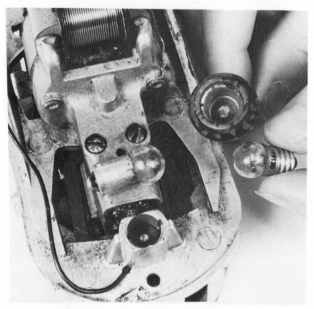

A comparison of a screw-type socket and bulb (held in the fingers) and a bayonet bulb and matching socket in the diesel locomotive. Bayonet bulbs, which, are held under spring tension in the socket, resist loosening from vibration better than screw base bulbs.

point of the bulb so that electrical contact may be restored.

Assuming that the replacement bulb also does not function in your passenger car socket, at least you know that the circuit is complete from the transformer to the track since the lights in the other cars are functioning. So the problem is somewhere between the track and the bulb. The hot half of this circuit is in the path from the center rail of the track, through the passenger car pickup roller, through the wire to the end of the socket, and finally into the end of the bulb. You can readily test the continuity of the hot line by touching a wire hooked to the ground circuit to various key points along the hot line. If there is a spark at these points, then the circuit is completed.

For example, if you take a ground wire and lightly touch the soldered connection at the end of the bulb socket and there is a spark, then you know that the circuit is completed all the way from the transformer to the socket. If there is not a spark, take the ground wire back to the

Cotton swabs are very handy for cleaning out the brush holders. A little alcohol or Carbona on the swab increases its cleaning efficiency.

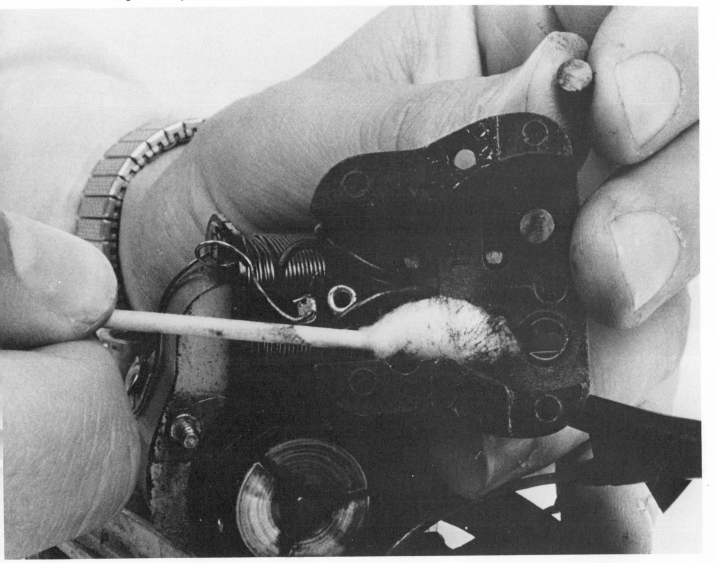

pickup roller bracket. If there is no spark here, then the pickup shoe may not be making contact with either the track or its bracket. Sometimes, due to oxidation, the roller's contact with its bracket is inadequate. Or perhaps the contact shoe and the bracket may have become bent in such a way that they no longer reach the track.

It is also possible that the bulb's ground circuit may have broken. You can easily reverse the process and touch a hot wire to each key point along the ground line. The major problem areas along the ground line are the point at which the truck joins the body of the passenger car, and the connection between the light bulb bracket and the body. Inadequate contact at both spots can be caused by excessive paint, corrosion, or the effects of vibration.

This same procedure and logic can be applied to more complicated pieces of equipment, such as locomotives and various accessories. In the case of a locomotive, it is possible to trace both the ground and the hot lines and determine precisely where the circuit is broken. It is vital to remember that frequently the locomotive frame and chassis form part of the ground line.

Using a toothpick to clean the slots between the commutator sections. The commutator slots fill with an oily mixture of carbon and dirt, which causes the engine to loose efficiency.

TOY TRAINS AND THEIR MOTORS

Toy train motors have several major parts. The armature is the unit that moves in the center of the motor; it usually has three parts, each consisting of a series of metal plates insulated from each other. Around each of these three parts (or "wings") is wrapped many turns of copper wire. Although the copper wire appears bare, it actually is insulated by a thin coating of clear enamel. On the armature also are found three copper plates (or round copper segments on the earlier motors). These copper plates are called the commutator.

The copper plates are connected to the coils of wire. Electrical contacts are made with these copper plates by little pieces of carbon that are called brushes. Surprisingly, carbon is a good conductor of electricity and simultaneously lubricates the contact points with the copper plates.

In each toy train motor there is also another set of copper windings known as the field coil. This field coil is wrapped around a portion of the iron laminations that cover three sides of the armature.

The field winding is electrically connected

A grimy F3 Lionel diesel motor. Note the deposits on the brushes. The three copper commutator sections and the slots separating these sections are readily visible.

to the armature through the brushes and the commutator. Toy train motors usually are "series wound;" this means that one side of the armature is connected through brush No. 1 with one side of the field coil (F-2) while the other side of the field coil (F-1) is hooked to the transformer post and the other end of the armature is hooked through brush No. 2 to the transformer.

As the carbon brushes rub onto the commutator, the carbon slowly coats the commutator surface and, more significantly, gradually fills the slots between the copper segments. Since carbon conducts electricity so well, these insulated slots slowly evolve into conductors, interfering with the electric circuit, causing excess heat and eventually a breakdown. Fortunately, the carbon residue can be easily removed from the slots. Simply use a pointed cuticle stick (or similar wooden item) to clean out these slots; make sure you use wood, since a metal device will damage the soft copper parts.

Through continual use, the carbon brushes, which are held against the commutator by springs, wear down and become shorter. Eventually, the brushes become too short and contact with the commutator becomes intermittent. The result of this is electrical "arching," which causes more oxidation and further consumption of the carbon brushes. The motor is about to stop completely.

The brushes should be replaced before they wear out. To determine if you have sufficient length to your brushes (and adequate spring pressure) use a pencil or stick to gently push down on both brushes while the motor is running. If the motor speeds up appreciably, then either your brushes are too short or your springs are too weak.

Toy train motors turn on a shaft known as the armature shaft, which usually protrudes from both sides of the motor. One end of the shaft is usually supported by the brush plate and a sleeve or bearing of some type; the other end is usually supported by the motor sideplate (and a sleeve or bearing). This shaft requires regular lubrication since it turns very rapidly and bears the stress of the motor. The lubrication, however, must be applied with great caution since the shaft is so close to the commutator and brushes. If there is too much oil on the armature shaft near the brush plate, the shaft will rapidly disperse oil onto the face of the commutator, thus reducing the contact between the brushes and the commutator. The oil also will spread into the brush holders and reduce the electrical contact between the brushes, holders, and springs. The efficiency of your motor will be greatly reduced.

To repeat: the armature shaft needs regular lubrication with a thin oil, perhaps as often as once every hour of operation. But only a small drop is needed, and it should be applied very carefully.

When you acquire used locomotives, it is common for the brushes and the brushes holder, the commutator and the slots to be glazed with a grimy mixture of oil and carbon that interferes with electrical contact and inhibits the motor's efficiency. This can be easily remedied; the first step is to remove the motor from the loco chassis. (If it is possible to remove the brushes holder without removing the motor, then leave the latter in the chassis.)

The brushes holder usually is held in place by two screws. When you loosen these, sometimes the brushes and the springs will fall out; it is advisable to work on a large table or another spot where you will not lose the springs and brushes. Next, you should remove the brush plate. Apply some rubbing alcohol or contact cleaner to a paper towel and place the brushes in the towel; rub and turn the brushes with moderate pressure to clean them. Then take a cotton swab dipped in alcohol or cleaner and rub out the brush holders.

Now use your toweling or swabs to clean the face of the commutator, but be careful not to scratch or damage the commutator; excess pressure will cause the copper segments to come loose. Use a pointed stick to clean the slots between the copper plates, and remember not to use any sort of abrasive on the face of the commutator; your contact cleaner (or alcohol) is powerful enough to remove the grime. (Even very fine steel wool will cause small scratches which will increase the amount of electrical arching and aggravate brush wear and commutator pitting. If your commutator has become badly grooved or pitted, you should place it on a lathe and smooth it down, or replace the entire unit.)

Occasionally, a lead wire to one of the brushes becomes disconnected. If you are going to resolder this connection, make sure that the areas to be joined are immaculately clean. Use emery paper or steel wool to gently buff the wire and the brush contact. There may already be sufficient solder on the contact to complete the job.

The other lead wire that occasionally becomes disconnected is the hot line soldered to the inside of the fiber plate on the bottom of the motor. This fiber plate provides support for the pickup rollers. Unfortunately, most modern Lionel motors have their sides riveted into place. This makes it very difficult to get to the other side of the fiber plate where the solder has come loose. You should not try to bend the sides of the motor; they will not bend back properly to their original shape. The solution is to use a screwdriver to pry out the fiber plate. With the fiber plate removed, it will be possible to resolder the leads on the inside of the plate.

These few pages should provide you with

an adequate introduction to diagnosing toy train problems. Soon you will be making the repairs with confidence.

SUGGESTIONS FOR REPAIRS FROM THE LIONEL SERVICE MANUAL

The following pages will offer much more detailed instructions for repairing Lionel equipment. Although less than comprehensive, this section will suggest methods for approaching and solving problems. The pages originally were published in the *Lionel Service Manual*. Although the original manual is no longer available, the Greenberg Publishing Company does offer a reproduction of the entire manual.

Representative pages have been selected from the manual which provide a working understanding of the various mechanisms and circuits which Lionel commonly has used, as well as the types of problems you are likely to encounter with this equipment.

For example, the milk car is a complicated mechanical device actuated by a special track. Most of its problems occur in the mechanical linkage; the instructions provide numerous suggestions. The cattle car is mechanically a very simple device, but it requires a very fine tuning of its vibrator to function properly.

The service manual section on transformers explains the theory behind transformers and offers suggestions for operation, as well as providing solutions for the most common problems. Track switches offer added excitement for a model railroad layout in addition to headaches for most operators. Lionel's most elaborate switches, the O-22 series, are delightful when they are working properly. They are dependent on several complicated mechanical and electrical relationships which unfortunately do not always work smoothly. This section should provide solutions to most of your switch problems.

There are also sections toward the end on disassembly and servicing of Lionel locomotives (and tips on troubleshooting) and on the Lionel remote control whistle, one of the company's finest inventions.

Figure 2- Circuit Diagram of a Typical Steam-Type
Locomotive and Tender

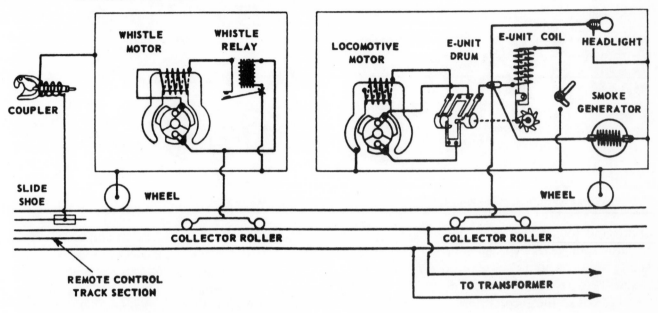

Figure 1- Typical Spur-Gear Motor (First Type)

DESCRIPTION OF LIONEL LOCOMOTIVES

Although Lionel locomotives in external appearance may resemble any of the several popular types of railroad locomotives, such as steam, steam turbine, electric, or diesel, they are all electrically propelled and contain much the same essential components. They are powered by a series-wound universal a.c.-d.c. motor, which picks up low voltage electric current from the center rail by means of a collector roller or shoe and is grounded to the outside rails through the locomotive body and driving wheels. The main parts of a Lionel motor are a

stationary motor field, a three-pole armature which spins inside the field structure and the copper-graphite brushes which ride on the segmented copper surface of the armature commutator and interconnect the field with the armature.

The motor normally consumes approximately 1 to 1.5 amperes and develops about 4,000 r.p.m. under normal train load. Power developed by the motor is transmitted to the driving wheels either through a series of spur gears, or through a worm and worm wheel arrangement. In order to obtain scale train speed of approximately 100 m.p.h. a gear reduction ratio of 8 to 1 is usually employed, but for locomotives with larger drivers, such as the 773 Hudson, a reduction ratio as large as 18 to 1 may be used.

Locomotive Motors

Although all Lionel motors are similar electrically, three main types have been developed which differ structurally. The first type, used principally in the smaller steam-type locomotives is constructed integrally with the locomotive framework and drivers. The armature is located transversely to the locomotive and is

Typical Worm-Shaft Motors (Second Type)

'Scout' Motor (Third Type)

connected to the geared driving wheels by a train of spur gears. The ends of the armature shaft project on both sides of the locomotive and require fairly frequent lubrication.

Motors of the second type, used in diesel, electric and the large steam-type locomotives, are separate assemblies held to the locomotive framework or to motor trucks by screws. They are mounted longitudinally or vertically and drive the locomotive by means of a worm which meshes with a worm wheel mounted on the driving axle. The armature shaft of these motors usually runs in a lubricant-filled reservoir and therefore does not require frequent lubrication. In the case where one end of the armature shaft runs in a bushing inserted in the brush plate, an oil-soaked wick is provided for lubrication.

A third type of motor, developed for use in 'Scout' locomotives, resembles the first type in the transverse position of its armature, but differs from standard Lionel motors in its reversing mechanism.

In order to reverse their direction standard Lionel motors are interconnected with the 'E-Unit', a solenoid-and-pawl operated three-position switch which changes the direction of the armature rotation by reversing the connection of the brushes in relation to the motor field winding.

Magne-Traction

Recently developed Lionel 'Magne-Traction' locomotives incorporate the use of permanent magnets to obtain greater adhesion of the locomotive drivers to the track. The number, shape and location of the magnets depend upon the structure of the locomotive and the amount of magnetic force which can be used without overloading the locomotive motor. The degree of improvement in locomotive performance due to the use of Magne-Traction usually varies with the type of locomotive, but the average Magne-Traction locomotive should pull a normal 4 or 5 car train up a 10% grade, while its draw-bar pull on level track is about double that of its non-Magne-Traction counterpart.

In those Magne-Traction locomotives where the magnets are placed externally to the driving axles, the axles themselves are made of non-magnetic type of stainless steel and should not be replaced with ordinary steel axles which would short-circuit the magnetic flux. In some of the locomotives the magnets are cemented to the locomotive frame or the motor truck. If such magnets become loosened or shift from their position so that they rub against the wheel, the entire truck should be replaced. It is impractical to attempt to recement the magnets because the cement used requires a special application technique.

In operating or servicing Magne-Traction locomotives care should be taken to keep screws, nails, paper clips or other small iron objects from jamming the wheels or drive action parts of the locomotive.

Whistles and Horns

Following actual railroading practice most

Arrangement of Working Parts in No. 681
Locomotive

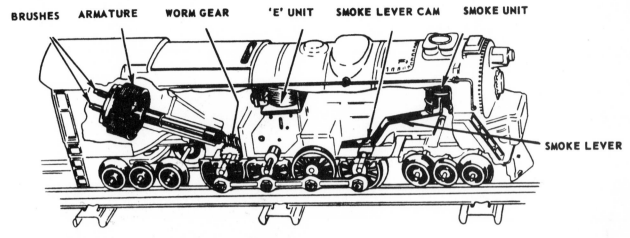

BRUSHES   ARMATURE   WORM GEAR   'E' UNIT   SMOKE LEVER CAM   SMOKE UNIT

SMOKE LEVER

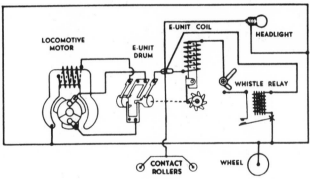

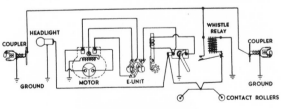

Figure 8 - Diagram of a 622 Diesel
Switcher Converted to 'Tele-Dyne'
Coupling. Note that the Whistle
Relay Must be Insulated from the
Locomotive Frame.

Lionel steam-type locomotives are equipped with a two-tone whistle. The whistle mechanism is carried in the tender and is powered by a separate motor. Electric and diesel locomotives carry a vibrating-type horn, usually powered by a size 'D' flashlight dry cell inserted in the locomotive. Both types of signals are controlled by a d.c. relay which is unaffected by the normal a.c. track voltage but which responds to a d.c. pulse superimposed upon the track circuit by

the whistle controller mechanism built into Multi-Control transformers or by separate No. 167 Whistle Controllers.

Other Applications of Whistle Relay

The d.c. whistle relay may be used for remote control of other model railroad functions instead of the locomotive whistle.

As in the 'Magic Electrol' locomotives produced by Lionel some years ago, the ground side of the E-Unit coil can be connected to the fixed contact of the relay in order to control locomotive reversing by d.c. pulse. In this way two trains can be independently operated on the same layout, one being stopped and reversed by normal interruptions of the track current, while the other is stopped and reversed by pressing the 'Whistle' control.

Another application of the whistle relay, known as the 'Tele-Dyne,' was used to achieve uncoupling of a switching locomotive anywhere on the track. This was done by connecting the coupler leads to the fixed contact of the relay. For this application the relay itself must be insulated from the locomotive body.

Direct Current Operation

While Lionel locomotives are usually operated on alternating current supplied by a step-down transformer, they can also be run on direct current obtained from storage batteries, a 'power pack,' a 32-volt d.c. generator of the type

Mounting Locomotive Wheels in a Lathe

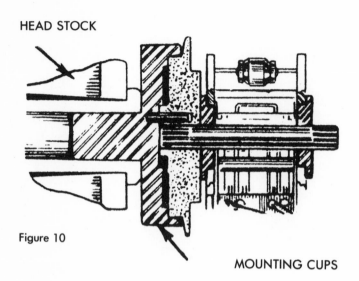

HEAD STOCK

Figure 10

MOUNTING CUPS

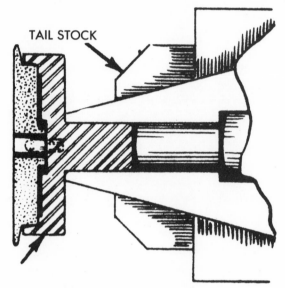

TAIL STOCK

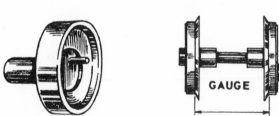

Figure 11
Left: Typical Wheel Mounting Cup
Right: Proper Way of Measuring Wheel Gauge

GAUGE

used in some rural areas, or any other d.c. power supply. The only locomotive component that will not operate properly on d.c. track supply is the whistle relay, which will remain closed, causing the whistle or horn to sound continually.

The d.c. operating voltage of Lionel motors is 2-3 volts lower than the equivalent a.c. voltage. Unless the d.c. power supply is provided with some means of varying its output voltage a rheostat must be used to control train speed. Taper wound Ohmite Model MT-14 rheostat is especially designed for this use. Also the d.c. source should be provided with some means of protection against overloads resulting from train derailment, etc. A 5-ampere Heinemann instantaneous-type circuit breaker, or equivalent, can be inserted in the track circuit for this purpose.

DISASSEMBLY AND SERVICING OF LOCOMOTIVES

From the experience of most service men, the largest single cause of poor locomotive performance is poor contact between the brushes and commutator due to an over-enthusiastic and careless use of lubricant and the consequent accumulation of caked grease, carbon dust, etc.

For this reason, examination and thorough cleaning of the brush plate, brush wells, brushes, and commutator surface and slots is generally a routine service performed on every locomotive.

On some locomotives the brush plate, held by two screws, is accessible from the locomotive cab but in majority of cases the locomotive body must be taken off in order to reach and remove the brush plate.

Taking off Locomotive Body

While the precise method of taking off the locomotive body naturally depends on type of locomotive, the following general description may be helpful. Most steam-type locomotives using a spur gear motor (Figure 1) have a one piece boiler and cab casting which is attached to the motor by means of an oval recessed head mounting screw running vertically from the top of the casting into one of the motor crossbars

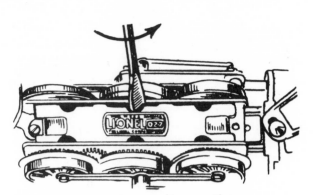

Figure 14- How to Remove Contact Plate

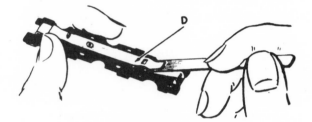

Figure 13- How to Remove Contact Slider

Figure 15- Adjusting Tension of Contact Spring

and by a transverse threaded or swedged mounting pin running from the side of the locomotive through the back of the motor side plates. Before removing the motor it is usually necessary to take off one or both of the trucks and to disconnect the crosshead supports and the valve gear assemblies from the locomotive casting.

Steam-type locomotives using a worm-shaft motor (Figure 2) have a motor frame casting on which the motor is mounted and which is held to the boiler and cab casting by screws (usually three in number) running upward from the bottom of the locomotive. In locomotives of this type the boiler casting can be removed while leaving the motor mounted on the locomotive frame. In some diesel-type engines, such as the 622 switcher, the body is held to the frame by means of two pivoted lock plates which can be turned with a screwdriver.

Removing Locomotive Drivers

Removing and replacing locomotive driving wheels should be done with particular care in order to maintain them properly lined up and quartered and correctly gauged.

While the older type zinc die-cast wheels can be removed by tapping the axle out of the wheel with a drive punch of suitable diameter, modern sintered iron powder wheels are best removed by means of a Lionel ST-301 Wheel Puller. To aid in replacing the wheels in proper quarter a guide line should be scribed across the end of the axle and the wheel hub.

Zinc die-cast wheels can generally be re-used. Used powder-iron wheels, however, do not have the same retentivity on the axle and frequently loosen up after being replaced. If the locomotive has ordinary steel axles, loosening of the wheels can be prevented by deepening the swedged grooves in the axle ends with giant nippers. If hard stainless steel axles are used, however, as in Magne-Traction locomotives, this cannot be done and new wheels should be used.

Wheels should be pressed onto the axle in a vise, arbor press, or a lathe. Best and fastest method is to use wheel mounting cups, illustrated in Figures 10 and 11, which support the wheel around the wheel rim and at the wheel hub. The cups are chucked in the lathe, the locomotive and the wheel to be mounted properly positioned and quartered, the lathe gears locked to prevent shifting, and the wheel pressed on by winding the tail stock in. While wheel mounting cups are at present not available as Lionel service tools an adequate set can be easily made on your own lathe or in a local machine shop.

When mounting wheels be careful to maintain the original distance between wheel flanges. The precise distance depends on the length of the locomotive and varies from 1.265″ in 'Scout' locomotives to 1.235″ in 773 Hudsons.

Removing Pinion Gears

If occasion arises to remove the pinion gear from the end of the armature shaft be careful not to strike the end of the shaft with a hammer or you may bend the shaft or upset the shaft end. The recommended way to remove the pinion is to apply a pair of giant nippers to the side (between teeth) of pinion until the pinion is loose. Once the pinion has been removed from the shaft it should not be reused but must be replaced with a new one. Otherwise it may eventually loosen on the shaft.

Locomotive Contact Rollers

Locomotive contact rollers and contact shoes are subject to considerable amount of normal wear and should usually be replaced when the locomotive is overhauled for the sake of appearance, as much as for proper operation.

Most 'O-27' spur-gear type motors are equipped with rollers or sliding shoes mounted on a fibre or plastic plate held between the sides of the motor. Downward tension on the sliders is maintained by a leaf spring mounted on the inside surface of this plate. To remove the sliding shoe insert a thin metal strip between the shoe and the spring 'D', as shown below and bend the spring upward to release the hook of the shoe from the slot in the spring. Then ease the shoe out. Be careful not to overbend the spring. To replace the shoe reverse the procedure.

If the spring loses its tension the best repair procedure is to spring the plate out of the motor frame with a screwdriver (Fig. 14). Tension is restored by bending the contact spring as shown in Fig. 15. The plate is snapped back into the motor frame by fitting one side into the slots in the motor side and then levering the other side into place with a screwdriver. To facilitate this operation the projections on one side of the

plate may be filed down slightly. It is not advisable to attempt to spread the motor sides with any spreading tool, since distortion of the motor sides can throw the axle bearings out of alignment and result in a permanent damage to the motor. This is particularly true of Magne-Traction motors of this type which have aluminum sides and can be distorted rather easily.

Most of the 'O' and the larger 'O-27' locomotives use a contact roller mounted on the end of the collector arm. In earlier locomotives the roller shaft is part of the roller and is free to turn in the holes in the collector arm. This type of roller tends eventually to elongate the holes in the collector arm and requires thorough lubrication. A later type of roller is made with a hole running lengthwise through the roller and turns on a stationary pin riveted to the side of the collector arms. Rollers of this type are made from sintered metal powder and are permeated with an adequate amount of lubricant. No additional oil or lubricant should be applied to these rollers because an excess may interfere with proper electrical contact and may cause the E-Unit to trip to neutral when the locomotive traverses a switch.

TROUBLE SHOOTING ANALYSIS

While the following trouble shooting analysis is not intended to be exhaustive and does not attempt to enumerate difficulties which are sometimes peculiar to specific locomotives, it lists the great majority of troubles which, in the experience of Lionel Service Department, are common to all locomotives.

Short Circuits

If the locomotive refuses to run when placed on test track and shows evidences of a short circuit, such as blinking of red signal on transformer, heavy sparking, or dimming of headlight, look for the following possible trouble spots:

1. Frayed or broken insulation on connecting wires, or a wire caught between the locomotive body and locomotive frame.

2. High solder point, such as the solder lug of the E-Unit touching the inside of the locomotive

body. Protect possible contact points with a piece of tape.

3. Bent roller arm touching the locomotive casting when locomotive is on the track.

4. Broken or distorted lamp lead washer causing lamp lead to touch the lamp socket.

5. Back of the armature winding rubbing against motor frame in spur-gear type motors. This is comparatively rare, but difficult to spot. A spacer washer between the pinion and the gear plate will remedy this condition.

Open Circuits

If the locomotive doesn't show evidence of a short circuit look for the following:

1. Broken wire lead from contact roller assembly, or any other disconnected wires.

2. Brush jammed in the brush well, failing to make contact with the commutator, or a broken or damaged brush spring.

3. Defective E-Unit with one of the spring contacts failing to make contact with the drum.

4. Open field winding, particularly at the ground end.

Lack of Power

If the locomotive operates slowly or lacks power the trouble may be either mechanical or electrical. Among electrical troubles there may be the following:

1. Clogged commutator slots, oil-soaked or worn-out brushes, or burned or weak brush springs. Make sure that the brushes move in and out of the brush wells freely and that the brush springs have sufficient and equal tension to hold brushes against the armature. Uneven spring pressure will cause the motor to run faster in one direction than the other.

2. One of the armature coils shorted to the armature shaft, or 'open' entirely. To check for 'shorts' touch one transformer lead to the armature shaft and the other lead to each of the commutator segments in turn. If no sparks appear the armature is not shorted. To check for 'opens' touch one transformer lead to one commutator segment and the other lead to each of the remaining segments in turn. There should be a spark.

Among possible mechanical troubles the most common are:

1. Worn out gears.

2. Pinion gear loose on the armature shaft.

3. Loose gear mounting stud causing the gears to wobble and jam against each other.

4. On some locomotives a jammed smoke lever.

5. On Magne-Traction locomotives a small iron object jammed in the wheels of the running gear.

Poor Reversing Action

If the locomotive reverses involuntarily or fails to reverse properly when desired look for:

1. One of the rollers or shoes failing to make proper contact with the center rail, particularly while crossing switches. Excessive lubricant on powder iron rollers will sometimes form an insulating coat producing this effect. Powder iron rollers should not be lubricated.

2. A defect in the E-Unit such as a bent or burned out contact spring, distorted or damaged E-Unit drum, loose E-Unit switch, or tight plunger due to collapsed coil spool.

MOTORS AND E-UNITS: A PRIMER
by Stan Shantar

The motors used in Lionel locomotives are the "universal" type, which means that either alternating or direct current may be used for power. Of course, it has been common practice to operate tinplate trains with alternating current (AC) from a transformer ever since the development of the first electric trains in the 1900's. At that time, there were no small, practical permanent magnetic DC motors. Besides, even if such motors had been available, there was no inexpensive way to obtain low voltage direct current of sufficient amperage to power toy locomotives. It wasn't until after World War II that these two obstacles had been overcome. By then the use of alternating current was too firmly entrenched among toy train operators to permit a swing over to DC. However, the then-emerging scale model railroading hobby (particularly HO scale) quickly adopted DC as its standard power source. This was probably the first significant delineation between "scale" and "tinplate" model railroading. (Remember, the first commercially produced true scale locomotive was Lionel's 700E, which ran on 3 rail track!)

Both AC and DC have certain advantages and disadvantages as model railroad current supplies. The main advantage of DC is that a locomotive's direction may be changed by simply reversing the polarity of the current. Therefore, a polarity reversing switch on the DC "power pack" (which is basically a constant voltage transformer, a rectifier, and a rheostat) is all that's needed to control the direction of a train.

DC Advantages

It isn't that simple with AC motors. Since alternating current changes polarity many times a second (typically, 60), an AC motor must maintain rotation in the same direction regardless of polarity. This is done by using an electromagnet for the motor's magnetic field, rather than a permanent magnet as on DC motors. This electromagnet (called the field winding) is wired in such a way that the magnetic polarity of the field changes *each time* the polarity of the armature winding changes. In this way the motor's field "leads" the armature, causing it to turn in the same direction regardless of the polarity of the current supply. Since the important factor in the operation of an AC motor is the relationship of the field polarity to the armature polarity, such a motor will work on AC or DC (hence, the term "universal"). On the other hand, a DC motor will not work on AC, for it will attempt to change direction each time the current polarity changes. At 60 cycles per second, this will result in no net motion at all, and eventually the armature will overheat and burn out.

To reverse an AC motor either the brush connections must be interchanged or a second field winding, wound in opposition to the first, must be switched in. In either case the motor's field will "lead" the armature in the opposite direction. The first means employed to reverse a tinplate locomotive was a switch mounted on the locomotive. This reversing switch changed connections to the brushes. However, this ar-

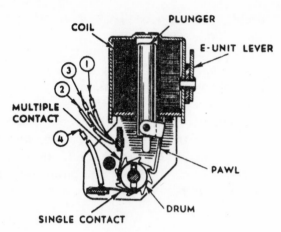

Figure 3

rangement left much to be desired. Therefore, a remote control reversing device was developed. Known as an E-unit, this solenoid-type device changes motor connections whenever track current is interrupted. This setup is often called "sequence reversing." Lionel's early E-units were the "pendulum" type, which were less satisfactory than the "drum" type, pioneered by Ives. When Lionel acquired Ives, the "drum" type E-unit became the standard reversing device for all Lionel locos. In 1957, Lionel introduced a very simple two position E-unit on some inexpensive locos. Instead of interchanging brush connections, the two position E unit switches between two oppositely wound field windings.

The Scout Reversing Unit

In the late 40's Lionel developed a sequence reversing system that did not employ a separate E-unit. This unique system was found on "Scout" locomotives. In a "Scout" motor, the field winding acts also as a solenoid, pulling down a hinged section of the field core each time current is applied. This motion is mechanically linked to rotating brush holders which effectively interchange connections each time current is interrupted. What Lionel saved by not having an E-unit they more than made up for with a Rube Goldberg style mechanism! This "Scout" reversing system was found to be very

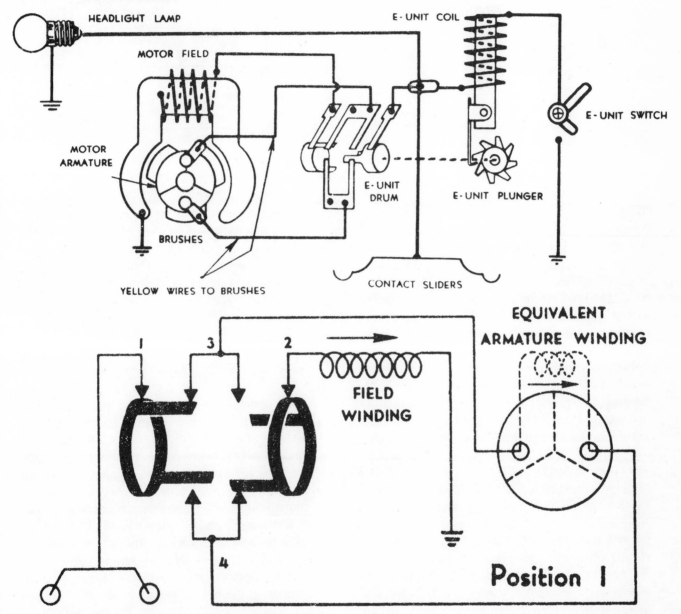

Figure 2- Schematic Wiring Diagram of a Typical E-Unit Installation

HEADLIGHT LAMP

E- UNIT COIL

MOTOR FIELD

E- UNIT SWITCH

MOTOR ARMATURE

E- UNIT DRUM

E- UNIT PLUNGER

BRUSHES

YELLOW WIRES TO BRUSHES

CONTACT SLIDERS

EQUIVALENT ARMATURE WINDING

FIELD WINDING

Position I

troublesome, and Lionel limited its use to the most inexpensive locos.

AC Advantages

Even though reversing an AC powered locomotive requires an additional (and sometimes erratic) E-unit or a complicated (and definitely erratic) "Scout"-type mechanism, AC does have some advantages over DC. First of all, low speed performance is generally better

with AC motors and transformers. By contrast, HOers have started using increasingly sophisticated power packs and/or flywheels to improve the low speed performance of their DC powered locomotives. In addition, the universal characteristic of the AC motor enabled Lionel to develop an on-board remote control whistle. The heart of the whistle system is a relay which responds *only* to DC. This relay is connected to

117

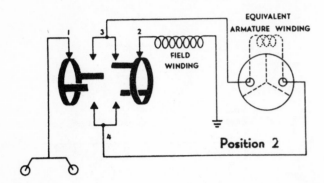

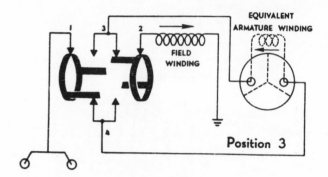

the whistle motor, allowing the operator to blow the whistle while the locomotive is running by momentarily changing the track current from AC to DC. The whistle relay had two other innovative applications in the late prewar era. The first of these was known as "Magic Electrol." In this system a locomotive's E-unit solenoid was connected to a whistle relay instead of the usual direct connection to the center rail pickup. A "Magic Electrol" loco would not reverse when the track current was interrupted; rather, it would reverse only when the whistle control was operated. This system provided independent direction control of two locos—one with standard sequence reversing, the other with "Magic Electrol"—on the same layout. The other prewar application of the whistle relay was advertised as "Teledyne Couplers." In this application the electromagnetic (coil) couplers of a locomotive were connected to a whistle relay instead of the usual connection to sliding shoes. The operation of the whistle control would open the locomotive's couplers *anywhere* on the track. Although relatively few locomotives were ever produced with "Magic Electrol" or "Teledyne Couplers," it is easy to convert many Lionel engines to either system if you desire. Remember, if you use either system, you forfeit the on-board whistle.

Interestingly, America's three major manufacturers of tinplate trains have introduced DC powered models at various times since World War II. American Flyer led the way with an entire line of S gauge trains with DC motors in the late 1940's. Lionel has had a DC powered

starter set in their line each year since 1973. A few years back Marx introduced DC powered O-27 starter sets which used a lantern battery in a controller housing rather than a power pack. However, none of these DC tinplate trains made much of an impact, and the familiar sound of sequence reversing is still an integral part of tinplate railroading.

LIONEL "E-UNITS"[1]

The E-Unit is a solenoid-operated rotary sequence switch used to reverse locomotive motors by interchaging the connections of the motor armature with respect to the motor field. The E-Unit is mounted in the locomotive and consists of a solenoid coil connected across the track, a plunger-and-pawl assembly, a rotating plastic drum equipped with copper contact inserts and a central toothed wheel, and an arrangement of solid silver contact springs riding on the drum. The E-Unit is also equipped with a lever-type switch or a plug-and-jack connection which is used to open the solenoid coil circuit, thus disconnecting the E-Unit. A typical wiring diagram of the E-Unit circuit is shown schematically in Figure 2.

Normally, i.e. when the solenoid circuit is closed and the solenoid coil is energized by track voltage, the plunger-and-pawl assembly remains drawn into the upper end of the solenoid tube, as shown in Figure 3, p. 116. When track voltage is interrupted for any reason, or when it drops below the minimum 'holding' voltage of the solenoid (4-5 volts), the plunger drops and the pawl engages the next tooth on the drum. When the voltage is reapplied (7-8 volts

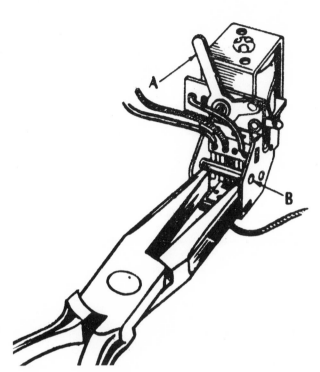

Figure 4- How to Open E-Unit

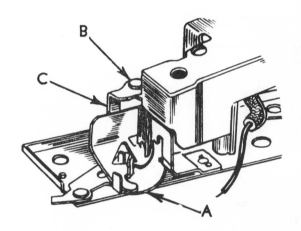

minimum), the plunger is drawn into the tube and the pawl rotates the drum into a new position. A cycle of operation consists of four positions: Forward, Stop, Reverse, Stop. Since the coil rotates 45 degrees with each movement of the plunger, one complete rotation of the drum produces two full cycles.

In position 1 the drum is turned so that contact springs 1 and 3 are connected by a metal insert on top of the drum while contact springs 2 and 4 are similarly connected by an insert in the bottom of the drum. Current from center rail follows the path in the direction of the arrows through contacts 1 and 3 to the motor armature and then through contacts 4 and 2 to the motor field and to the outside or 'ground' rail. In this position the direction of the current through the field and the armature is the same so that the motor turns 'forward.'

In position 2 the drum is turned 45 degrees so that the connection between contact springs 1 and 3 and between 4 and 2 is broken. The motor circuit is open and the train remains standing in 'neutral.'

In position 3 the drum is turned so that connection is made between contact springs 1 and 4 and between 3 and 2. The current from the center rail now follows the path through contacts 1 and 4 to the motor armature and then through contacts 3 and 2 to the motor field and from there to the 'ground' rail. In this position the direction of the current through the field is opposite to that through the armature so that the motor turns in 'reverse.'

The fourth position of the drum again opens the connection between the field and the armature putting the motor again into 'neutral.' Note that when the E-Unit lever is open the drum cannot be turned electrically and the train will rontinue to operate in the same direction, or will remain standing in 'neutral' despite current interruptions.

With the exception of Nos. 726-51 and 2333M-10, which operate on a slightly higher

119

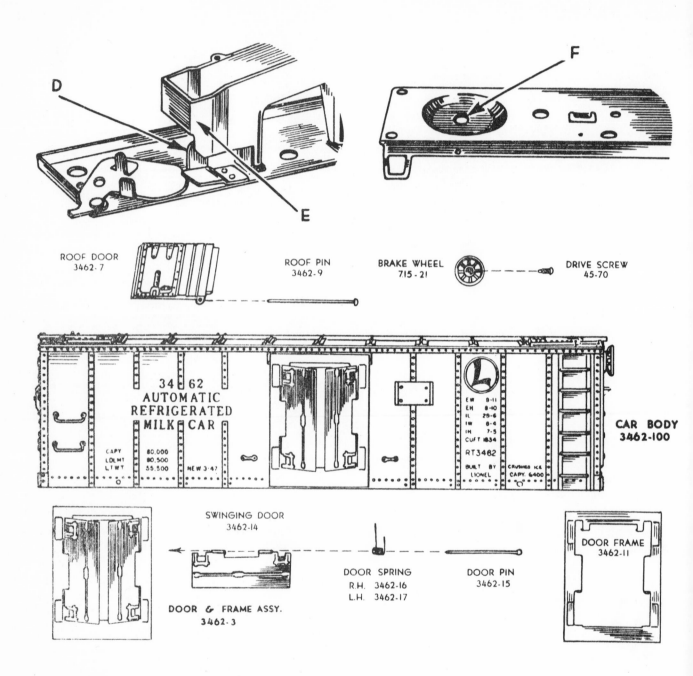

ROOF DOOR
3462-7

ROOF PIN
3462-9

BRAKE WHEEL
715-21

DRIVE SCREW
45-70

34 62
AUTOMATIC
REFRIGERATED
MILK CAR

CAPY. 80,000
LDLMT 80,500
LTWT 55,500   NEW 3·47

EW   8-11
EH   8-10
IL   29-6
IW   8-4
IH   7-5
CUFT 1834
RT3462
BUILT BY
LIONEL   CRUSHED ICE
CAPY. 6400

CAR BODY
3462-100

SWINGING DOOR
3462-14

DOOR FRAME
3462-11

DOOR SPRING
R.H. 3462-16
L.H. 3462-17

DOOR PIN
3462-15

DOOR & FRAME ASSY.
3462-3

voltage, all E-Units are electrically alike, differing only in the lengths of leads and the location and length of the lever. E-Units Nos. 671-50 and 726-51 which are mounted in the locomotive horizontally and cannot have a gravity return, have, in addition, a spring to return the plunger to its indexing position.

While E-Units usually control but one motor, it is possible, to control as many as four motors simultaneously by connecting them to a single E-Unit in parallel.

Servicing E-Units

If the locomotive fails to reverse properly, the E-Unit is probably at fault. First make sure that the E-Unit lever is closed and makes good contact, then check the wiring connections. Remove the E-Unit from the locomotive frame and check the continuity of the solenoid coil by

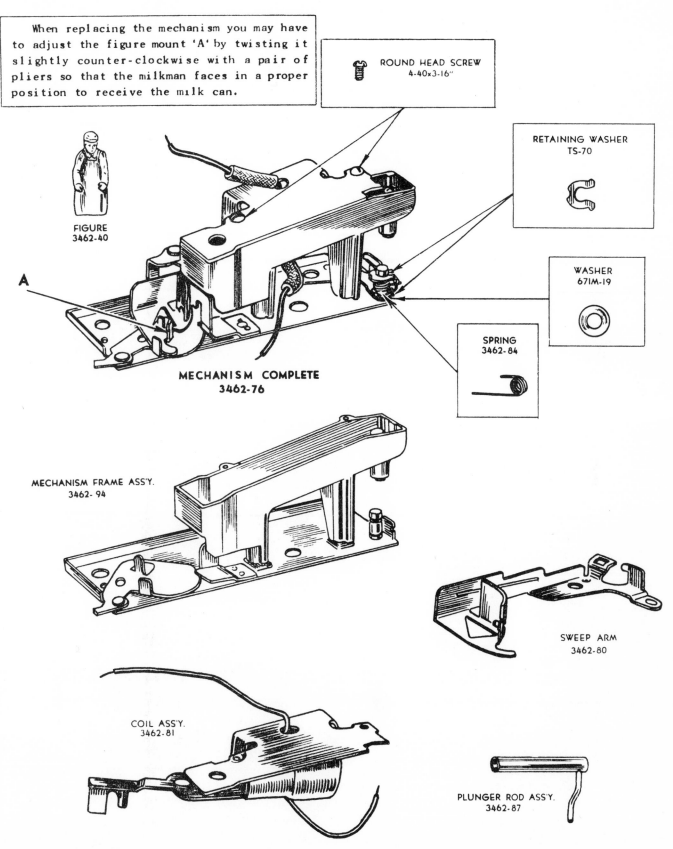

When replacing the mechanism you may have to adjust the figure mount 'A' by twisting it slightly counter-clockwise with a pair of pliers so that the milkman faces in a proper position to receive the milk can.

ROUND HEAD SCREW
4-40x3-16"

RETAINING WASHER
TS-70

WASHER
671M-19

SPRING
3462-84

FIGURE
3462-40

A

MECHANISM COMPLETE
3462-76

MECHANISM FRAME ASS'Y.
3462-94

SWEEP ARM
3462-80

COIL ASS'Y.
3462-81

PLUNGER ROD ASS'Y.
3462-87

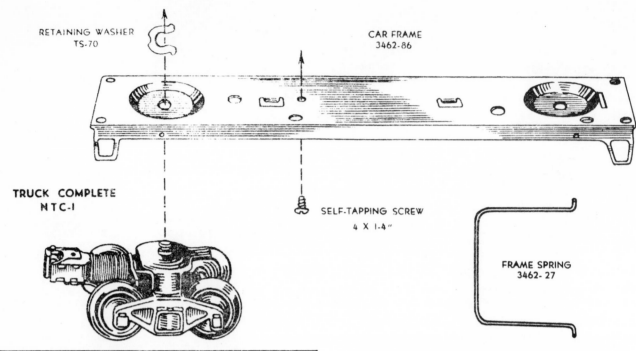

RETAINING WASHER
TS-70

CAR FRAME
3462-86

TRUCK COMPLETE
N T C - I

SELF-TAPPING SCREW
4 X 1-4"

FRAME SPRING
3462- 27

See section on coupler trucks for the complete breakdown of this assembly.

Coupler trucks are sold without the associated lead. Use a 6" lead for the front truck (away from the mechanism) and a 3-1/2" lead for the rear truck.

To separate car body and car frame move spring down and compress sides slightly.

PLATFORM STEPS
3462P-8

PLATFORM
3462P-14

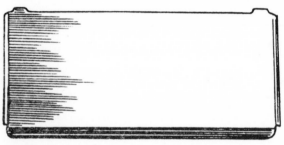

PLATFORM COMPLETE
3462P -1

"A"
"B"

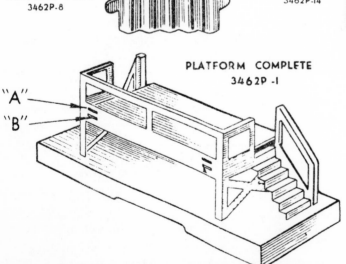

MILK CAN SET
3462-70

No. 3462-70 MAGNETIC MILK CANS
No. 3462 AUTOMATIC MILK CAR

'A' and 'B' are the slots for adjusting platform for the height of the track. Use 'A' slots for '0' Gauge and 'B' slots for '0-27'.

Milk cans are sold only in sets of seven packaged as illustrated above. Note that a small magnet is pressed into the bottom of each can to help keep it upright on the unloading platform.

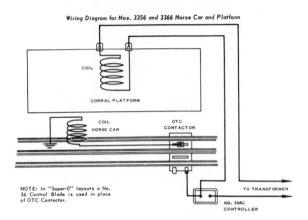

Wiring Diagram for Nos. 3356 and 3366 Horse Car and Platform

COIL

CORRAL PLATFORM

COIL
HORSE CAR

OTC
CONTACTOR

NOTE: In "Super-0" layouts a No.
36 Control Blade is used in place
of OTC Contactor.

TO TRANSFORMER

NO. 364C
CONTROLLER

touching the transformer leads to both ends of the coil. Apply 7-8 volts. If the plunger operates the coil is good. (Gravity-operated E-Units will function only in upright position.)

To remove the drum and the contact assemblies, spread the E-Unit cheeks apart with a pair of pliers, as shown in **Figure 4**. Clean the contact springs and the drum well with carbon tetrachloride (Carbona) to remove all grit and oil. Replace all worn parts. *Make sure that the contact springs have sufficient tension.* Reassemble unit and fasten tightly by tapping the end of stud 'B' with a ball peen hammer. When reassembling the E-Unit back into the locomotive make sure that solder joints or bare wires do not touch the locomotive frame or the cab casting.

Most "E" Units vary only in the length and location of the E-Unit lever and in the length and color of the wire leads. To simplify servicing, the "E" Units which differ only in the length of leads have been grouped together and a single replacement specified for each group. With the exception of horizontally-mounted units, the component replacement parts of all "E" Units are identical. Horizontally-mounted units require a special Plunger & Pawl Assembly to retain a plunger return spring.

LIONEL TWO-POSITION "E-UNITS"

The 101 series of two-position reversing units was initiated in 1957. This permits either forward or reverse operation and eliminates the intermediate "stop" position.

Motors equipped for two-position opera-

tion have double-wound fields connected to the armature through the reversing unit. Depending on the position of the contact arm either half of the field is connected to the armature thus changing the direction of its rotation.

Since the plunger of this reversing unit depends on gravity to return to its "ready" position, this unit must be mounted vertically. Part numbers of this type will differ because of various formings of the lever.

Split-field motors can be converted to the regular three-position reverse. In this case only one of the fields (either green or copper-colored), should be wired into the circuit. The two leads of the other field coil should be insulated or cut short.

This two-position unit has proven itself to be almost completely trouble-free and component parts of it are not required.

MILK CAR NO. 3462

Like all Lionel remote-control unloading cars No. 3462 Milk Car operates through the agency of a solenoid-type electromagnet which, energized, attracts an iron plunger linked to the operating mechanism. The return of the plunger and the mechanism to the normal position is accomplished by means of a spring.

As in all operating cars the solenoid leads are connected to the truck collector shoes which make contact with the control rails of a remote control track section. The solenoid is energized by positioning the car on the remote control track section (RCS, 1019 or 6019) and then pressing the 'unload' button of the controller connected to that track section.

The Automatic Milk Car can be operated on either 'O' or 'O-27' track but since the two tracks differ in the height of the rails the unloading platform which receives the miniature milk cans must be adjusted to the proper height corresponding to the track used.

The mechanism of the 1948 model of the No. 3462 Automatic Milk Car, described in this section has been completely redesigned and is, therefore, for the most part not interchangeable with the mechanism of the 1947 model.

NO. 3356 AND NO. 3366 HORSE CAR AND CORRAL

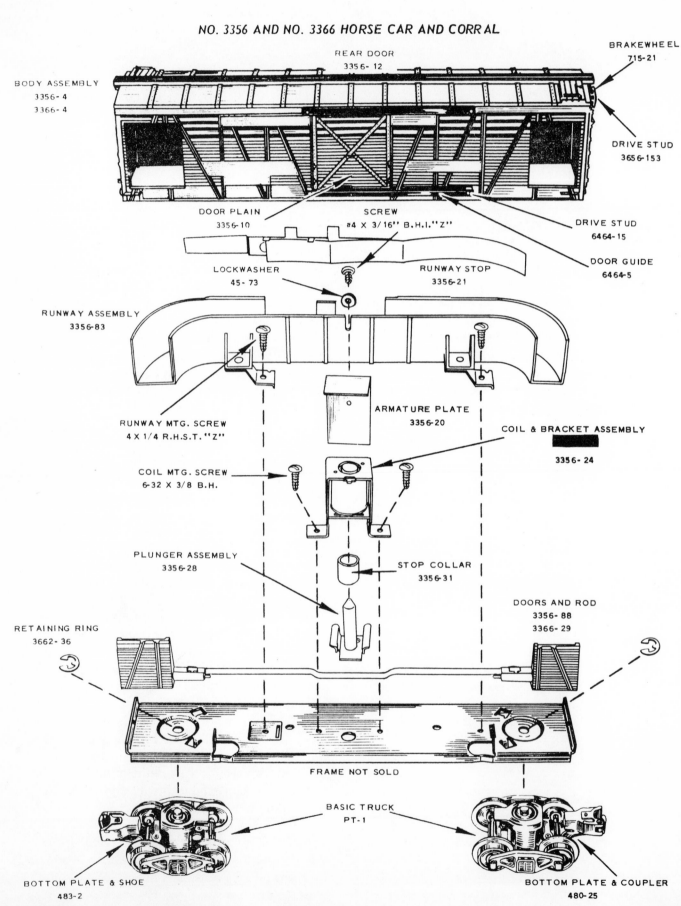

BRAKEWHEEL
715-21

REAR DOOR
3356-12

BODY ASSEMBLY
3356-4
3366-4

DRIVE STUD
3656-153

DOOR PLAIN
3356-10

SCREW
#4 X 3/16" B.H.I. "Z"

DRIVE STUD
6464-15

DOOR GUIDE
6464-5

LOCKWASHER
45-73

RUNWAY STOP
3356-21

RUNWAY ASSEMBLY
3356-83

RUNWAY MTG. SCREW
4 X 1/4 R.H.S.T. "Z"

ARMATURE PLATE
3356-20

COIL & BRACKET ASSEMBLY

3356-24

COIL MTG. SCREW
6-32 X 3/8 B.H.

PLUNGER ASSEMBLY
3356-28

STOP COLLAR
3356-31

DOORS AND ROD
3356-88
3366-29

RETAINING RING
3662-36

FRAME NOT SOLD

BASIC TRUCK
PT-1

BOTTOM PLATE & SHOE
483-2

BOTTOM PLATE & COUPLER
480-25

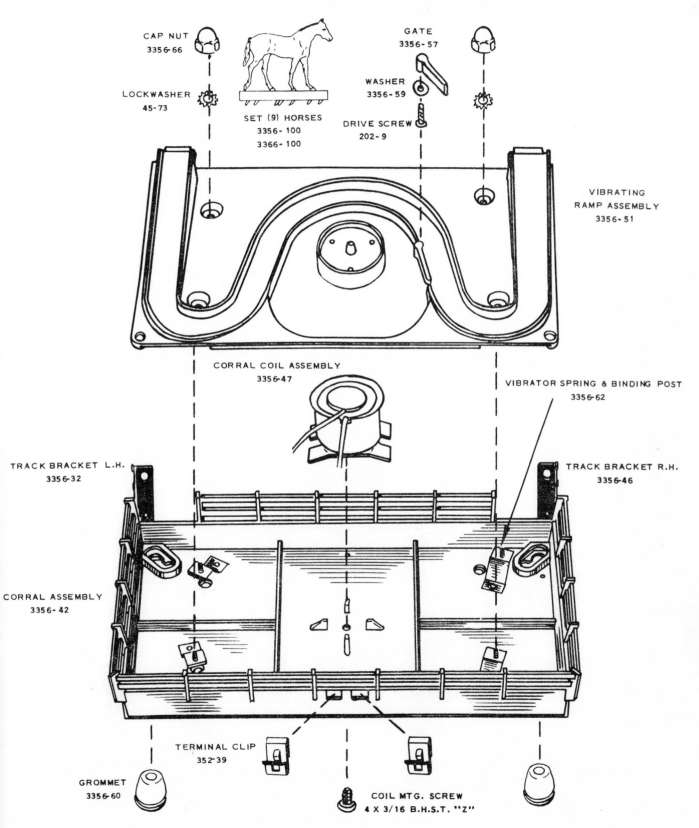

NO. 3356 AND NO. 3366 HORSE CAR AND CORRAL

CAP NUT
3356-66

LOCKWASHER
45-73

SET (9) HORSES
3356-100
3366-100

GATE
3356-57

WASHER
3356-59

DRIVE SCREW
202-9

VIBRATING
RAMP ASSEMBLY
3356-51

CORRAL COIL ASSEMBLY
3356-47

VIBRATOR SPRING & BINDING POST
3356-62

TRACK BRACKET L.H.
3356-32

TRACK BRACKET R.H.
3356-46

CORRAL ASSEMBLY
3356-42

TERMINAL CLIP
352-39

GROMMET
3356-60

COIL MTG. SCREW
4 X 3/16 B.H.S.T. "Z"

Service Hints

Any trouble that may develop in the operation of the Automatic Milk Car may be either electrical or mechanical in nature. It is, of course, extremely difficult to foresee and describe all the possible difficulties that may arise in the operation of the mechanism but the following specific examples are typical and may help you in determining and solving the problem.

Electrical Troubles: Most of these are caused by a short between the coil circuit and the metal frame of the car or coupler truck.

1. Check to see that the insulating sleeving on the coil leads is in place.

2. The insulating paper on the coil may be broken allowing the bare solder joint to ground against the chute cover. Twist the coil around and repair the insulation.

3. The bare end of the wire lead soldered to the coupler coil may be bent upward so that it 'shorts' against the truck frame. Push the bare wire down away from the frame as shown by arrow in the illustration below.

Mechanical Troubles: Improper functioning of the mechanism may be due to burred edges of moving metal parts, too tight or too loose riveting or to bent or distorted parts. Check the mechanism carefully to discover the place where any binding or interference occurs.

1. The moving platform fails to return to normal position. This may be due either to a burred edge or to a slight distortion of the platform slide. Smooth the edges of the metal and bend the slide 'A' up slightly by prying up gently. Also failure of the platform slide to come out far enough or to return to normal position may be caused by improper tension of the spring, 3462-84.

2. The last can fails to drop from the chute. This may be caused by burred edges of the chute opening, or excess metal on the guide rib on bottom of chute. File clean and tap down the rib gently.

3. The can fails to come into proper position in front of figure. This may be due to (a) Tight riveting of can sweep arm, (b) distortion of vertical flap of the can sweep arm, (c) interference between arm slot and vertical portion of the bracket support. To adjust (a) loosen rivet 'B' slightly, (b) adjust arm flap 'C' inward by bending slightly with a pair of pliers, (c) bend vertical section of bracket 'D' so that it is in the center of the arm slot.

4. Cans fail to drop through slot in chute. Chute may be too wide allowing the cans to move diagonally across slot. Tap side of chute at point 'E' to reduce width.

5. Platform slide hits the edge of unloading platform. This may be due to excessive rocking of car body during operation. Reduce play between car body and truck by inserting a thin metal washer or an additional retaining washer at 'F'.

NOS. 3356 AND 3366 HORSE CARS

The operating principle of No. 3356 Car and Corral is similar to that used in No. 3656 Stock Car. Both the car and the corral are equipped with vibrator coils which cause the runway inside the car and the floor of the corral to vibrate rapidly. The interaction between these vibrating surfaces and miniature rubber "fingers" on the base of the animals cause the figures to move forward in the corral and car runways.

This operating car and platform is designed for use with "O", "O-27" and "Super-O" track. However, since these tracks vary in rail height the platform is provided with four rubber feet which may be inverted to raise or lower the platform.

The car runway is equipped with a slide assembly to hold horses in the runway. This slide assembly is operated by the rear center door which is opened to hold the horses within the car while they are being loaded from the corral to the car.

The vibrator coil in the car is also provided with a plunger which is linked to the end doors of the car. As the coil is energized the doors drop down converting to ramps connecting the car to the corral.

Unlike most operating cars No. 3356 and 3366 cars have only one slide shoe which is

WIRING DIAGRAM OF NO. 3656 STOCK CAR AND PLATFORM

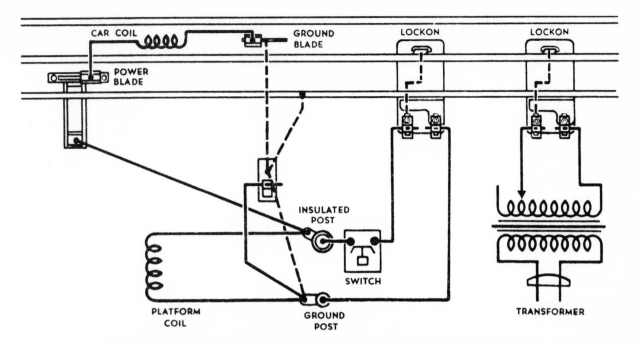

Note that when the corral platform is assembled to the track, the electrical circuit is completed not only through the ground post which is wired to the track lockon, but also directly through the frame to the outside rails, as indicated by dotted lines,. For this reason the car and platform will operate even if the grounding wire is omitted. Consequently the controller switch, in order to be effective, must be inserted in the 'high' side of the circuit.

connected to the "high" side of the coil. The other side of the electric circuit is grounded through the metal framework and truck wheels of the car to the outside track rails. This type of wiring is used so that the car will operate only when properly oriented on the track with its drop doors facing the corral.

The vibration of the car runway is regulated by adjusting the air gap between the coil bracket and its armature. The screw which holds the armature is located in line with the rear door and is reached by removing the car body.

The vibrator of the corral ramps is adjusted by adjusting the four Cap Nuts which hold the corral platform to the mounting springs riveted to the base.

Service Notes. The Corral Platform has locating arms to hold the platform to the trackside. The rivet holding each cannot be replaced. A sheet metal screw together with a washer will make a suitable replacement.

Care must be taken to adjust the operating doors so that they lower fully and evenly to the corresponding lip of the corral runway.

NO. 3656 STOCK CAR

The motion of the miniature animals in the No. 3656 Stock Car and along its corral platform is produced by rapid vibration of the "floating" floor of the platform and the cattle runway in the car. Vibration is produced by solenoids mounted underneath the car and the platform. Electric current for the two solenoids is supplied through the two binding posts on the end of the platform.

Since it is impractical to stipulate a precise voltage for operating a vibrating mechanism of the type employed, the platform binding posts should be connected to a source of variable voltage—such as the track itself—so that voltage may be readily adjusted for best performance.

Current for the car solenoid is fed through two blades which project from the track base and which make contact with the sliding shoes beneath the car trucks. The blades are so located that the car can be energized only when it is within ¼" of its precise operating position in front of the platform. The circuit diagram of the car and the correct platform is shown below.

Note that because the platform, when assembled to the layout, is in addition grounded through the outside track rails, the controller switch must be inserted on the 'high' side, as shown.

The Stock Car outfit can be operated with either 'O' or 'O-27' gauge track provided that proper adjustment is made in the height of the corral platform and the correct contact blades are used to compensate for the difference in the heights of the two types of track.

It is important that the track is mounted on platform track base correctly, according to instructions, or the car will be tilted and either fail to make proper electrical contact with the base, or interfere with the action of the platform bridge.

SERVICE HINTS

1. Sticking Overhead Doors. Relieve friction along sides of door frames by scraping off excess paint, burrs, etc. Failure of overhead doors to operate properly may be caused by poor adjustment of the spring lever. Adjust as follows: Overbend spring lever upward. Then, holding overhead doors closed, reach the plunger through the sliding door and push it down several times until doors rise enough to clear cattle and close completely. Readjustment of lever may be necessary when replacing or remounting the overhead doors or the cattle runway. To prevent interference with spring level, anchor the coil lead to floor of car with a bit of scotch tape.

2. Replacing Overhead Doors. When replacing overhead doors it may be necessary to remove any rough spots and round off the sharp corner at the center 'cam' portion of the bar joining the two doors. Clean out the pivot holes in the ends of the bar by hand-reaming with a No. 55 drill.

3. Tight Solenoid Plunger. May cause poor vibration and improper action of overhead doors. Most often due to misalignment between the plunger and the brass plunger tube. Correct by bending or twisting plunger support care-

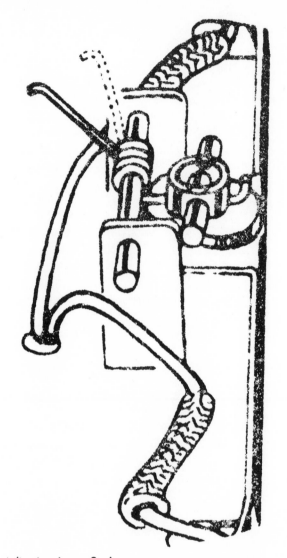

Adjusting Lever Spring

fully, as needed (at right). To obtain more positive operation of overhead doors replace hollow plunger with solid plunger 3656-145 and plunger return spring 2020M-34.

4. Loose Sliding Door. If sliding door is too loose it may be pushed open by the moving cattle so that it will be impossible to load the car. Increase friction, when necessary, by bending the cattle stop bar so that it rubs against wall of car.

5. Short Circuit in Coil. Coil leads may be short-circuited by being jammed against each other or against coil housing. Remove coil by unsoldering spring pin and straightening the four 'fingers' holding housing to car floor. Lo-

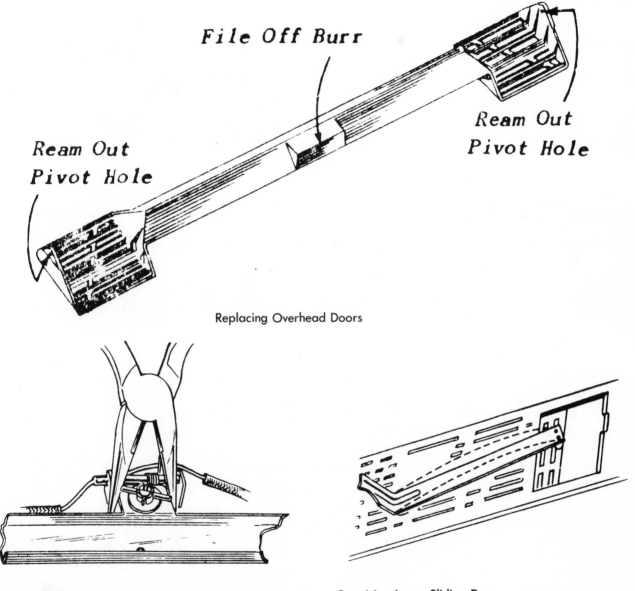

File Off Burr

Ream Out Pivot Hole

Ream Out Pivot Hole

Replacing Overhead Doors

Adjusting Plunger Alignment

Repairing Loose Sliding Door

cate coil in housing so that the leads lie in the widest part of housing (front).

6. *Replacing Cattle Runway*. Clean out adhesive grommet seats in car floor thoroughly, scraping out residue and using carbon tetrachloride (Carbona). To apply adhesive grommets, dip them in carbon tetrachloride, then set them into the seats and place runway on top using the aligning holes (see **page 130**) as guides. Do not depend on these holes to give perfect

alignment, but check by moving the plunger in the plunger tube.

7. *Removing Car Trucks*. Since alignment of the runway is fairly difficult try to disturb it as little as possible when removing or replacing car trucks. One of the trucks (at the entrance end of the runway) can be removed and replaced by using long-nose pliers without disturbing the runway. To remove the other truck, lift off that end of the runway only.

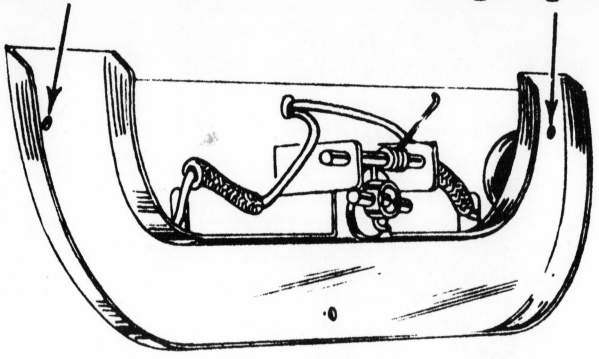

Aligning Hole

Aligning Hole

Aligning Cattle Runway

SERVICING THE PLATFORM

1. Aligning Platform Bridge. Bridge ramps must align with the car floor. To adjust remove front fence and, holding the center of the connecting bar with a pair of pliers, adjust one of the bridges to proper height. Then bend the finger of the other bridge (at right) until it makes contact with the floor of the platform when the bridge is lowered. The finger serves to transmit vibration from the floor of the platform to the bridge.

2. Platform Vibration. Check to see that the platform 'floats' in the frame at all four points of suspension. Adjust the grommeted tips by bending them slightly to free platform at points where vibration seems to be poor. In the earlier production models initial adjustment of platform vibration can be made through an adjustment nut in the bottom of the platform. Resting platform on blocks to reach the nut with a socket wrench, adjust for best performance while applying 12-15 volts. After adjustment the nut should be sealed with Sauereisen cement. In later production models no adjustment is necessary and the nut is merely brought up tight.

3. Interference With Motion of Cattle. In the earlier production models possible sources

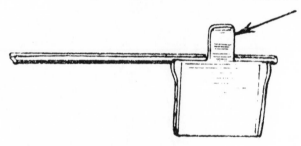

Finger Must Touch Platform

Adjusting Bridge Vibration

of interference are sharp corners of the corral fence bases. Bend them back slightly.

NO. O22 REMOTE CONTROL SWITCH

No. O22 Remote Control Switches are made for use with 'O' gauge track and are generally sold in sets consisting of a right hand switch, a left hand switch and a pair of No. O22C controllers. Each switch is operated by its own controller connected to it by means of a three-conductor cable.

The mechanism of the switch, commonly called the switch 'motor', is activated by two solenoid coils assembled end to end over a common tube and plunger. The plunger is linked

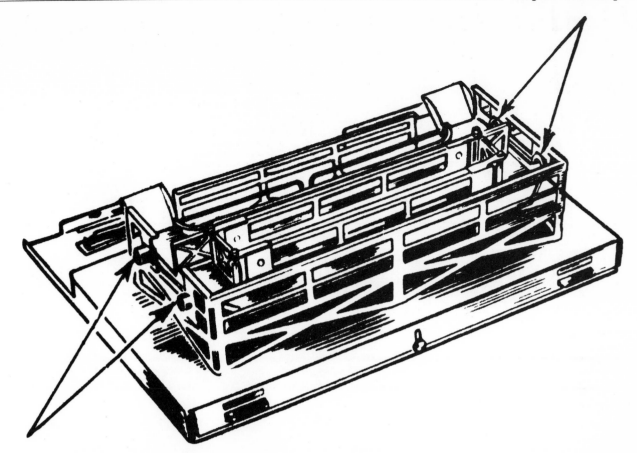

Check Platform Suspension

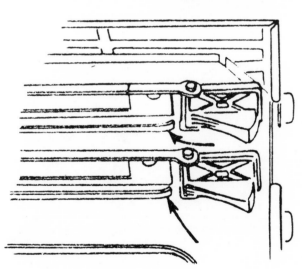

Eliminate Sharp Corners in Passage

mechanically to the swivel rail and other parts of the switch mechanism. When either coil is energized the plunger is pulled into that coil moving the swivel rail and the rest of the switch mechanism.

The current for the switch 'motor' and for the lamps in the switch and the controllers is usually obtained from the center rail of the track through a contact spring which projects from the bottom of the switch frog rail. It is also possible, however, to obtain power directly from the transformer by using the Fixed Voltage Plug which is inserted over the booster pin of the switch. Insertion of the plug automatically separates the pin from the spring and disconnects the track power supply.

The diagram of the switch motor and controller circuit is illustrated below. The plunger and consequently the swivel rail and the moving contact assembly have two alternate positions. In the position illustrated, the swivel rail will be set for the train to proceed along the curved branch on the rail. In this position the right spring contact connects end of coil 'A' to terminal 'A' and to the red lamp in the controller, so that current flowing from the booster pin, through coil 'A' and cable will light the red lamp. This current, however, is not large enough to operate the plunger and the switch remains undisturbed. When the lamp is shorted out by moving the controller lever a surge of current operates the plunger moving the switch mechanism and the contact assembly to the alternate position in which the swivel rail is set for the train to proceed along the straightaway and the

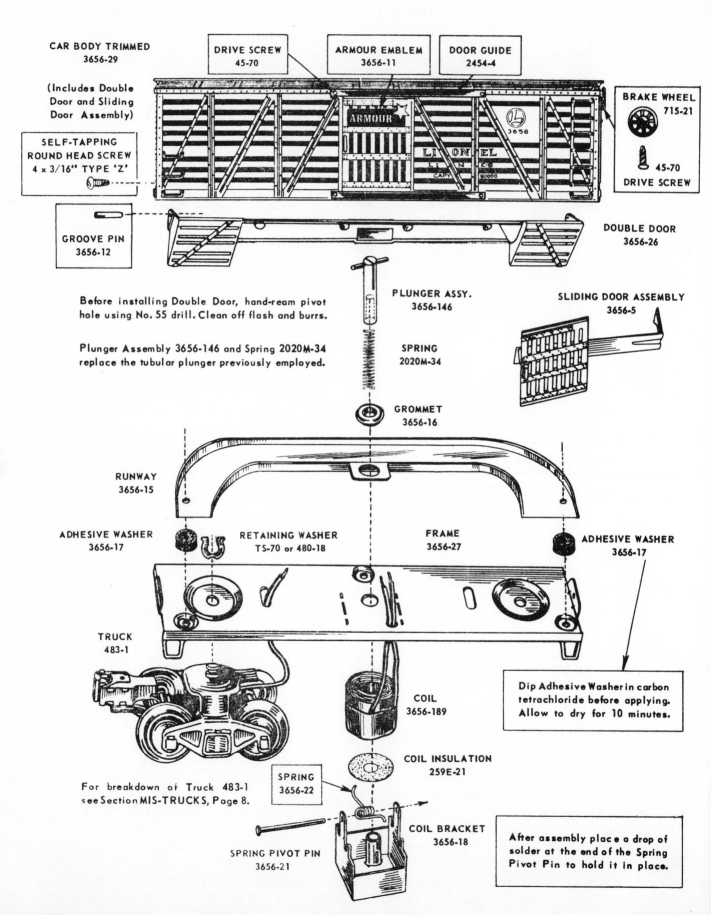

CAR BODY TRIMMED
3656-29

(Includes Double
Door and Sliding
Door Assembly)

DRIVE SCREW
45-70

ARMOUR EMBLEM
3656-11

DOOR GUIDE
2454-4

BRAKE WHEEL
715-21

45-70
DRIVE SCREW

SELF-TAPPING
ROUND HEAD SCREW
4 x 3/16" TYPE 'Z'

GROOVE PIN
3656-12

DOUBLE DOOR
3656-26

Before installing Double Door, hand-ream pivot
hole using No. 55 drill. Clean off flash and burrs.

Plunger Assembly 3656-146 and Spring 2020M-34
replace the tubular plunger previously employed.

PLUNGER ASSY.
3656-146

SPRING
2020M-34

SLIDING DOOR ASSEMBLY
3656-5

GROMMET
3656-16

RUNWAY
3656-15

ADHESIVE WASHER
3656-17

RETAINING WASHER
TS-70 or 480-18

FRAME
3656-27

ADHESIVE WASHER
3656-17

TRUCK
483-1

Dip Adhesive Washer in carbon
tetrachloride before applying.
Allow to dry for 10 minutes.

COIL
3656-189

COIL INSULATION
259E-21

For breakdown of Truck 483-1
see Section MIS-TRUCKS, Page 8.

SPRING
3656-22

SPRING PIVOT PIN
3656-21

COIL BRACKET
3656-18

After assembly place a drop of
solder at the end of the Spring
Pivot Pin to hold it in place.

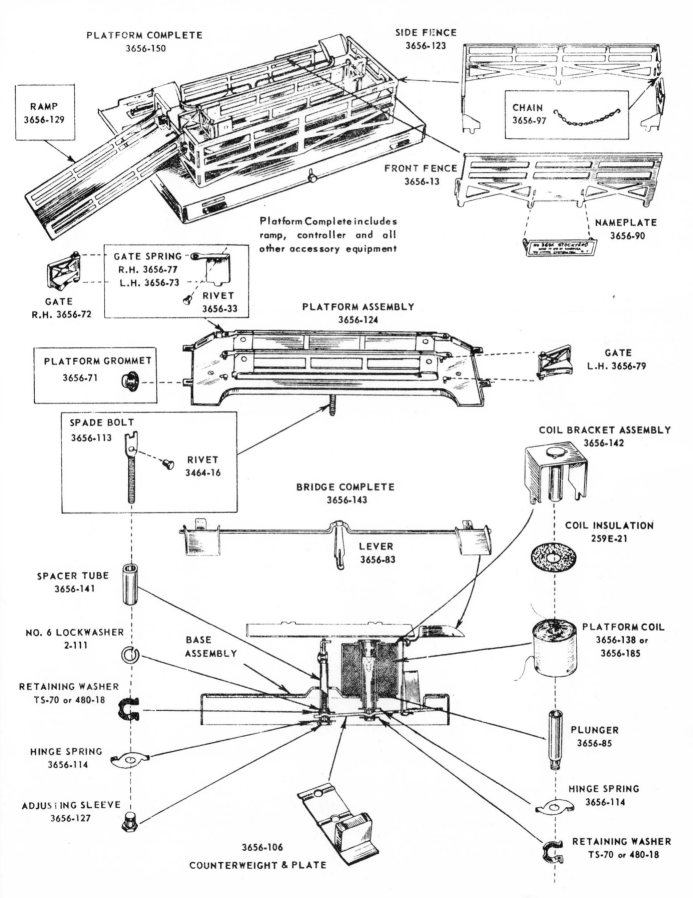

PLATFORM COMPLETE
3656-150

SIDE FENCE
3656-123

RAMP
3656-129

CHAIN
3656-97

FRONT FENCE
3656-13

NAMEPLATE
3656-90

Platform Complete includes ramp, controller and all other accessory equipment

GATE SPRING
R.H. 3656-77
L.H. 3656-73

RIVET
3656-33

GATE
R.H. 3656-72

PLATFORM ASSEMBLY
3656-124

PLATFORM GROMMET
3656-71

GATE
L.H. 3656-79

SPADE BOLT
3656-113

RIVET
3464-16

BRIDGE COMPLETE
3656-143

COIL BRACKET ASSEMBLY
3656-142

COIL INSULATION
259E-21

LEVER
3656-83

SPACER TUBE
3656-141

PLATFORM COIL
3656-138 or
3656-185

NO. 6 LOCKWASHER
2-111

BASE
ASSEMBLY

RETAINING WASHER
TS-70 or 480-18

PLUNGER
3656-85

HINGE SPRING
3656-114

HINGE SPRING
3656-114

ADJUSTING SLEEVE
3656-127

RETAINING WASHER
TS-70 or 480-18

3656-106

COUNTERWEIGHT & PLATE

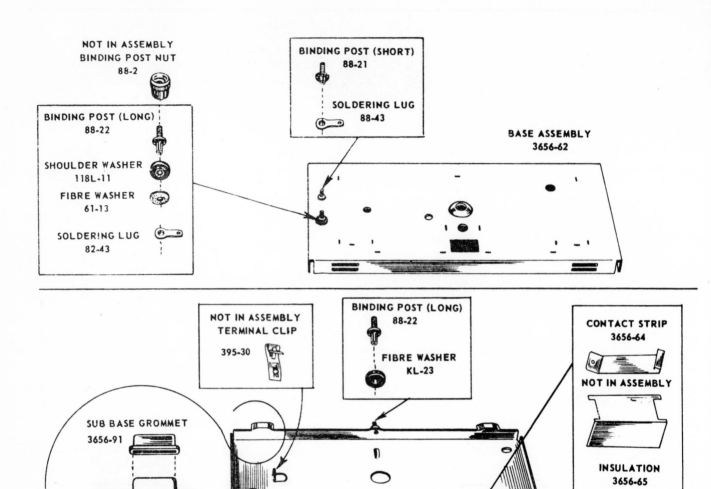

NOT IN ASSEMBLY
BINDING POST NUT
88-2

BINDING POST (LONG)
88-22

SHOULDER WASHER
118L-11

FIBRE WASHER
61-13

SOLDERING LUG
82-43

BINDING POST (SHORT)
88-21

SOLDERING LUG
88-43

BASE ASSEMBLY
3656-62

NOT IN ASSEMBLY
TERMINAL CLIP
395-30

BINDING POST (LONG)
88-22

FIBRE WASHER
KL-23

CONTACT STRIP
3656-64

NOT IN ASSEMBLY
3656-65

INSULATION
3656-65

SUB BASE GROMMET
3656-91

SUB BASE ASSEMBLY
3656-54

RIVET
3656-59

POWER CASING
3656-63

In the early part of production the four metal guides in the sub-base were straight and used Sub-base Grommets 3656-91, as illustrated in the inset. In later production metal guides were shaped as shown and grommets were eliminated.

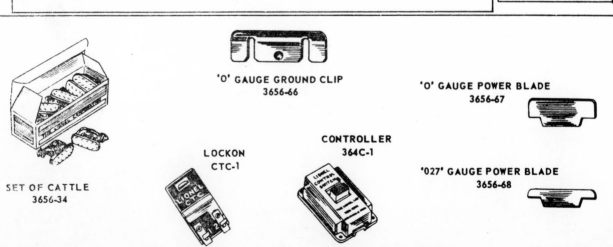

SET OF CATTLE
3656-34

'O' GAUGE GROUND CLIP
3656-66

LOCKON
CTC-1

CONTROLLER
364C-1

'O' GAUGE POWER BLADE
3656-67

'027' GAUGE POWER BLADE
3656-68

NO. 3656 CORRAL PLATFORM (1950 MODEL)

The 1950 model of the Corral Platform, also produced the following year, differs considerably from the previous model. The vibrating mechanism, the method of mounting the vibrating platform and the electrical contact system were all simplified and completely redesigned. Consequently, most of the component parts of the two Corral Platform models are not interchangeable.

Wiring Diagram of No. 3656 Corral Platform (1950 Model)

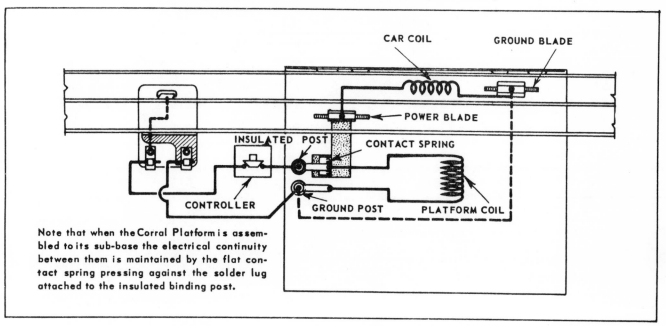

Note that when the Corral Platform is assembled to its sub-base the electrical continuity between them is maintained by the flat contact spring pressing against the solder lug attached to the insulated binding post.

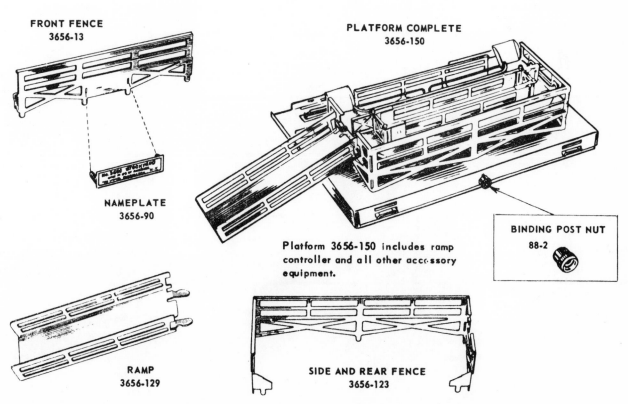

FRONT FENCE
3656-13

NAMEPLATE
3656-90

PLATFORM COMPLETE
3656-150

Platform 3656-150 includes ramp controller and all other accessory equipment.

BINDING POST NUT
88-2

RAMP
3656-129

SIDE AND REAR FENCE
3656-123

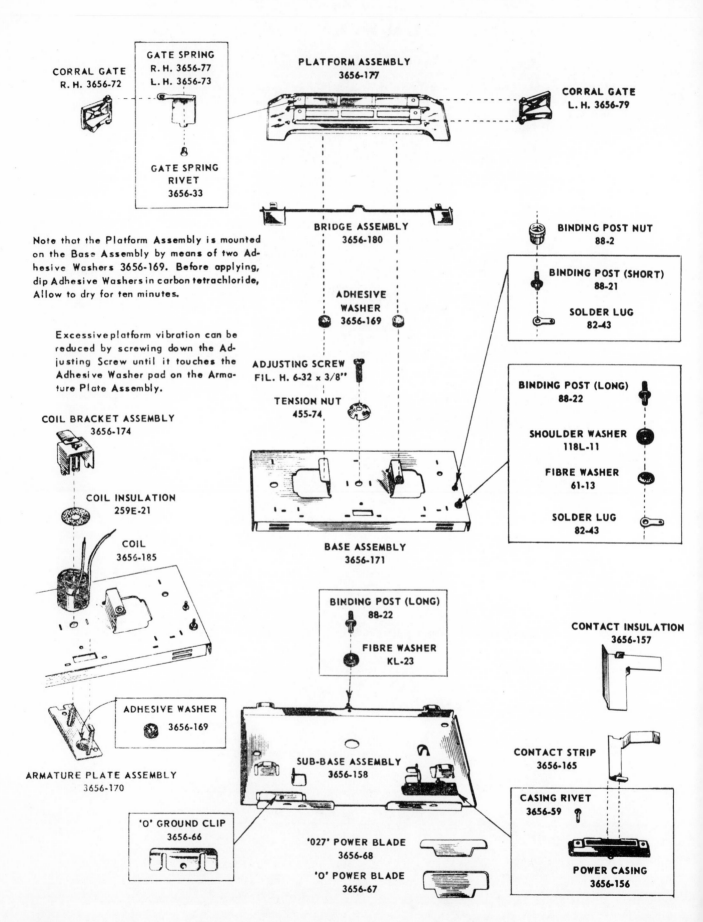

CORRAL GATE
R. H. 3656-72

GATE SPRING
R. H. 3656-77
L. H. 3656-73

GATE SPRING
RIVET
3656-33

PLATFORM ASSEMBLY
3656-177

CORRAL GATE
L. H. 3656-79

BRIDGE ASSEMBLY
3656-180

BINDING POST NUT
88-2

BINDING POST (SHORT)
88-21

SOLDER LUG
82-43

Note that the Platform Assembly is mounted on the Base Assembly by means of two Adhesive Washers 3656-169. Before applying, dip Adhesive Washers in carbon tetrachloride, Allow to dry for ten minutes.

ADHESIVE
WASHER
3656-169

Excessive platform vibration can be reduced by screwing down the Adjusting Screw until it touches the Adhesive Washer pad on the Armature Plate Assembly.

ADJUSTING SCREW
FIL. H. 6-32 x 3/8"

TENSION NUT
455-74

BINDING POST (LONG)
88-22

SHOULDER WASHER
118L-11

FIBRE WASHER
61-13

SOLDER LUG
82-43

COIL BRACKET ASSEMBLY
3656-174

COIL INSULATION
259E-21

COIL
3656-185

BASE ASSEMBLY
3656-171

BINDING POST (LONG)
88-22

FIBRE WASHER
KL-23

CONTACT INSULATION
3656-157

ADHESIVE WASHER
3656-169

ARMATURE PLATE ASSEMBLY
3656-170

SUB-BASE ASSEMBLY
3656-158

CONTACT STRIP
3656-165

CASING RIVET
3656-59

'O' GROUND CLIP
3656-66

'027' POWER BLADE
3656-68

'O' POWER BLADE
3656-67

POWER CASING
3656-156

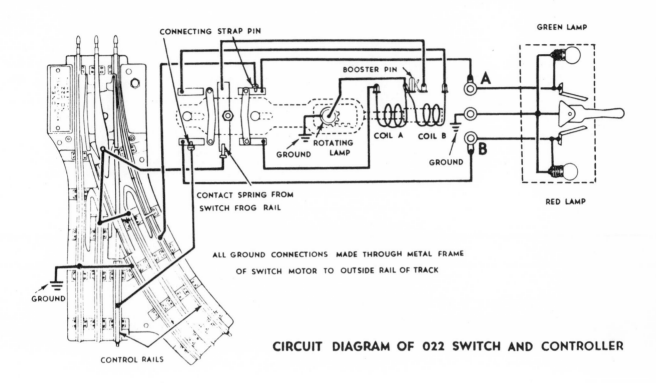

CIRCUIT DIAGRAM OF 022 SWITCH AND CONTROLLER

end of coil 'B' is connected to terminal post 'B' and to the green controller lamp.

In order to prevent a train from running into an 'open' switch and thus derailing itself, No. O22 switches are provided with 'control' rails which automatically throw the switch to a correct position for the passage of the approaching train.

It is obvious from the circuit diagram that the two control rails, which are insulated from the rest of the track layout by means of fibre pins, are connected in parallel with the switch terminals and perform a similar function. In the illustration, if an approaching locomotive should enter on the curved control rail, its wheels would ground the control rail and thus short out the green controller lamp. This would pull the plunger to the left and set the swivel rail to correct position for the train to pass through, and at the same time lighting the red lamp in the controller.

All electrical connections between the switch 'motor' and the switch itself are made by means of pressure contacts, when the motor and the switch are assembled together. The connections between the switch 'motor' and the control rails are made by two pins riveted to the connecting straps on the under side of the switch, the ground contact is made through the spring brass ground link and the power connection is made by means of contact spring projecting from the frog rail of the switch. (See illustration of the under side of the switch.)

SERVICING NO. O22 SWITCH

To test the operation of the switch, apply 12-14 volts to ends of center and outside rails, then simulate the action of the controller by shorting the center binding post to each of the outside binding posts in turn. Test the automatic operation of the non-derailing control rails by shorting each of the control rails to the opposite

137

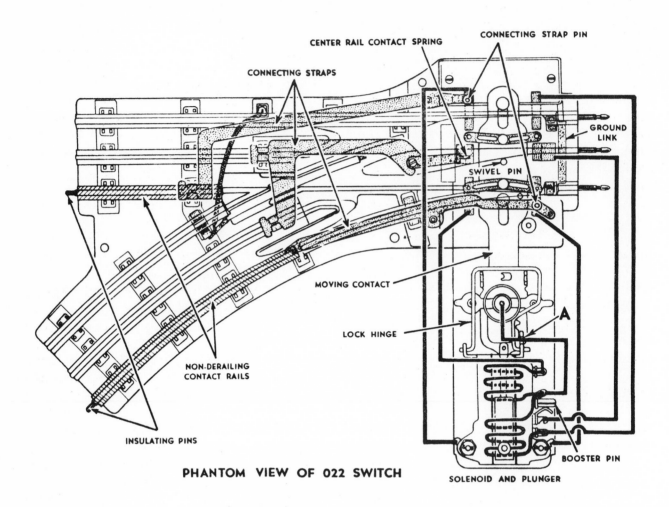

CONNECTING STRAPS

CENTER RAIL CONTACT SPRING

CONNECTING STRAP PIN

GROUND LINK

SWIVEL PIN

MOVING CONTACT

LOCK HINGE

A

NON-DERAILING CONTACT RAILS

INSULATING PINS

PHANTOM VIEW OF 022 SWITCH

SOLENOID AND PLUNGER

BOOSTER PIN

outside rail, simulating the shorting action of locomotive wheels. Plier handles make a convenient testing instrument for this purpose.

The swivel rail should lock securely in both positions. Failure to lock may cause train derailment and is due to improper operation of hinge lock. The hinge lock should drop into place to lock the sliding mechanism at the end of both strokes. If it does not it may be adjusted by bending the front bar slightly. Make sure the hinge bar spring is unbroken and in proper place.

To check for possible mechanical interference operate the switch mechanism manually by rotating the lamp frame by hand. Possible sources of interference may be a bent swivel pin

rubbing against the swivel rail slot, or a distorted lamp frame which might cause the lamp cover to rub against the switch cover. Interference with the action of the hinge lock might also be caused by the lamp lead unless it is properly located in the slot provided for this purpose in the coil frame (A in above).

Checking the Motor

If the switch fails to work at all, check the continuity of the electrical circuit of the switch motor. Look for loose solder joints, broken wires, or poor contact between the spring and the booster pin. Check the continuity of the two solenoid coils. Check for possible shorts in the lamp socket or between the common center rail and the swivel rail pin. Check for loose riveting of the outer binding posts which may cause the solder lugs to turn so as to short against the coil frame supporting posts.

If the switch works irregularly or in one direction only, the trouble may lie in the sliding contact assembly. Examine the riveting of the springs to their insulating base and of the insulating base to the rest of the assembly. Loose riveting at any of these points may cause a shifting of the parts so that proper contacts are not made.

Clean the contact surfaces with alcohol or carbon tetrachloride (Carbona) to remove dirt, carbon deposit, or soldering flux. Check the tension of the springs to see that proper contact is made at all four points of contact.

Adjustment of spring tension is a delicate operation and should be done carefully. Too great a tension will create too much drag. Insufficient tension will result in uncertain or irregular operation and arcing at the contact points. Too great a bend in the spring may cause mechanical interference with the switch base. If the springs are too badly distorted it is advisable to replace the entire sliding assembly by removing the two retaining shoulder rivets.

Checking Switch Base

If the switch motor is in good operating condition examine the rail connections in the switch base. Check the connecting straps to see that they are properly soldered to the control rails but do not short against the rail fingers of any of the other rails. If the control rails are shorted to ground rails, the switch will 'chatter' continuously when the power is on. Remove all rust and corrosion spots which may act as insulation and prevent the proper electrical contact. Tighten the common center rail strap screw and check the riveting of the common center rail. Loose riveting at this point will result in an uncertain electrical contact.

When reassembling the switch don't forget to insert the insulating paper between the switch base and its metal bottom plate. Bend up the soldered ends of the contacting strips on the switch motor to make sure they make proper contact with the connecting strap pins project-

ing from the switch base. Bend out the ground link connecting the outside rails of the switch to make sure it makes a good ground to the motor frame. Make sure that the swivel rail pin fits into the swivel rail slot before you tighten the screws holding the switch base to the switch motor. Otherwise you may fail to get proper electrical contact between the two parts of the switch.

LIONEL TRANSFORMERS

All Lionel equipment operates on low voltage, ranging from 8 to 18 volts, depending on the size and type of the locomotive and the number of cars in the train. Since the house voltage generally available is 115 volts a.c., a *step-down* transformer must be used to reduce it to the required voltage.

A transformer consists essentially of two coils of insulated copper wire wound on a common iron core. Although the two coils are completely insulated from one another, an alternating voltage imposed on one of the coils (which is then termed the *primary* coil) electromagnetically induces a voltage in the other, or *secondary*, coil. The relation between the two voltages depends on the ratio of the number of turns in the two coils. In *step-down* transformers the secondary winding has fewer turns than the primary winding and, consequently, the secondary voltage is lower than the primary or line voltage in the same ratio.

The primary winding of the transformer is connected to line voltage by plugging the line cord into any convenient wall outlet; the low voltage is then obtained from the secondary winding of the transformer which is brought out to the binding posts on the transformer case.

Lionel transformers are designed specifically to provide low voltage for operation of model railroad equipment and are therefore equipped with a means to vary the secondary voltage in order to control the speed of the train.

Two voltage ranges are usually provided by tapping the secondary winding (an exception to this are the Types V and Z transformers which have but one broad continuously variable voltage range) of the transformer at different

TOP VIEW

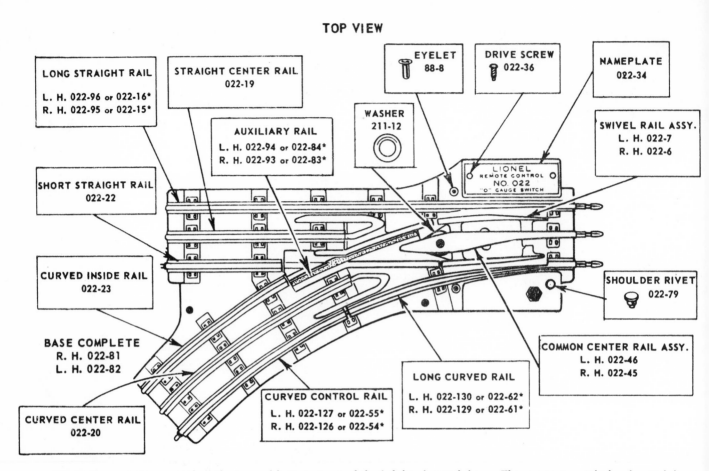

LONG STRAIGHT RAIL
L. H. 022-96 or 022-16*
R. H. 022-95 or 022-15*

STRAIGHT CENTER RAIL
022-19

EYELET
88-8

DRIVE SCREW
022-36

NAMEPLATE
022-34

WASHER
211-12

AUXILIARY RAIL
L. H. 022-94 or 022-84*
R. H. 022-93 or 022-83*

SWIVEL RAIL ASSY.
L. H. 022-7
R. H. 022-6

SHORT STRAIGHT RAIL
022-22

CURVED INSIDE RAIL
022-23

SHOULDER RIVET
022-79

BASE COMPLETE
R. H. 022-81
L. H. 022-82

COMMON CENTER RAIL ASSY.
L. H. 022-46
R. H. 022-45

CURVED CENTER RAIL
022-20

CURVED CONTROL RAIL
L. H. 022-127 or 022-55*
R. H. 022-126 or 022-54*

LONG CURVED RAIL
L. H. 022-130 or 022-62*
R. H. 022-129 or 022-61*

Illustrations on this page show the top and bottom views of the left-hand switch base. The companion right-hand switch base is its mirror image except for the location of the steel track pins and the section which makes contact with the switch motor. In 1950 a number of changes were made to facilitate production. However, the old parts, marked by asterisks, may be used interchangeably with the new parts except as noted.

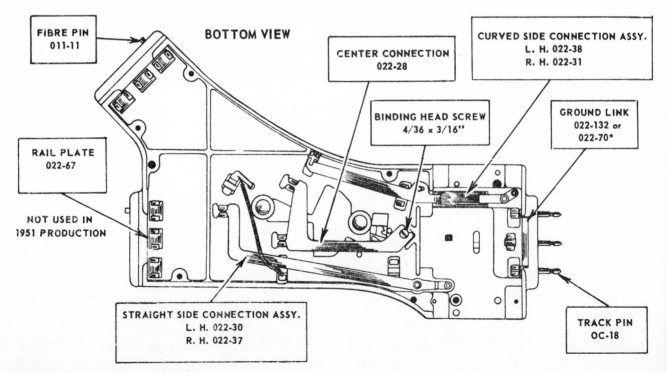

FIBRE PIN
011-11

BOTTOM VIEW

CENTER CONNECTION
022-28

CURVED SIDE CONNECTION ASSY.
L. H. 022-38
R. H. 022-31

BINDING HEAD SCREW
4/36 x 3/16"

GROUND LINK
022-132 or
022-70*

RAIL PLATE
022-67

NOT USED IN
1951 PRODUCTION

STRAIGHT SIDE CONNECTION ASSY.
L. H. 022-30
R. H. 022-37

TRACK PIN
OC-18

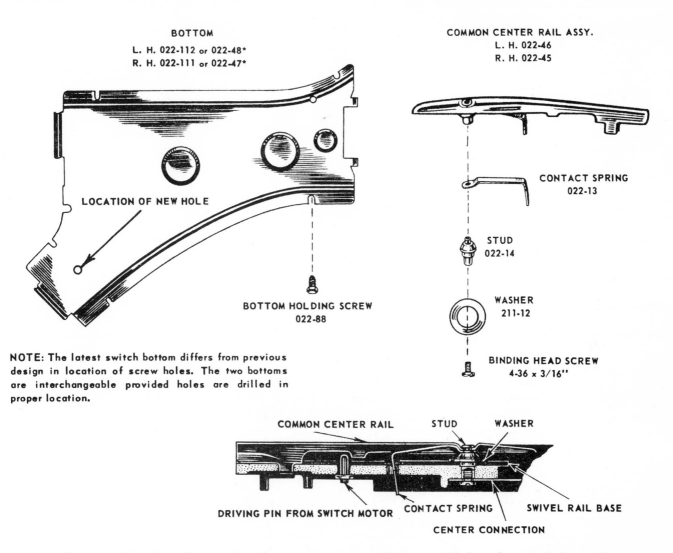

BOTTOM
L. H. 022-112 or 022-48*
R. H. 022-111 or 022-47*

COMMON CENTER RAIL ASSY.
L. H. 022-46
R. H. 022-45

LOCATION OF NEW HOLE

CONTACT SPRING
022-13

STUD
022-14

WASHER
211-12

BOTTOM HOLDING SCREW
022-88

BINDING HEAD SCREW
4-36 x 3/16''

NOTE: The latest switch bottom differs from previous design in location of screw holes. The two bottoms are interchangeable provided holes are drilled in proper location.

COMMON CENTER RAIL   STUD   WASHER

DRIVING PIN FROM SWITCH MOTOR   CONTACT SPRING   SWIVEL RAIL BASE
CENTER CONNECTION

Cross-section view showing how the common center rail is assembled to the switch base. The driving pin which is shown engaged to the swivel rail is part of the motor switch assembly not shown in the illustration.

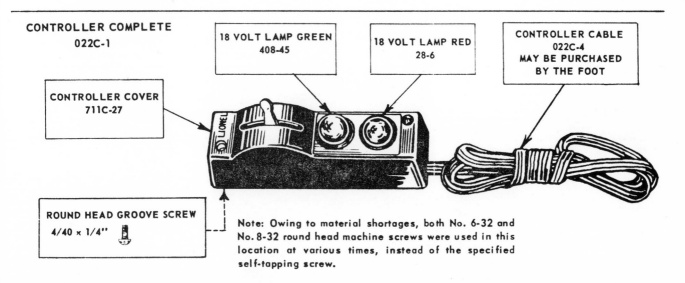

CONTROLLER COMPLETE
022C-1

18 VOLT LAMP GREEN
408-45

18 VOLT LAMP RED
28-6

CONTROLLER CABLE
022C-4
MAY BE PURCHASED
BY THE FOOT

CONTROLLER COVER
711C-27

ROUND HEAD GROOVE SCREW
4/40 x 1/4''

Note: Owing to material shortages, both No. 6-32 and No. 8-32 round head machine screws were used in this location at various times, instead of the specified self-tapping screw.

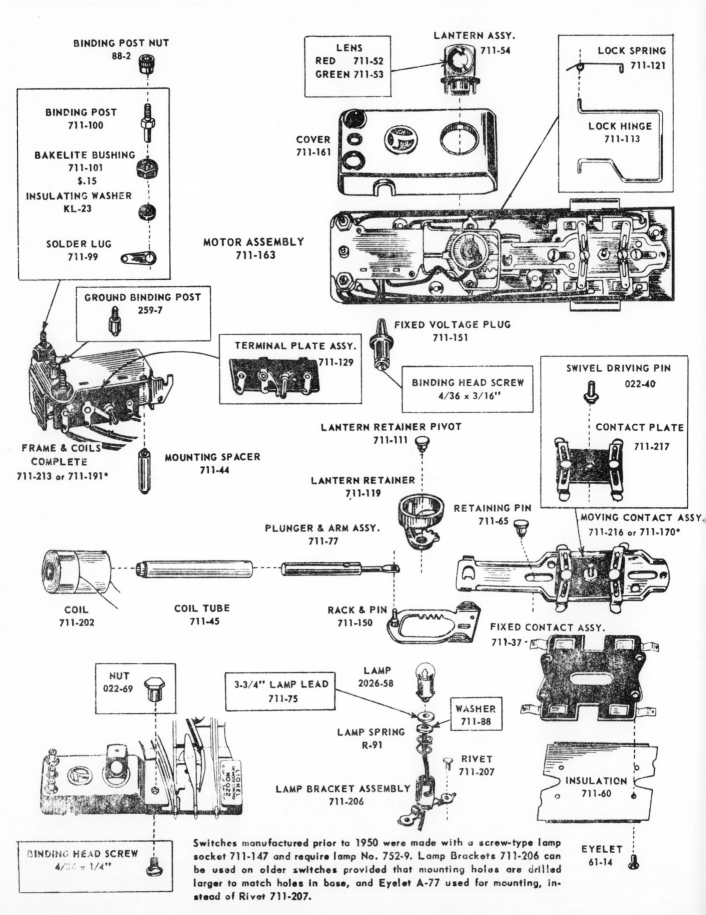

BINDING POST NUT
88-2

BINDING POST
711-100

BAKELITE BUSHING
711-101
$.15

INSULATING WASHER
KL-23

SOLDER LUG
711-99

GROUND BINDING POST
259-7

FRAME & COILS
COMPLETE
711-213 or 711-191*

MOUNTING SPACER
711-44

COIL
711-202

COIL TUBE
711-45

NUT
022-69

BINDING HEAD SCREW
4/36 x 1/4''

LENS
RED   711-52
GREEN 711-53

LANTERN ASSY.
711-54

COVER
711-161

MOTOR ASSEMBLY
711-163

FIXED VOLTAGE PLUG
711-151

TERMINAL PLATE ASSY.
711-129

BINDING HEAD SCREW
4/36 x 3/16''

LANTERN RETAINER PIVOT
711-111

LANTERN RETAINER
711-119

PLUNGER & ARM ASSY.
711-77

RACK & PIN
711-150

RETAINING PIN
711-65

3-3/4'' LAMP LEAD
711-75

LAMP
2026-58

LAMP SPRING
R-91

LAMP BRACKET ASSEMBLY
711-206

WASHER
711-88

RIVET
711-207

LOCK SPRING
711-121

LOCK HINGE
711-113

SWIVEL DRIVING PIN
022-40

CONTACT PLATE
711-217

MOVING CONTACT ASSY.
711-216 or 711-170*

FIXED CONTACT ASSY.
711-37

INSULATION
711-60

EYELET
61-14

Switches manufactured prior to 1950 were made with a screw-type lamp socket 711-147 and require lamp No. 752-9. Lamp Brackets 711-206 can be used on older switches provided that mounting holes are drilled larger to match holes in base, and Eyelet A-77 used for mounting, instead of Rivet 711-207.

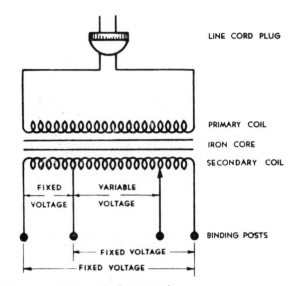

LINE CORD PLUG

PRIMARY COIL

IRON CORE

SECONDARY COIL

FIXED VOLTAGE   VARIABLE VOLTAGE

BINDING POSTS

FIXED VOLTAGE

FIXED VOLTAGE

Schematic Diagram of a Transformer

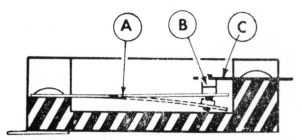

Lionel Circuit Breaker

points. Each range is continuously variable from its minimum to maximum voltages by means of a knob or arm which moves a sliding or rolling contact across a bared portion of the secondary winding, thus, in effect, tapping it at any desired turn. In this way, the voltage delivered to the track can be gradually changed without interrupting the flow of current at any time.

In addition to the variable voltage ranges, most Lionel transformers also provide several fixed low voltages in order to operate accessory equipment. Fixed voltages are obtained by tapping the secondary winding.

While the majority of Lionel transformers are designed to work on 115 volts 60-cycle alternating current, other transformers are available for 220 volts 50-60 cycles and for 115 volts 25 cycles. A 60-cycle transformer cannot be used on 25-cycle line because it will overheat and burn out. *No transformer should ever be plugged into a direct current line* because it will either blow the fuses or burn out immediately.

Wattage Rating

Transformers are rated not only for the voltage and frequency of the power lines on which they can be used, but also for the wattage. The wattage of a transformer is technically the amount of power taken from the power lines when delivering its maximum effective output, or, in other words, the measure of its ability to furnish power without overheating and too great a drop in its output voltage. The larger the amount of current required by the model railroad the greater should be the wattage of the transformer used. If a transformer is 'overloaded' by drawing from it too great a current, it will overheat and its output voltage will drop.

The largest transformer currently made by Lionel is Type Z, rated at 250 watts, which is more than adequate to run any moderate size model railroad system. In exceptionally large layouts it is advisable, however, to use auxiliary transformers for lights, operating accessories, insulated spur tracks, etc.

In order to estimate the power requirements of a model railroad system the table below lists the power used by some of the more common individual components. In estimating the size of the transformer needed it is important to remember that its rated wattage represents the power drawn from the line rather than power delivered to the track. To prevent overheating and unnecessary power loss, transformers should not be loaded continuously at more than 75% of their rated wattage.

Circuit Breakers

To protect them from overheating and damage due to 'overloads', most Lionel transformers are equipped with built-in, automatically operating, circuit breakers. Whenever the current drawn from the transformers exceeds a certain limit the circuit breaker opens, cutting off the output of the transformer. The circuit

"O-27" Gauge locomotive; no whistle	15-25	Automatic Accessories	12-15
"O" Gauge locomotive with whistle	25-35	Operating Accessories	15
"O" Gauge locomotive; no whistle	20-25	Each 6-volt lamp	1.5
"O" Gauge locomotive with whistle and lamp-type smoke unit	30-35	Each 12-volt lamp (small)	2.0
		Each 12-volt lamp (large)	3.0
"O" Gauge locomotive with whistle	35-40	Each 18-volt lamp	5.0
No. 167 Whistle Controller	5-10		

breaker will cool down and reset itself in a few seconds, but if the reason for the overload, such as a short circuit on the track, still exists, the circuit breaker will open again. This sequence will continue without damage to the transformer until the trouble is remedied.

The most frequent cause of a short circuit is a derailed car or locomotive where a wheel or a truck makes direct connection between the center power rail and the outside ground rails. A less easily discovered short circuit may be caused by broken insulation between the center rail and the track tie, or by an internal short in the locomotive or some of the accessory equipment.

The above wattages are drawn by locomotives when pulling the average number of cars. In the case of passenger outfits, add the power used by lamps within the cars.

It is important to understand that the circuit breakers are designed to protect the transformers themselves and not necessarily any of the other equipment which might be damaged by the short-circuit current. For example, the circuit breaker contained in the Type Z transformer will carry 15 amperes without opening, while the breaker in the No. 1642 transformer will open if more than 4.5 amperes are drawn from the transformer. It is therefore possible, particularly when large transformers are used, for a short circuit to exist on the track without causing the circuit breaker to open. In such a case, no damage will result to the transformer itself although the operation of the other equipment might be impaired.

Illustrated below is a typical circuit breaker used in Lionel transformers. The strip 'A' is made of thermostatic material which bends to

the dotted position when heated for a few seconds by excessive electric current passing through it and breaks contact at 'B'. Since the action of the circuit breaker is not instantaneous momentary short circuits on the track will not affect the operation of the trains. Minor time adjustments can be made on the circuit breakers by adjusting the strip 'C' to give more or less pressure on the contact points. Some circuit breakers have an adjusting screw for that purpose. Do not bend or distort the thermal strip 'A' or you will destroy its calibration completely.

The power requirement for automatic couplers and operating cars need not be added in the total since power for that purpose is used only for an instant and, in the case of operating cars, only when the train is not running.

Multi-Control Transformers

The name 'Multi-Control' is applied to those Lionel transformers which are equipped with built-in controls for operating the train whistle and for reversing the direction of the train.

As in the accessory No. 167 Whistle Controller, the built-in whistle controller converts a portion of the transformer a.c. output into d.c. voltage to operate the whistle relay in the tender. This is accomplished by means of a copper-oxide rectifier disc which is switched into the circuit as you operate the whistle control. As in the 167 Whistle Controller two d.c. voltages are supplied: a momentary 4-5 volt 'pick-up' surge to close the whistle relay, then a steady 'holding' voltage of 2-3 volts which maintains the relay in closed position. This voltage depends largely on the transformer load: a 'weak' relay which 'drops out', when the locomotive is standing still, will work satisfac-

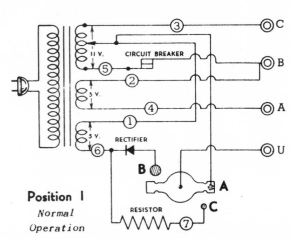

Position 1
*Normal
Operation*

Figure 1- Schematic Wiring Diagram of 'Multi-Control' Transformers Nos. 1032, 1033, 1032M

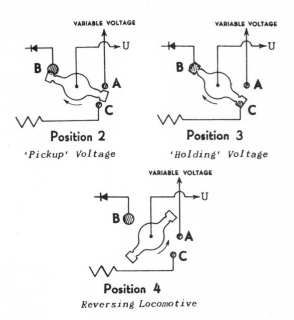

Position 2
'Pickup' Voltage

Position 3
'Holding' Voltage

Position 4
Reversing Locomotive

torily if a couple of lights are added to the layout.

An important feature of 'Multi-Control' transformers is a compensating winding which is switched into the circuit automatically to make up for the voltage drop in the rectifier and for the load of the whistle motor.

The sketches below illustrate the action of the switch which operates the built-in whistle controller in No. 1033 'Multi-Control' transformer. While mechanical details of the switches may vary, the principle of operation is the same in all 'Multi-Control' transformers.

Position 1. In the normal position the spring contact of the whistle control switch connects the variable voltage winding at contact rivet 'A' to the transformer output binding post.

Position 2. As the switch is rotated clockwise, the contact spring first makes contact with rivet 'B' and then breaks contact with 'A'. This places the auxiliary transformer winding and rectifier in series with the main variable voltage winding and produces the momentary high d.c. 'pickup' surge to close the whistle relay. If the spring loses contact with 'A' *before* touching 'B' the current to the track will be interrupted and may cause the reversing E-Unit in the locomotive to trip and stop the train.

Position 3. At the end of the swing the contact spring makes contact with rivet 'C' thus connecting the resistor wire in parallel with the rectifier. In this position most of transformer current by-passes the rectifier leaving enough d.c. 'holding' voltage to keep the relay closed. Unless this contact is continuous high current passing through the rectifier may overheat and damage it.

Turning the control arm in counter-clockwise direction, shown in *Position 4*, disconnects the transformer output from the output binding post causing the locomotive reversing unit to operate.

SERVICING TRANSFORMERS

The following service notes will prove useful in making mechanical repairs on transformers similar to Types 'R', 'A', etc.

1. To Remove Voltage Control Knobs

Use two screwdrivers placing each one on opposite sides of knob as far under the body of the knob as possible. Lift both screwdrivers simultaneously pulling handles upward as shown in Figure 1.

2. To Remove Transformer Cover

First remove all voltage control knobs. Then, turning transformer bottom upward remove the four screws holding the cover to the base. Hold down line cord and lift cover until

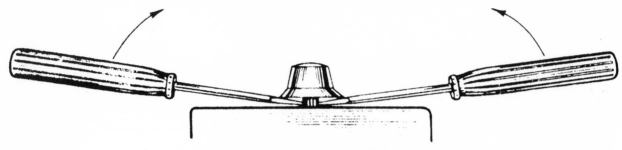

Figure 1   Removing bearing plate

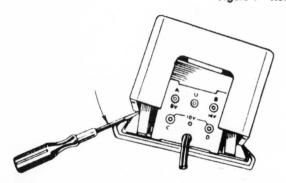

Figure 2   To Remove Transformer Cover

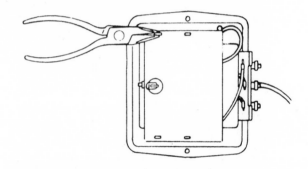

Figure 3   To Remove Bearing Plate Assembly

terminal plate in back of the transformer disengages from the cover. Place screwdriver under lower side and pry cover outward very gently. See Figure 2.

3. To Remove Bearing Plate Assembly

After knobs and transformer cover are removed straighten out the four twisted fingers which project through the bearing plate. Use a flat nose pliers as shown in Figure 3. The plate can then be lifted off.

4. To Repair a Loose Voltage Knob

Remove bearing plate assembly as described above and place it on a wooden block (See Figure 4) so that the collar of the die cast stud is supported by the block as shown in Figure 5. Tap the die cast stud at points (A) to rivet the assembly more tightly.

5. To Repair a Tight Voltage Knob

Resting the bearing plate on the wooden block as before check point (B), Figure 5. If the contact link binds against the locating fibre washer bend or pry them gently apart with a small screwdriver or knife blade.

If after this is done the arm is still tight the assembly has been riveted too tightly. Invert the wooden block so that the ¾″ hole faces upward and place the bearing plate on it so that the die cast stud fits into the hole (See Figure 7). Apply a punch at the center of the stud, as shown, and tap very lightly with a hammer just enough to loosen the riveting. Be very careful not to strike too hard or you will drive the stud out of the assembly.

6. To Replace the Contact Arm

If the contact arm or any other part of the assembly has to be replaced, support the bearing plate in the ¾″ hole of the wooden block and drive the stud out of the assembly by striking it with a punch as shown in Figure 7. Replace parts in proper order as shown in the assembly drawing, making sure that the contact arm lines up with the ribs on the die cast stud. Rest the bearing plate in the ½″ hole of the wooden block and rivet the assembly together by striking lightly at points (A), Figure 5.

7. To Repair 'Dead' Spots on Coil Winding

The output voltage of the transformer should vary gradually and steadily over the

Figure 5

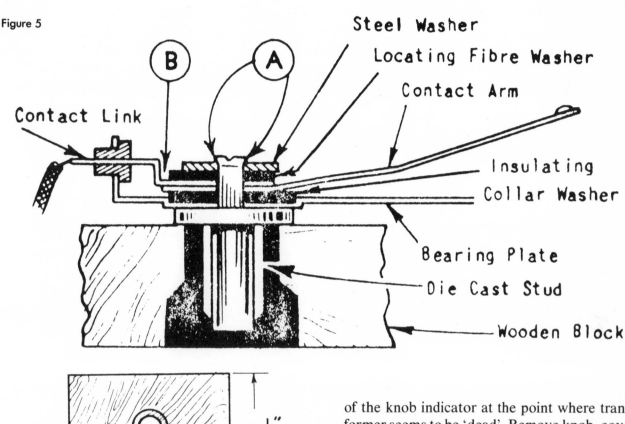

Figure 4   Block for repairing transformer.

entire range of movement voltage control knobs. If the transformer output drops at any point this may indicate that the contact arm fails to make proper contact with the bared portion of the secondary winding at that point. To repair this condition proceed as follows:

Gauge approximately, by eye, the position of the knob indicator at the point where transformer seems to be 'dead'. Remove knob, cover and bearing plate and examine the cleaned portion of the winding indicated by the position of the contact arm. Look for particles of foreign matter or a section of wire that may still be covered by a varnish coating. Clean the spot with a piece of fine sandpaper (No. 0) to remove varnish, etc. Be sure that the transformer is thoroughly clean before reassembling.

8. To Repair Shorted Turns in Coil

Excessive no load watt loss may be due to a shorted turn in the secondary winding. The short may be caused by distorted contact arm, or by one turn of wire crossing over another, particularly at the end of the winding. In the latter case it is possible to repair the coil by removing the last turn of wire and resoldering to the brass terminal plate.

9. To Repair Loose Switch Shaft

Improper function of whistle controlling apparatus may be due to a loose switch shaft assembly. To repair, remove contact plate by straightening bent frame fingers (See Figure 3).

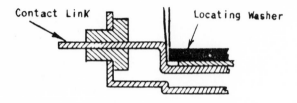

Figure 6- Adjusting contact link

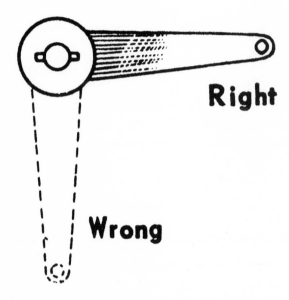

Right

Wrong

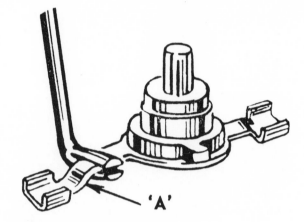

Figure 8 - Adjusting Spring Tension

Invert plate on a wooden block resting the shaft within a ½″ hole and tap down retaining sleeve to increase tension on centering spring. (A hollow punch for the purpose may be made out of a piece of ⅛″ pipe or tubing.)

To increase tension of the contact spring increase bend at point 'A', in Figure 8, using Lionel Spring Adjusting Tool No. ST-302.

CIRCUITS WITH COMMON GROUND

In model railroading there are numerous occasions when it is desirable to apply different voltages to accessories or track components which are connected or are in contact with the outside rails of the track system and thus have a common electrical ground. Examples of this usage are fixed voltage plugs of No. O22 switches, remote control track sections operating on fixed voltage, insulated track blocks used in multiple train operation, upgrade or

downgrade portions of track requiring higher or lower voltage than level track, No. 456 Coal Ramp, etc.

To prevent short circuit condition in all such cases it is important to select transformer circuits which also have a common ground. The chart below lists various circuit combinations which are available in modern Lionel transformers. The voltages specified are the nominal or 'no load' voltages and will, of course, crop somewhat under operating conditions, depending on the load and the rated wattage of the transformer.

REMOTE CONTROL WHISTLE

The Lionel whistle is composed of three units: (1) a whistle casting containing a high and a low pitch resonating air chamber, (2) motor and impeller, and (3) a direct current relay. The entire whistle assembly is mounted in the tender.

The circuit of the whistle is shown in sketch below. When a small amount of direct current is fed to the track the relay coil closes the relay contacts. When the circuit is complete the whistle motor and its impeller rotate at a high rate of speed sending a stream of air against the lips of the air chambers producing the whistle.

The d.c. voltage is obtained by means of a rectifier enclosed in the Whistle Controller which converts a portion of the alternating cur-

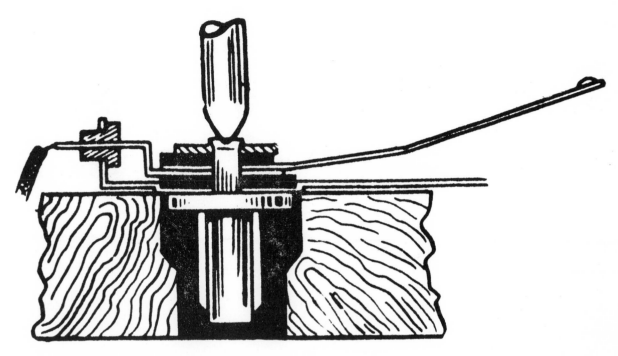

Figure 7- How to Loosen Riveting

rent supplied by the transformer into direct current and then feeds it to the power rails.

There are two types of whistles used in the current production of whistle tenders. Whistle WS-85 is used for 'O' Gauge outfits; whistle WS-75 is used for 'O-27' outfits. The two whistles are identical mechanically but differ in the winding of the motor field so that the WS-85 whistle operates at approximately 11 volts while the WS-75 works at 9 volts.

Servicing the Whistle

If the whistle does not blow, the cause of the trouble may be either in the whistle itself, the Whistle Controller, or both. To check the whistle, therefore, use a Whistle Controller which is know to be satisfactory. Remove the body of the Whistle Tender and set it on the track, to which a transformer and a whistle controller are connected in the usual way. Set the transformer voltage at 12 volts for an 'O-27' whistle and on 14 volts for 'O' whistle. (The 3 volt drop caused by the whistle controller will lower the track voltage to the proper testing voltage for the whistles.) If the whistle fails to blow when the 'whistle' button is pressed, first check the external electric connections.

Examine the roller collector on the tender to make sure that it bears on the center rail with sufficient pressure to give good electrical contact. Rail and roller must be clean. Worn rollers should be replaced. All wire connections to roller collector brackets must be cleanly soldered. Check over all whistle wiring for connections that may be broken, poorly soldered, or shorted.

Whistle Relays
1. Method of Operation

A relay is considered satisfactory if it picks up on 1.1 volts d.c. and remains closed on .5 volts d.c. when in the presence of 10 volts a.c., but does not close on less than 28 volts 60 cycle a.c. alone. On less than 60 cycles, the relay will close on proportionately lower a.c. voltage. On 25 cycles, for example, it will close at 12 volts a.c. causing the whistle to blow continuously when used with most Lionel outfits. This is why the remote control whistle cannot be used on 25-cycle current.

149

CIRCUITS WITH COMMON GROUND

In model railroading there are numerous occasions when it is desirable to apply different voltages to accessories or track components which are connected or are in contact with the outside rails of the track system and thus have a common electrical ground. Examples of this usage are fixed voltage plugs of No. 022 switches, remote control track sections operating on fixed voltage, insulated track blocks used in multiple train operation, upgrade or downgrade portions of track requiring higher or lower voltage than level track, No. 456 Coal Ramp, etc.

To prevent short circuit condition in all such cases it is important to select transformer circuits which also have a common ground. The chart below lists various circuit combinations which are available in modern Lionel transformers. The voltages specified are the nominal or 'no load' voltages and will, of course, drop somewhat under operating conditions, depending on the load and the rated wattage of the transformer.

Transformer	With this as Common or Ground Post	These are the Fixed Voltage Posts	And these are The Variable Voltage Posts
'A', 'A220', 'Q'	A	C 14 V. / B 8 V.	U 14-24 V.
	B	A 8 V. / C 6 V.	U 6-16 V.
	U	None	A 14-24 V. / B 6-16 V.
'AX'	A	E 20 V. / C 10 V.	U 15-20 V.
	B	E 15 V.	U 10-15 V.
	C	E 10 V. / A 10 V. / D 5 V.	U 5-10 V.
	D	C 5 V. / E 5 V.	U 0-5 V.
	E	A 20 V. / B 15 V. / C 10 V. / D 5 V.	None
	U	None	A 15-20 V. / B 10-15 V. / C 5-10 V. / D 0-5 V.
'KW' Multi-Control	U	D 20 V. / C 6 V.	A 6-20 V. / B 6-20 V.
	C	D 14 V. / U 6 V.	A 0-14 V. / B 0-14 V.
'R', 'R220'	A	D 14 V. / B 8 V.	C 14-24 V. / F 14-24 V.
	B	E 16 V. / A 8 V.	C 6-16 V. / F 6-16 V.
	D	A 14 V. / E 10 V.	None

Transformer	With this as Common or Ground Post	These are the Fixed Voltage Posts	And these are The Variable Voltage Posts
'RW' Multi-Control	A	D 19 V. / C 9 V.	U 9-19 V.
	B	D 16 V. / C 6 V.	U 6-16 V.
	D	A 19 V. / B 16 V. / C 10 V.	None
	U	None	A 9-19 V. / B 6-16 V.
'RWM' 'R250' Multi-Control	A	D 16 V. / C 8 V.	U 8-16 V.
	B	D 14 V.	U 6-14 V.
	D	A 16 V. / B 14 V. / C 8 V.	None
	U	None	A 8-16 V. / B 6-14 V.
'RX'	A	D 18 V. / C 8 V.	U 12-18 V.
	B	D 14 V.	U 8-14 V.
	C	D 10 V. / A 8 V.	U 4-10 V.
	D	A 18 V. / B 14 V. / C 10 V.	U 5-0 V.
	U	None	A 12-18 V. / B 8-14 V. / C 4-10 V. / D 6-0 V.
'S' 'S220' Multi-Control	A	C 19 V. / B 5 V.	U 10-19 V.
	B	C 14 V.	U 5-14 V.
	C	A 19 V. / B 14 V.	None
	U	None	A 10-19 V. / B 5-14 V.
'V' 'Z' 'V220' 'Z220'	U	None	A 6-25 V. / B 6-25 V. / C 6-25 V. / D 6-25 V.
'VW' 'ZW' Multi-Control	U	None / *With Internal Whistle Control	A* 6-20 V. / B 6-20 V. / C 6-20 V. / D* 6-20 V.
1032, 1033 1233, 1032M Multi-Control	A	C 16 V. / B 5 V.	U 5-16 V.
	B	C 11 V.	U 0-11 V.
	C	A 16 V. / B 11 V.	None
	U	None	A 5-16 V. / B 0-11 V.
1034	A	C 20 V. / B 6 V.	U 10-20 V.
	B	C 14 V. / A 6 V.	U 4-14 V.
	C	A 20 V. / B 14 V.	None
	U	None	A 10-20 V. / B 4-14 V.

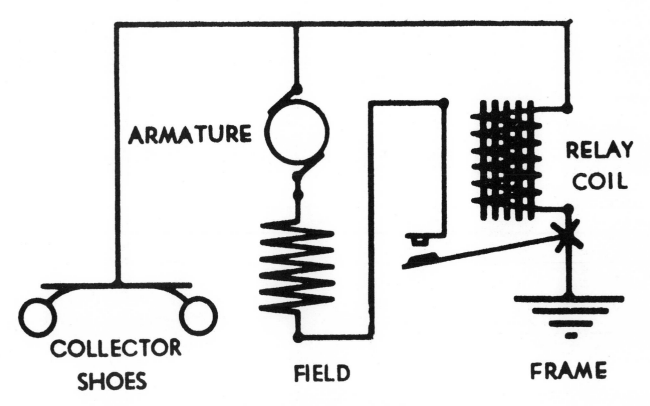

Figure 1- Remote Control Whistle Circuit

2. Relay Armature Fails to Close

If relay fails to close when whistle button is pressed, either the relay coil is 'open' or the relay armature is 'sticking' or 'binding'. To check for 'open' coil, remove the two wire connections at points (3) and (8). Do not cut wires but loosen solder with a soldering iron. Check with a continuity meter, or flash through with a battery and flashlight bulb. When a coil is defective, the entire relay should be replaced.

If the armature is tight, it will lift slightly and make an effort to close, but will not bring the contact points close enough together to complete the circuit. Try closing the contacts by hand to see if whistle motor operates. If it does, bend the armature contact spring at point (7) Figure 3, to provide adequate contact. Avoid closing contact too far as this will cause armature to 'chatter.' It may be necessary to adjust the spring slightly at point (6) to lessen the tension so armature closes easily. Make sure that the silver contact points are clean. Use a piece of fine grade sandpaper for cleaning.

3. Relay Jams in Closed Position

If the whistle blows continuously when placed upon the test track, the relay armature is jammed in a closed position. Adjust the face plate, (9), Figure 2, to allow the armature to drop down to its normal position. It should make contact only when the circuit is closed, that is, when the controller 'Whistle' button is pressed.

If damaged due to accident or tampering, the entire relay armature with contact and spring should be replaced.

Whistle Motor

1. Relay Closes but Motor Does Not Run

If the motor does not run although the relay closes the trouble may be caused by any of the following:

a. Brushes worn
Replace with new brushes.

151

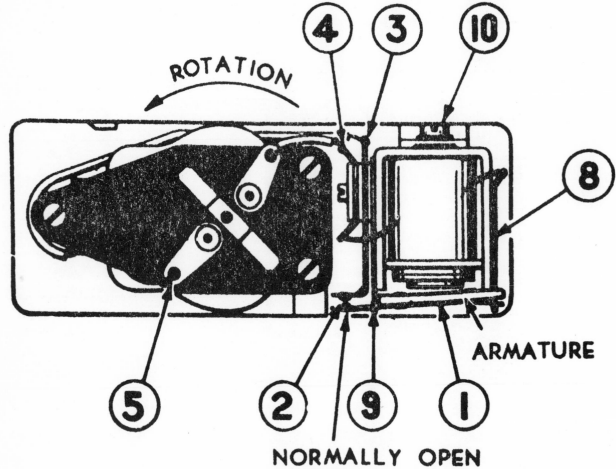

ROTATION

ARMATURE

NORMALLY OPEN

Figure 2- Complete Whistle Showing Motor and Whistle Relay Mounted on the Whistle Casting

b. Brushes stuck in brush holder

Remove brushes and clean brush holders.

c. Brush springs collapsed

If brush springs overheat because of clogged commutator slots, or some other reason, they may weaken and collapse. They will then give insufficient pressure on the commutator face and will result in a slow running motor. Remove weakened springs and replace with new ones.

d. Open field coil

Connect a pair of 6-volt leads to points (3) and (5), Figure 2, to check the continuity of field winding. If wire is broken there will be no spark.

e. Grounded field coil

Connect one 6-volt lead to point (3), Figure 2, and touch the other lead to the field laminations. If field winding is grounded there will be a spark. When a field is discovered to be defective, the best procedure is to replace the entire whistle unit.

f. Open armature

Expose commutator face by removing brush plate. Touch any two adjacent commutator segments with two 6-volt leads. There should be a flow of current indicated by a spark, unless the winding is open. Check all three combinations in the same way, noting the intensity of the spark which should be approximately the same for each pair of segments. An a.c. ammeter of 0-5 amperes can be used to good

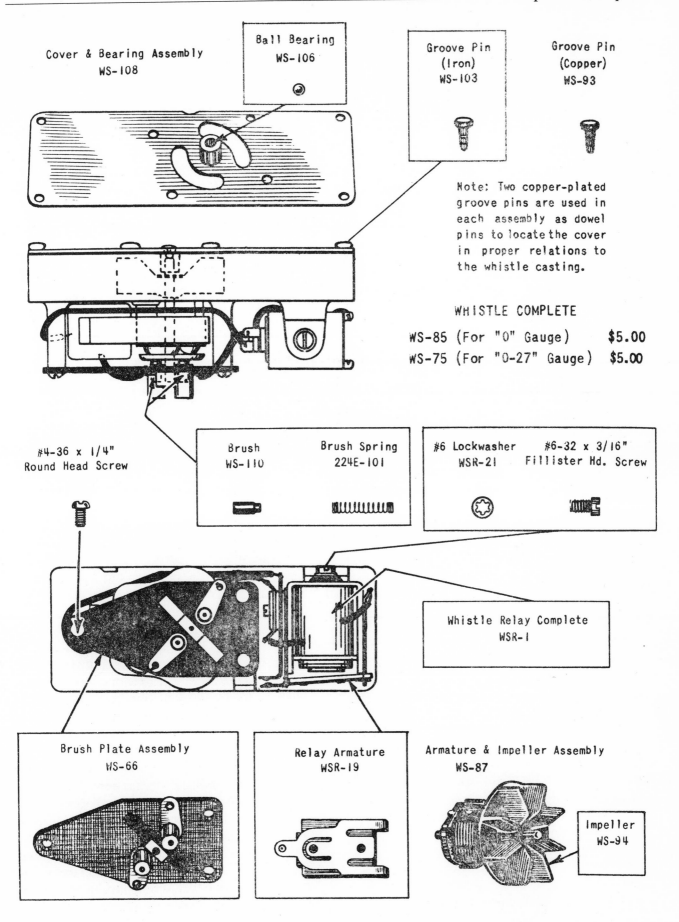

Cover & Bearing Assembly
WS-108

Ball Bearing
WS-106

Groove Pin
(Iron)
WS-103

Groove Pin
(Copper)
WS-93

Note: Two copper-plated
groove pins are used in
each assembly as dowel
pins to locate the cover
in proper relations to
the whistle casting.

WHISTLE COMPLETE

WS-85 (For "0" Gauge) $5.00
WS-75 (For "0-27" Gauge) $5.00

#4-36 x 1/4"
Round Head Screw

Brush
WS-110

Brush Spring
224E-101

#6 Lockwasher
WSR-21

#6-32 x 3/16"
Fillister Hd. Screw

Whistle Relay Complete
WSR-1

Brush Plate Assembly
WS-66

Relay Armature
WSR-19

Armature & Impeller Assembly
WS-87

Impeller
WS-94

153

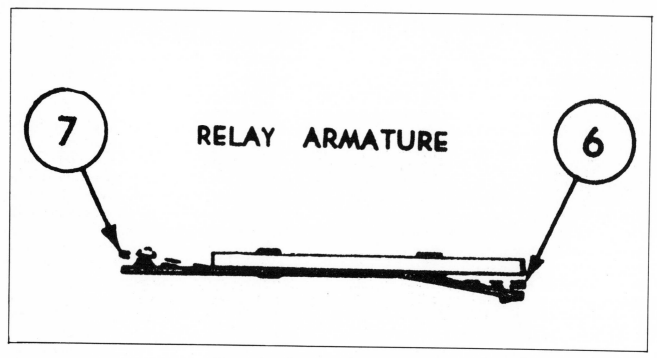

Figure 3- Adjustment of Relay Armature

advantage for this test and should show equal deflections for each pair of segments. If armature is 'open,' replace the entire armature-impeller assembly.

g. Grounded armature

Place one of the 6-volt leads on a commutator segment and the other lead on the armature axle. Repeat with each segment. If any of the segments is grounded, as shown by a spark, replace the entire armature impeller assembly.

h. Dirty commutator

A dirty commutator face will result in a slow-running motor which will give little if any sound. Expose armature, as described above, and polish the commutator face with a piece of '00' grade (or finer) sandpaper. Remove carbon accumulated in the commutator slots with any small sharp-pointed instrument being careful not to cause any sharp burrs which would cut brushes.

2. Motor Operating in Wrong Direction

Motor should run in a counter-clockwise direction when viewed from the brush plate side. (See Figure 1.) If motor is running in the opposite direction, there will be little if any whistle sound. To correct make sure that wires (3), (4), and (5), Figure 2, are connected as shown.

3. Motor Operating But No Whistle

a. Broken or Slipping Impeller

A broken or slipping impeller will not produce sufficient volume of air to blow the whistle. If you discover that the impeller is broken, or if it slips on the armature shaft, replace the armature-impeller assembly. To do this remove the 8 groove-pins which hold the metal cover plate and gasket to the whistle casting. Use a pair of side-cutting pliers to get under the head of the groove-pin, close the pliers enough to wedge up the head, then extract the pin. Be careful not to clip off the head of the pin. The armature assembly will slide out when cover plate is removed. After assembly has been replaced with a new one, replace gasket and cover plate and reassemble groove-pins by pressing or tapping them into place.

b. Leaking Air Chamber

If impeller is not broken or slipping, lack of sound may be due to a leaky gasket. Seal the seam between the cover plate and casting with lacquer, asphaltum, or a quick-drying paint. It is important that the tone chambers be practically air-tight and the mouth of the pipes free from obstruction.

4. Noisy Motor

A noisy motor may be due to a worn bearing on the cover plate of a worn or mis-shapen hole in the brush plate which may cause the armature to hit the field laminations as it revolves. In either case, replace the worn part. When replacing the brush plate assembly make sure that the wire connections are resoldered in the correct order or the motor will turn in wrong direction.

Cleaning and Lubrication

All whistles returned for service should be carefully cleaned and lubricated. In addition to the commutator face and contact points, previously mentioned, other parts of the whistle such as the brush plate, bearings, brushes, etc., which tend to collec. dust should be thoroughly cleaned with a small brush.

Lubricate well, but *sparingly*. A few drops of oil properly applied are of much more value than a bath of lubricant which only collects dust and impedes the proper functioning of the working parts. Only two points on the whistle require lubrication: (1) the oil retainer on the brush plate, and (2) the phosphor bronze bearing in the whistle chamber cover. The latter bearing may be oiled externally because it is porous and a drop or two of oil applied on the outside will gradually work into the interior.

Use a good grade of light machine oil, SAE 10 for bronze bearings. Lionel No. 925 Lubricant is well adapted for use in retainers.

Do not apply any lubricant either to the brushes or commutator face.

SOURCES OF SUPPLY

If you are not blessed by having a first-rate hobby store in your community, you may wish to acquire the equipment and information necessary for model railroading through the mails. Many high-quality toy train items and publications are available through the mail only; the first step is to find out who is offering what for how much.

Accordingly, the following is a beginner's list of various sources of supply for the model railroad enthusiast, regardless of the section of the country in which he lives.

Alvin Levin (of Maryland) offers fine used Lionel trains for sale, but does not publish a listing of his selections. He is always interested in purchasing toy train collections, whether they are Marklin, Lionel, or Ives. He is very reliable and highly recommended. Mr. Levin may be reached at telephone number 301-358-0916. His address is 3501 Shelburne Rd., Baltimore, Maryland 21208.

The Greenberg Publishing Company offers the world's largest selection of Lionel, American Flyer, and Marx publications, as well as an enormous selection of other model railroad and prototype railroad publications. Send $2 for its 64-page catalog. The address is 605 Gaither Road, Sykesville, Maryland 21784. Telephone: 301-442-1130.

Williams Reproductions Ltd. offers superb reproductions of classic Lionel equipment, including the O-gauge streamline passenger cars, the Irvington series of brown coach cars, the GG-1 "Pennsy" electric locomotive, and the prewar No. 256 locomotive. In standard gauge, Williams offers the No. 9, the No. 381, and the No. 408. Williams also offers a fine O-gauge original model of the Amtrak E-60 electric locomotive, and has plans for reproducing the Amtrak Metroliner. The company's current catalogue costs $2 and can be obtained by writing to 7925 Hammond Parkway, Laurel, Maryland 20810. Telephone: 301-776-6758.

Bill Eddins (of Virginia) offers a huge selection of new Lionel trains at very attractive prices. Mr. Eddins is one of the leading specialists in Lionel variations and his current listing can be obtained by sending a self-addressed stamped envelope to 8916 Virginia Avenue, Manassas, Virginia 22110.

Al Cox (of Washington State) offers an extensive selection of used toy trains of all kinds. He issues several lists each year, each of which costs $2. Mr. Cox takes special pains to describe his equipment carefully and accurately. He also offers many train parts which are available nowhere else; he "creates" these parts by disassembling high-quality used equipment. Mr. Cox, who can be contacted at 18025 8th Avenue NW, Seattle, Washington 98177, is highly recommended.

Harry Gordon (of Connecticut) offers a wide selection of original and reproduction parts for Lionel and American Flyer trains. Mr. Gordon's $2 listing, which is recommended, can be obtained by writing to 465A Congress Avenue, New Haven, Connecticut 06519.

Model Engineering Works (of California) offers an extensive selection of prewar parts for Lionel, American Flyer and Ives trains. Their list can be purchased for $2 by writing to MEW, Box 261, Monrovia, California 91016.

Tony Hay (of West Virginia) produces a valuable list of available used trains several times a year at a cost of $1. Mr. Hay can be reached at Box 9274, Huntington, West Virginia 25704.

Al Franceschetti (of Maryland) has an expansive line of used parts for various toy train lines, many of which are available nowhere else. His $1 list can be obtained by writing to 7910 Poplar Hill Drive, Clinton, Maryland 20735.

Estes Hobbies (of Pennsylvania) offers finely rematched spray paints for those of you who wish to make your own toy train restorations. Send a self-addressed stamped envelope for a list of available colors and prices to 1733 Markley Street, Norristown, Pennsylvania 19401.

Also offering fine spray paints for restoration jobs is Charles Wood, of 2538 East Market Street, Warren, Ohio 44483. Send him a self-addressed stamped envelope for his list or call 216-392-6306.

The M. B. Klein Hobby Shop (of Baltimore) offers a very large selection of new and used toy trains at very attractive prices in O-gauge, HO-gauge and N-gauge. You should write them for price quotes (enclosing a self-addressed stamped envelope) since they do not offer price lists. Their address is 162 N. Gay Street, Baltimore, Maryland.

Stanley Orr (of New York) offers a wide selection of parts and reliable service. His list costs $1 and can be obtained through Indian Pass Road, Stormville, New York 12582.

Another New Yorker, George Tebolt, has a far-ranging selection of original and reproduction parts available, as well as reliable service. His catalogue can be obtained by sending $1 to 130 Eastchester Road, New Rochelle, New York 10801.

Colonel Gordon Bragg (retired in California) offers a semiannual listing of various toy train equipment which costs $1. His address is 644 S. Valley Street, Anaheim, California 92804.

R. S. Baibak (of Michigan) collects and sells unusual Lionel train items of all kinds. Send him an SASE at Box 1321, Lansing, Michigan 48904.

Howard Godel (of New York) also buys and sells high-grade Lionel trains. The author of *Antique Toy Trains*, Godel is very knowledgeable and can be contacted at 38 Robinson Ave.,

Bedford Hill, N.Y. 10507.

John Davanzo (of New York) is the manufacturer of "Pride Lines," a handsome line of reproductions and custom trolley cars in Standard gauge. For a copy of his catalogue, send $1 to 87-A Argyle Avenue, Babylon, New York 11702. His telephone number is 516-587-4548.

Larry Battley (of suburban Washington, D.C.) offers a tumbling machine for the restoration of metal toy train parts. For information on this device, send a self-addressed stamped envelope to 2780-A N. Quincy St., Arlington, Virginia 22207.

The Bowers Hobby Shop (of Pennsylvania) has many pieces of new Lionel equipment for sale at quite attractive prices. Dan Bowers will send you his list in your self-addressed stamped large envelope if you write to 815 Flintlock Ridge, Mechanicsburg, Pennsylvania 17055.

Jim Pierce (of Washington, D.C.) does excellent restoration work on toy trains. When making inquiries, send your letters and SASE's to 2309 36th Street S.E., Washington, D.C. 20020.

Bob McCoy (of Washington State) produces his own ready-to-run equipment for Standard gauge. His catalogue can be obtained for $1 from P.O. Box 444, Kent, Washington 98031. Telephone: 206-852-5595.

Andrew Kriswalus (of New York) produces toy train track in the O-72 gauge and Standard-72 gauge, as well as O-gauge and Standard-gauge motors for locomotives. Send your SASE for Kriswalus' information to 121-A Smithfield Drive, Endicott, New York 13760.

Jerry Butler (of California) offers rubber stamps for restoring the lettering on toy trains. He also has reproduced the oil labels for the bottoms of prewar freight cars. Send a SASE for his list to P.O. Box 862, San Fernando, California 91341.

Ed Kraemer (of New Jersey) offers very precise decal reproductions and plates for many Lionel engines. For information, send a SASE to 105 Hollywood Avenue, Fairfield, New Jersey 07006. (check this zip code)

Peter Bianco (of New York) sells reproduction cabs for many of Lionel's diesel and electric locomotives. $1 will buy you his catalogue if you send it to 1510 Avenue M, Brooklyn, New York 11230. Telephone: 212-998-4226.

Old railroad movies of prototype activities can be purchased from Richard Nadel, of 1213 Cardinal Lane, Cherry Hill, New Jersey 08003. He requests an SASE for return information.

Dan Olson (of Washington State) produces American Flyer decal reproductions. Send a request for his listing and an SASE to Olson at 7209 Woodlawn Avenue NE, Seattle, Washington 98115.

Dana Lee Barlow (of Florida) is the manufacturer of Standard-gauge 4-8-4 Northern locomotives. These engines, which are made with twin motors for three-rail track, are pictured in Barlow's $1 catalogue, which can be obtained from 11920 35th Terrace S.W., Miami, Florida 33175.

John Knepper (of Oregon) cuts gears for Lionel and other toy trains, and will send information in an SASE from 5428 Shattuck Road S.W., Portland, Oregon 97221.

Choo-choo Charlie Burt (of Detroit) rewinds and rebuilds the armatures, commutators, and fields of various toy train motors. Send a SASE to Charlie at 8924 Crosley Street, Detroit, Michigan 48239. Telephone: 313-535-3060.

You may also wish to write to several of the major toy train clubs and associations to inquire about membership and/or information about equipment. The addresses of the major clubs are listed below.

The Train Collectors Association, National Headquarters and Museum, P.O. Box 248, Strasburg, Pennsylvania 17579. The TCA is the nation's largest organization of toy train enthusiasts, with more than 10,000 members. The TCA publishes a magazine and a quarterly newsletter (which includes classified advertising), and also sponsors numerous train shows every year.

The Toy Train Operating Society maintains its national business office at 25 West Walnut Street, Suite 305, Pasadena, California 91103. The TTOS also sponsors many train shows nationwide, and publishes a monthly magazine with classified ad columns.

The Marklin Enthusiasts of America issue a newsletter (with classified ads) and also sponsor shows for their members. For more information, contact Pete Texier at P.O. Box 189, Beverly, New Jersey 08010.

The Lionel Collectors Club of America also has a monthly newsletter with classified ads, and sponsors train shows for its members. Albert Otten, of 3 Raquet Court, Little Rock, Arkansas 72207, can provide more information.

GLOSSARY OF TERMS AND MODEL RAILROADING JARGON

AC—this abbreviation stands for "alternating current," which is the most common current available to household consumers of electricity in the United States. The polarity of the circuit (between the positive and the negative terminals) changes 60 times each second.

alligator clips—small metal electrical clips which are attached to the bare ends of wires (one clip per wire) to make electrical connections. When pinched into the open position (resembling the open jaws of an alligator) the clips can easily be attached to or disconnected from electrical posts on transformers, etc.

amperes—a term used in electricity as a unit of measurement to determine the level of flow of electricity within a circuit.

ballast tamper—a railroad track installation device used to push into place the rock fragments which ballast (or hold) the track ties tightly in position on the roadbed. Lionel manufactured a small motorized unit, roughly modeled after prototype ballast-tamper units. Previously, the railroad workmen had pushed the prototype rocks into place with large iron tampers.

bell wire—a solid light wire usually covered with an insulating plastic, commonly used for the circuits of household door bells (between 12 and 15 volts). Bell wire is frequently used in model railroad wiring because it is inexpensive, readily available, and an appropriate thickness (most frequently 18- or 20-gauge).

blocks—sections of model railroad track which are insulated from adjoining sections of track. A block may be composed of as few as 3 or 4 sections of track, or it may be substantially longer. Blocks permit one train to be operated independently of another.

"C" clamp—metal thumbscrew clamps common in carpentry for temporarily adjoining two or more pieces of wood which are being glued. The pieces to be joined are fitted together within the mouth of the clamp and the thumbscrew is used to apply the necessary pressure. These clamps are helpful in the construction of model railroad table layouts.

cab control—the process of switching control of blocks (or sections) of track on a model train layout so that two or more transformers control different blocks on the layout. The blocks under control of a specific transformer change sequentially as the train controlled by that transformer travels the track.

circuit breaker—an electrical device which prevents excessive current from flowing through the track circuit. Many Lionel transformers have built-in circuit breakers which "open" when excessive current flows through them. Circuit breakers suitable for low voltage AC common in toy train operation (6–20 volts) are commercially available.

clockwork engines—mechanically-powered toy train locomotives, commonly manufactured by

Marx Toys and other companies from the 1930s to the 1950s. These engines had internal spring-and-gear motors which were wound up with a spring, similar to a clock, and are considered safer for young children.

closed-top—the type of model railroad layout design which incorporates a single flat surface as the foundation for roadbed, scenery and landscaping, buildings, and accessories. A large plywood sheet on top of a wooden frame with legs is the most common closed-top design.

common ground—the use of one ground wire (or ground rail from the track) to electrically operate several train accessories. This one lead substitutes for numerous leads heading back to the transformer.

commutator—the part of a locomotive motor armature which maintains contact with the brushes, and thereby completes the circuit. Two kinds of commutators commonly are found in toy train motors: the flat type with three copper segments, and the drum type with copper segments curved to fit the exterior surface of the armature.

cracking tower—a large vat common in chemical and oil refineries in which crude oil is heated to transform the liquid into a gas. At different temperatures, a variety of different gases are given off by the crude oil; these are captured and ultimately produce different chemicals.

DC—direct current of electricity in which the positive pole remains positive and the negative pole remains negative throughout the circuit.

Flashlight batteries, for example, produce direct current.

die-cast—a process in which powdered metal is subjected to great heat to convert it into a strengthened solid form within a "die" or mold. This process allows much greater detail in the metal than does stamping; the metal boilers of Lionel steam locomotives have been die-cast since 1945.

diodes—switchlike electrical devices which convert AC (alternating current) into DC (direct current).

E-unit—Lionel's name for the three-position reversing unit within its engines and locomotives, similar in function to an automobile transmission.

emery paper—a mildly abrasive paper with a fine texture used to polish metal and remove rust.

4-6-4—these numbers are the Whyte designation for a particular configuration of locomotive wheels. The first number, 4 represents the total number of pilot wheels (two on each side of the locomotive). The 6 represents the total number of driving wheels (three on each side). The last 4 represents the wheels in the trailing truck (two on each side). A 4-6-4 locomotive commonly is called a Hudson, since this was the name given to 4-6-4's by the New York Central Railroad. An 0-4-0 designation would indicate an engine with two driving wheels on each side and no pilot wheels or trailing truck, as was common in switchyard steam engines.

160

grade—the degree to which railroad track rises from a flat surface over a given distance.

homosote—a soft, relatively inexpensive insulation board which can be purchased in large sheets and often works adequately as a foundation for model railroad table tops.

hot line—the positive side of an electrical circuit. By convention, the A and B terminals of Lionel transformers provide the "hot line" and the U terminal provides the negative or "ground line." Wires leading from the transformer's A or B terminals are called "hot lines."

Hydrocal—a powdery substance which, when combined with water and made into a pasty mixture, is commonly used in the construction of model railroad mountains and scenery. Hydrocal's virtues include its durability, the quickness with which it dries into solid form, and its lightness.

joist—a carpentry/construction term for the long strips of wood which form the internal support for a frame. The joists on a model train table are the wooden strips running lengthwise beneath the table top.

kit-bashing—the process through which a standard mass-produced model railroad kit is altered in some major fashion to fit your personal preferences and needs.

lag screws—a heavy threaded screw with coarse threads to increase traction in the wood. The thread does not run the entire length of the screw.

lock-on—a Lionel device for connecting electrical wires to train track. The lock-on consists of two terminals connected to pressure plates by solid metal strips. The pressure plates make contact with two rails: the center rail and one of the outside rails.

magnetraction—a Lionel invention in which permanent magnets were inserted into the frame of the engine to create a magnetic attraction between the engine wheels and the track. First introduced in 1949 (but not publicly announced until 1950), magnetraction substantially enhanced the pulling-power of Lionel equipment and allowed greater speeds on curves without derailment.

N-gauge—next-to-the-smallest available size of model railroad equipment (the smallest being T-gauge). An average N-gauge locomotive stands about 1½ inches in height.

nipper—a small set of pliers with sharpened, pointed jaws commonly used to snip off the ends of wire and heads of thin nails and tacks.

O-gauge—a scale of model trains in which the models are about 1/48 the size of their prototypes, or with a scale of ¼ inch to the foot. O-gauge track is 1¼ inches between the rails. This gauge was introduced in about 1900 and most Lionel trains manufactured since 1945 were made in O-gauge. A circle of regular

O-gauge track is 33 inches in outside diameter.

O-27 gauge—This gauge of track was introduced in the mid-1930s by Lionel. The track has the same distance between the rails as O-gauge, but a circle of O-27 gauge is only 27 inches in diameter, making it somewhat difficult for O-gauge equipment to operate on O-27 curves. O-27 track is slightly less tall and lighter than O-gauge; but it is possible to use both gauges on the same train layout.

ohms—an electrical term describing a unit of measurement to determine the level of resistance within a circuit to the flow of electricity.

one-foot center—a method for measuring the distance between two or more units of construction. The distance between two wooden wall supports (studs), for example, is measured from the center of one stud to the center of the next stud. If the distance between the center of one train table joist to the center of the next joist is 12 inches, then the joists were assembled on a one-foot center.

open top—the type of model railroad layout design which incorporates a wooden frame with joists, supported by six or more legs, allowing the roadbed to rise and fall beneath the top level of the frame.

oxidation—the process by which the oxygen in air joins with other chemical agents to form another compound. Rust is one form of oxidation. The process inhibits the flow of any electricity and is quite common on aluminum and copper. The oxidation may be removed by emery paper or other abrasives.

papier-mâché—a substance consisting principally of water, flour, and newspaper strips which is commonly molded by model railroaders into mountains (with the help of wire screening) and other forms of scenery. The soaked strips are then allowed to dry and usually painted for landscaping effects.

pawl—a lever or rod equipped with a clip or catch for moving another mechanical device. Lionel requires the use of a pawl to turn the drum of its E-units.

phasing—the time relationship between the single waves of AC electric current. Most 120 to 220 volt current comes in single phases; there is only one surge of AC up and down. (However in heavy industrial use, perhaps at 230 volts, there are two separate flows of current usually 90 degrees apart; this type of current provides for much more efficient operation of heavy duty motors.)

prototype—the real thing. Genuine, life-size railroad rolling stock, equipment, structures, and paraphernalia.

rail joiners—flat metal plates usually bolted onto two adjoining track rails to secure the connection. Occasionally miniaturized to enhance the authenticity of model railroad track.

rectifying—the process in which alternating current (with its rapid shifting of polarity) is changed into direct current. Several different devices, including diodes, can make this conversion.

roadbed—the surface, usually raised in the form of a flattened ridge of rocks and earth, upon which railroad ties, ballast, and rails are laid to create a railroad track.

rollers—sometimes called pickup rollers. These small cylindrical devices are found beneath the motor of a toy train locomotive; they roll along the center rail of Lionel and Marx track, picking up electrical current to operate the motor.

rolling stock—any piece of model railroad equipment which operates along the rails, except for locomotives, engines, or tenders. Freight cars, cabooses, flat cars, tankers, passenger cars, and gondolas are all rolling stock.

roundhouse—a curved structure for housing locomotives, usually built facing the circumference of a turntable. A locomotive maneuvers onto the turntable, which turns it to a track leading into one of the roundhouse stalls, where major locomotive repairs are made. The roundhouse stalls usually comprise a semicircular building.

S-gauge—a size of toy trains and track created by the A.C. Gilbert Co. in 1946 to compete with Lionel's O-gauge. The two-rail track is somewhat narrower than O-gauge, and the American Flyer S-gauge trains were built at the smaller scale of $3/16$ inch to the foot (compared to ¼ inch for O-gauge).

scale—the relation between the prototype train's size and the size of the model. O-gauge is a ¼-inch scale (or roughly $1/48$ the size of the prototype).

scratch-building—the process of constructing scale toy train equipment from raw materials by hand. A model railroad coaling station fashioned from cardboard, paper, balsa wood, and glue is said to have been scratch-built.

sealed unit motor—a toy train locomotive motor which has been sealed, ostensibly to protect it from dust and grime. Such sealing, however, precludes home repairs by the model railroader. Some of the inexpensive Lionel engines of the 1950s and 1960s were equipped with such motors, preventing replacement of the brushes and commutator cleaning.

siding—a section of track leading off to the side of the main roadbed from a switch. Rolling stock may be shunted onto this track for purposes of delivery or to keep the right-of-way clear for other train movements.

skirting—the strips of wood attached to the side of a flat surface (such as a plywood train table top) for cosmetic and functional reasons.

sleepers—(a) the wooden ties used beneath track rails in prototype trackwork.
(b) a collector's term describing items available at modest cost but expected to substantially increase in value.

solderless connectors—plastic or ceramic cones which are open at one end and equipped with interior threading for the purpose of providing temporary connections of electrical wiring. After two bare wire ends have been wound together, a wireless connector is screwed down over the wires to firm the connection and provide insulation.

spanners—short pieces of wood attached between the joists of an open-top toy train table to support the roadbed as it rises and falls along the layout.

Standard gauge—a large gauge of toy trains, in which the three-rail track measures 2⅛ inches between the outside rails; the scale is approximately ⅜ inch to the foot. Lionel developed this gauge in 1906, and other producers of this "wide-gauge" track included American Flyer, Ives, and Dorfan. The track is still commercially available.

starter holes—small, shallow holes made in wood by a hammer and nail to facilitate the starting of a screw into the hole.

switchyard—a collection of track and sidings off the main right-of-way used to store unused boxcars and other rolling stock; an area of rendezvous and preparation for shipments and the building of trains.

tender—the piece of rolling stock positioned directly behind the locomotive or engine, for which it carries either coal or oil; formerly called the coal car.

throttle—the mechanical device which regulates the speed either of prototype locomotives (controlled by the engineer in the cab) or of toy trains (controlled by you at the transformer).

tinning—a process through which a thin coat of solder is applied to a bare piece of electrical wire or to the rail of a toy train track, or any two metal surfaces which are to be joined by solder. The two pieces of tinned metal are brought into contact with each other and heat is applied; the solder then melts again, forming a bond between the two pieces.

tinplate—steel which has been coated with a thin layer of tin to prevent rusting. Most toy train track is tinplated, and in earlier years much of the toy train rolling stock was tinplated and then painted. Lionel, American Flyer, Ives, and Marx trains often are referred to as tinplate trains.

track clips—devices designed to hold together pieces of sectional track, which normally are joined only by track pins. Track sections often tend to separate, unless fastened to the roadbed or joined by track clips.

trestle—a structure designed to carry train tracks above the ground. In prototype operations, trestles are constructed of wood or steel and often are built to span rivers, gulches, and valleys. Toy train trestles have been manufactured by Lionel, Marx, and American Flyer to suspend track above the train table.

trucks—the wheels, axles, and containing assemblies on railroad rolling stocks (both model and prototype).

turnbuckles—devices for tightening the pressure on rods or wire, normally consisting of a central threaded shaft with opposing sets of threads. As the central holding shaft is turned counterclockwise, the wires in each end of the shaft are drawn in toward each other, thus increasing the pulling pressure at the far ends of the wires. (Turnbuckles often are used to straighten screens and storm doors which have become warped; they also were common beneath the wooden foundation of old-time freight cars.)

turntable—a large mechanical device used by prototype railroads to turn around steam engines for operation in different directions. The turntable usually consisted of a short section of straight track on a platform which rotated within a shallow pit. Prototype railroads discontinued use of turntables with the advent of diesel engines after World War II. Lionel manufactured a model turntable in the 1950s.

UCS track—the uncoupling section of track which Lionel developed to uncouple cars as well as to operate its special accessory cars (such as the milk car).

uncoupling track—Lionel developed several different kinds of uncoupling sections of track for the remote control uncoupling of rolling stock.

wide gauge—the term used by American Flyer, Dorfan, and Ives to identify their Standard-gauge track and equipment.

windings—integral parts of a model railroad transformer consisting of long sections of copper wiring wound tightly around each end of an iron core within the transformer. The electrical current flows from the windings at one end of the core to the other end.

wye—a configuration of railroad track for reversing the direction of a steam engine without the use of a turntable. A wye is laid out in the shape of the alphabet letter Y with the top of the letter connected by a section of track.

volts—a unit of electrical measurement to determine the level of pressure behind an electrical current. The greater the number of volts (or voltage), the more powerful the current.

INDEX